THE LEAST
DANGEROUS BRANCH

*The Supreme Court
at the Bar of Politics*

Also by Alexander M. Bickel

THE UNPUBLISHED OPINIONS OF MR. JUSTICE BRANDEIS:
THE SUPREME COURT AT WORK (1957)

THE LEAST
DANGEROUS BRANCH

---

*The Supreme Court
at the Bar of Politics*

ALEXANDER M. BICKEL

Bobbs-Merrill Educational Publishing
Indianapolis

First Edition
Tenth Printing—1980

Library of Congress Catalog Card Number: 62–20685
ISBN 0–672–60757–3 (pbk.)
ISBN 0–672–51318–8

ACKNOWLEDGMENTS

I wish to record my indebtedness to Zane Klein, of the Yale Law School, Class of 1961, Sanford Jay Rosen and Paul Arthur Nejelski, of the Class of 1962, and Stephen Fraidin, of the Class of 1964. Although they are in no way to be held responsible for any errors committed herein, Messrs. Klein, Rosen, and Nejelski educated me on, respectively, the eighteenth-century law of sedition in England and the American colonies, which is relevant to the issue of prior restraints discussed in Chapter 4; the proceedings in the case of Caryl Chessman, to which I refer in Chapter 5; and early reaction to the decision in the *School Segregation Cases,* which I deal with in Chapter 6. Mr. Fraidin double-checked all my references to the source and prepared the Table of Cases.

My secretary, Mrs. Lillian Weitzler, made this book possible, as she generally makes it possible for me to function professionally; and Miss Gwendolyn Hatchette assisted with final typing chores.

Mrs. Meira G. Pimsleur prepared the index, expertly and promptly.

Dean Eugene V. Rostow, of the Yale Law School, made all other assistance possible. His capacity for marshaling the resources of the School in behalf of his faculty is a marvel and a blessing.

Some aspects of the thesis of this book have found expression over the past five years in notes and articles, signed and unsigned, that I have published in *The New Republic.* In a few instances I have borrowed my earlier phrasing, with the kind permission of the editor and publisher, Mr. Gilbert A. Harrison. Portions of Chapter 4 appeared, in an earlier version, in the November 1961 issue of the *Harvard Law Review* and are incorporated here by permission of the editors of that publication.

Finally, I am grateful to the editorial staff of my publisher for many helpful suggestions.

A.M.B.

New Haven, Connecticut
October 1962

Contents

"Whoever attentively considers the different departments of power must perceive, that, in a government in which they are separated from each other, the judiciary, from the nature of its functions, will always be the least dangerous to the political rights of the Constitution; because it will be least in a capacity to annoy or injure them. The Executive not only dispenses the honors, but holds the sword of the community. The legislature not only commands the purse, but prescribes the rules by which the duties and rights of every citizen are to be regulated. The judiciary, on the contrary, has no influence over either the sword or the purse; no direction either of the strength or of the wealth of the society; and can take no active resolution whatever. It may truly be said to have neither FORCE nor WILL, but merely judgment; and must ultimately depend upon the aid of the executive arm even for the efficacy of its judgments."

ALEXANDER HAMILTON,
in the 78th FEDERALIST,
"The Judges as Guardians
of the Constitution."

THE LEAST
DANGEROUS BRANCH

*The Supreme Court
at the Bar of Politics*

CHAPTER 1

Establishment and General Justification of Judicial Review

The least dangerous branch of the American government is the most extraordinarily powerful court of law the world has ever known. The power which distinguishes the Supreme Court of the United States is that of constitutional review of actions of the other branches of government, federal and state. Curiously enough, this power of judicial review, as it is called, does not derive from any explicit constitutional command. The authority to determine the meaning and application of a written constitution is nowhere defined or even mentioned in the document itself. This is not to say that the power of judicial review cannot be placed in the Constitution; merely that it cannot be found there.

Marbury v. *Madison*

Congress was created very nearly full blown by the Constitution itself. The vast possibilities of the presidency were relatively easy to perceive and soon, inevitably, materialized. But the institution of the judiciary needed to be summoned up out of the constitutional vapors, shaped, and maintained; and the Great Chief Justice, John Marshall—not singlehanded, but first and foremost— was there to do it and did. If any social process can be said to have been "done" at a given time and by a given act, it is Marshall's achievement. The time was 1803; the act was the decision in the case of *Marbury* v. *Madison*.

William Marbury's law suit against Secretary of State Madison

1

was an incident in the peaceful but deep-cutting revolution signaled by Jefferson's accession to the presidency. The decision was both a reaction and an accommodation to the revolution. It was, indeed, as Professor Robert G. McCloskey has written, "a masterwork of indirection, a brilliant example of Marshall's capacity to sidestep danger while seeming to court it, to advance in one direction while his opponents are looking in another." The Court was "in the delightful position . . . of rejecting and assuming power in a single breath"; although Marshall's opinion "is justly celebrated," "not the least of its virtues is the fact that it is somewhat beside the point."[1]

The opinion is very vulnerable. "It will not bear scrutiny," said the late Judge Learned Hand. And it has in fact ill borne it at the hands of Thomas Reed Powell and others. Marshall was one of the most remarkable figures in an astonishing generation of statesmen. He was not given, he at once created and seized, what Holmes called "perhaps the greatest place that ever was filled by a judge." In his superb brief *Life,* James Bradley Thayer made the just estimate that in constitutional law, Marshall was "preëminent—first, with no one second." But Thayer remarked also that the very common favorable view of the reasoning in *Marbury* v. *Madison* "is partly referable to the fallacy which Wordsworth once remarked upon when a friend mentioned 'The Happy Warrior' as being the greatest of his poems. 'No,' said the poet, 'you are mistaken; your judgment is affected by your moral approval of the lines.' "[2] It is necessary to analyze the reasoning and to abandon it where it fails us, however hallowed by age and incantation. For to rest the edifice on the foundation Marshall supplied is ultimately to weaken it, as opponents of the function of judicial review know well. There are sounder justifications of judicial review. And there is yet another purpose to be served by a hard analysis of the decision. Not only are the props it provides weak, and hence dangerous; they also support a structure that is not quite the one we see today. Marshall's proofs are not only frail, they are too strong; they prove too much. *Marbury* v. *Madison* in essence begs the question. What is more, it begs the wrong question.

William Marbury and some others sued Secretary Madison for delivery of their commissions as justices of the peace for the County of Washington in the District of Columbia, an office to which they had been appointed in the last moments of the administration of President John Adams. Marshall held that Marbury and the others were entitled to their commissions, but that the Supreme Court was without power to order Madison to deliver, because the section of the Judiciary Act of 1789 that purported to authorize the Court to act in such a case as this was itself unconstitutional. Thus did Marshall assume for his Court what is nowhere made explicit in the Constitution—the ultimate power to apply the Constitution, acts of Congress to the contrary notwithstanding.

"The question," Marshall's opinion begins, "whether an act repugnant to the Constitution, can become the law of the land, is a question deeply interesting to the United States; but, happily, not of an intricacy proportioned to its interest." Marshall's confidence that he could traverse the path ahead with ease is understandable, since he had already begged the question-in-chief, which was not whether an act repugnant to the Constitution could stand, but who should be empowered to decide that the act is repugnant. Marshall then posited the limited nature of the government established by the Constitution. It follows—and one may grant to Marshall that it follows as "a proposition too plain to be contested"—that the Constitution is a paramount law, and that ordinary legislative acts must conform to it. For Marshall it follows, further, that a legislative act contrary to the Constitution is not law and need not be given effect in court; else "written constitutions are absurd attempts, on the part of the people, to limit a power in its own nature illimitable." If two laws conflict, a court must obey the superior one. But Marshall knew (and, indeed, it was true in this very case) that a statute's repugnancy to the Constitution is in most instances not self-evident; it is, rather, an issue of policy that someone must decide. The problem is who: the courts, the legislature itself, the President, perhaps juries for purposes of criminal trials, or ultimately and finally the people through the electoral process?

This is the real question. Marshall addressed himself to it only partially and slightly. To leave the decision with the legislature, he said, is to allow those whose power is supposed to be limited themselves to set the limits—an absurd invitation to consistent abuse. Perhaps so, but the Constitution does not limit the power of the legislature alone. It limits that of the courts as well, and it may be equally absurd, therefore, to allow courts to set the limits. It is, indeed, more absurd, because courts are not subject to electoral control. (It may be argued that to leave the matter to the legislature is to leave it ultimately to the people at the polls. In this view the people as the principal would set the limits of the power that they have delegated to their agent.)

The case can be constructed where the conflict between a statute and the Constitution is self-evident in accordance with Marshall's general assumption. Even so, Marshall offers no real reason that the Court should have the power to nullify the statute. The function in such a case could as well be confided to the President, or ultimately to the electorate. Other controls over the legislature, which may be deemed equally important, are so confided. Courts do not pass on the validity of statutes by inquiring into election returns or into the qualifications of legislators. They will entertain no suggestion that a statute whose authenticity is attested by the signatures of the Speaker of the House and the President of the Senate, and which is approved by the President, may be at variance with the bill actually passed by both Houses.[3] Marshall himself, in *Fletcher* v. *Peck*,[4] the Yazoo Frauds case, declined to inquire into the "motives" of a legislature, having been invited to do so in order to upset a statute whose passage had been procured by fraud. Why must courts control self-corruption through power, a condition difficult of certain diagnosis, when they rely on other agencies to control corruption by money or like inducements, which is no less dangerous and can be objectively established?

So far Marshall's argument proceeded on the basis of a single textual reliance: namely, the fact itself of a written Constitution. But Marshall did go on to some more specific textual references. His first was to Article III of the Constitution, which establishes the judiciary and reads in relevant part as follows:

SECTION 1. The judicial Power of the United States, shall be vested in one supreme Court, and in such inferior Courts as the Congress may from time to time ordain and establish. The Judges, both of the supreme and inferior Courts, shall hold their Offices during good Behavior, and shall, at stated Times, receive for their Services a Compensation which shall not be diminished during their Continuance in Office.

SECTION 2. The judicial Power shall extend to all Cases, in Law and Equity, arising under this Constitution, the Laws of the United States, and Treaties made, or which shall be made, under their Authority;—to all Cases affecting Ambassadors, or other public Ministers and Consuls; —to all Cases of admiralty and maritime Jurisdiction;—to Controversies to which the United States shall be a Party;—to Controversies between two or more States;—between a State and Citizens of another State;—between Citizens of different States;—between Citizens of the same State claiming Lands under Grants of different States, and between a State, or the Citizens thereof, and foreign States, Citizens or Subjects.

In all Cases affecting Ambassadors, other public Ministers and Consuls, and those in which a State shall be a Party, the supreme Court shall have original Jurisdiction. In all the other Cases before mentioned, the supreme Court shall have appellate Jurisdiction, both as to Law and Fact, with such Exceptions, and under such Regulations as the Congress shall make.

Could it be, Marshall asked, that those who granted the judicial power and extended it to all cases arising under the Constitution, laws, and treaties meant that cases arising under the Constitution should be decided without examination and application of the document itself? This was for Marshall "too extravagant to be maintained." Note well, however, that what the Constitution extends to cases arising under it is "the judicial Power." Whether this power reaches as far as Marshall wanted it to go—namely, to reviewing acts of the legislature—is the question to be decided. What are the nature and extent of the function of the Court—the judicial power? Is the Court empowered, when it decides a case, to declare that a duly enacted statute violates the Constitution, and to invalidate the statute? Article III does not purport to describe the function of the Court; it subsumes whatever questions may exist as to that in the phrase "the judicial Power." It does not purport to tell the Court how to decide cases; it only specifies which kinds of case the Court shall have jurisdiction to deal with at all. Thus, in giving jurisdiction in cases "arising under . . . the Laws" or "under . . . Treaties," the clause is not read as prescribing the process of decision to be followed. The process varies. In cases "under . . . the Laws" courts often leave determination of issues of fact and even issues that may be thought to be "of law" to administrative agencies. And under both "the Laws . . . and Treaties," much of the decision concerning meaning and applicability may be received ready-made from the Congress and the President. In some cases of all three descriptions, judicial decision may be withheld altogether—and it is for this reason that it will not do to place reliance on the word "all" in the phrase "all cases . . . arising. . . ." To the extent that the Constitution speaks to such matters, it does so in the tightly packed phrase "judicial Power."

Nevertheless, if it were impossible to conceive a case "arising under the Constitution" which would not require the Court to pass on the constitutionality of congressional legislation, then the analysis of the text of Article III made above might be found unsatisfactory, for it would render this clause quite senseless. But there are such cases which may call into question the constitutional validity of judicial, administrative, or military actions without attacking legislative or even presidential acts as well, or which call upon the Court, under appropriate statutory authorization, to apply the Constitution to acts of the states. Any reading but his own was for Marshall "too extravagant to be maintained." His own, although out of line with the general scheme of Article III, may be possible; but it is optional. This is the strongest bit of textual evidence in support of Marshall's view, but it is merely a hint. And nothing more explicit will be found.

Marshall then listed one or two of the limitations imposed by the Constitution upon legislative power and asked whether no one should enforce them. This amounts to no more than a repetition of his previous main argument, based on the very fact of limited government established by a written Constitution. He then quoted the clause (significantly constituting Section 3 of Article III, the Judiciary Article) which provides that no person "shall be convicted of Treason unless on the Testimony of two Witnesses to the same overt Act, or on Confession in open Court." If the legislature were to change that rule, he asked, and declare that one witness or a confession out of court was sufficient for conviction, would the courts be required to enforce such a statute? In one aspect, this is but another restatement of the argument proceeding from the existence of limitations embodied in the written Constitution. But even if it were admitted that a court, in the treason case Marshall put, should apply the Constitution and not the contrary statute, this may mean only that it is the judiciary's duty to enforce the Constitution within its own sphere, when the Constitution addresses itself with fair specificity to the judiciary branch itself. The same might be true as well of other clauses prescribing procedures to be followed upon a trial in court and also of the provisions of Article III setting forth the jurisdiction of the courts. Such a provision was in question in *Marbury* v. *Madison* itself, and perhaps the result there might be supported in this fashion. The upshot would be that each branch of the government would construe the Constitution for itself as concerns its own functions, and that this construction would be final, not subject to revision by any of the other branches. Marshall himself, at this point in his argument, drew only the following conclusion: "From these, and many other selections [from the Constitution] which might be made, it is apparent that the Framers of the Constitution contemplated that instrument as a rule for the government of courts, as well as of the legislature." And of the legislature as well as of courts, so that when the Constitution addresses itself to the legislature, or to the President, or to the states, for that matter, each may be the final arbiter of the meaning of the constitutional commands addressed to it. The distinction would lie between such provisions as those empowering Congress "to regulate Commerce" or "to coin Money," on the one hand, and, on the other, such commands as that of the Sixth Amendment that, "In all criminal prosecutions, the accused shall enjoy the right to a speedy and public trial, by an impartial jury. . . ." To find such an arrangement textually permissible is not, of course, to advocate it or to vouch for its workability. I should make plain my disavowal of an analysis by Professor William Winslow Crosskey, which is in some respects similar but which is also quite different, having regard to its context and supports and to the purposes it is made to serve.[5]

But, Marshall continued, the judges, under Article VI of the Constitution, are "bound by Oath or Affirmation, to support this Constitution." Would it not be immoral to impose this oath upon them while at the same time expecting them, in upholding laws they deem repugnant to the Constitution, to violate what they are sworn to support? This same oath, however, is also required of "Senators and Representatives. . . . Members of the several State Legislatures, and all executive and judicial Officers, both of the United States and of the several States. . . ." Far from supporting Marshall, the oath is perhaps the strongest textual argument against him. For it would seem to obligate each of these officers, in the performance of his own function, to support the Constitution. On one reading, the consequence might be utter chaos—everyone at every juncture interprets and applies the Constitution for himself. Or, as we have seen, it may be deduced that everyone is to construe the Constitution with finality insofar as it addresses itself to the performance of his own peculiar function. Surely the language lends itself more readily to this interpretation than to Marshall's apparent conclusion, that everyone's oath to support the Constitution is qualified by the judiciary's oath to do the same, and that every official of government is sworn to support the Constitution as the judges, in pursuance of the same oath, have construed it, rather than as his own conscience may dictate.

Only in the end, and then very lightly, does Marshall come to rest on the Supremacy Clause of Article VI, which in later times has seemed to many the most persuasive textual support.[6] The Supremacy Clause is as follows:

This Constitution and the Laws of the United States which shall be made in Pursuance thereof; and all Treaties made, or which shall be made, under the Authority of the United States, shall be the supreme Law of the Land; and the Judges in every State shall be bound thereby, any Thing in the Constitution or Laws of any State to the Contrary notwithstanding.

"It is also not entirely unworthy of observation," Marshall wrote —and this was all he had to say on the point—that in declaring what is to be the supreme law of the land, this clause mentions the Constitution first and then not the laws of the United States generally but only those which shall be made in pursuance of the Constitution. Marshall left it at that, and what is to be concluded from this remark? First, it must be noted that nothing here is addressed to federal courts. Any command to them will have to be inferred, if there is to be one at all. Only as a forensic amusement can the phrase "Judges in every State" be taken to include federal judges, on the ground that some of them sit in the states. After all, the Supreme Court does not. The clause speaks to the constituent states of the federation and tells them that federal law will supersede any contrary state law. Further, it goes over the heads of the state governments and speaks to state judges directly, telling them that it will be their duty to enforce the supreme federal law above any contrary state law. State judges need enforce, however, only such federal law as is made in pursuance of the Constitution. Conceivably the reference here might be to more than just the mechanical provisions that describe how a federal law is to be enacted—by the concurrence of both Houses and with the signature of the President. Conceivably state judges were to be authorized to measure federal law against the federal Constitution and uphold it or strike it down in accordance with their understanding of the relevant constitutional provision. But such an arrangement, standing alone, would have been extraordinary, and it would have been self-destructive.

It is perfectly evident that the purpose of the clause is to make federal authority supreme over state. It is also certain that if state judges were to have final power to strike down federal statutes, the opposite effect would have been achieved, even though the authority of the state judges was drawn from the federal Constitution. The result is possible on the language, and there have been those who have contended for it precisely because it is destructive. The argument, known as interposition, is grounded in the oath provision discussed above as well as in the Supremacy Clause. And it is easily met. There is no call thus to upend the plain purpose of the clause. State judges must apply supreme federal law, statutory and constitutional, and must do it faithfully on their oaths. So much is unavoidable. But it fully meets all else that is compelling in the language of the clause simply to conclude that the proviso that only those federal statutes are to be supreme which are made in pursuance of the Constitution means that the statutes must carry the outer indicia of validity lent them by enactment in accordance with the constitutional forms. If so enacted, a federal statute is constitutional. That is to be taken as a given fact by state courts, on the authority and responsibility of the federal Congress and President who enacted the statute. No obstacle is thus raised to the exercise of the state judicial function. A court can just as well uphold the Constitution, thus performing its duty under the Supremacy Clause, by taking the meaning of the Constitution to have been settled by another authority and going on from there as by going to the trouble of parsing out the meaning of the document for itself.

Different considerations, however, govern the function (with which the state courts are also charged under the Supremacy Clause) of applying, not the federal Constitution against other federal laws, but federal statute and treaty law itself. Here, when a question of meaning arises, there will be no ready answer emanating from the fact of enactment or ratification. If a federal statute is said to conflict with the Constitution, and the question thus raised is, what is the meaning of the Constitution, that question can be said to have been answered by Congress and the President in favor of the validity of the statute which they enacted. But if the question is, what is the meaning of a statute or of a treaty as applied to a given situation, then there can be no similar, complete prior answer. Partial solution of, or guides to, the problem of interpretation and applicability may exist ready-made. But, barring the intervention of some other agency, the state court will in some measure have to construe the statute or the treaty for itself. The Supremacy Clause does not tell it to do otherwise, and it refers it nowhere else. Yet there is an obvious interest, if for no other reason than uniformity of application, in having federal law construed as well as declared by an institution of the general government. No single state should be empowered to lay down a uniform interpretation; only the federal government represents and can bind all. And a court is, in the very nature of things, the only agency that can be used to perform, in behalf of the general government, the ultimate task of lending uniformity and national authority to the construction and application of federal law in specific cases.

The option was open to set up a lower federal court system and to withdraw into it cases arising in the state courts which involved issues of the construction of federal law; or perhaps to withdraw into it only those issues themselves and remand the cases back to the state system once the issues had been decided. Another option was to set up in one Supreme Court appellate jurisdiction over state courts, again for the purposes of such cases or such issues. Is there anything in the Supremacy Clause to prevent either solution? Its drift, if anything, is equally in favor of either, and certainly not against. Article III, in turn, is also open to either solution. And Congress has in fact adopted a bit of both, although the chief reliance in the early days was on the appellate jurisdiction of the Supreme Court.

So much is reasonably clear. But from this starting point, many modern commentators take the Supremacy Clause on a giant leap. It would be just as absurd and destructive, it is said, for state courts to be authorized to render final constructions of the federal Constitution, in cases of alleged conflict with a federal statute, as it would be for them to have the last word on the meaning of such a statute itself, or of a treaty; indeed, more absurd. State courts are subjected to the reviewing authority of federal courts in their construction of statutes and treaties. By the same token, they ought to be subjected to the reviewing authority of federal courts when they construe the Constitution. Moreover, it would be silly to empower state judges, as courts of first instance, to construe and apply the Constitution in passing on the validity of federal statutes without so empowering federal judges also, in cases coming directly to them. What sense is there in allowing federal judges to function as spokesmen of the Constitution in cases coming from state courts but not in cases originating in the federal system itself? It follows that the Supremacy Clause addresses itself specifically to state judges only, because as to them there might have been some doubt, whereas it was regarded as obvious that the federal Constitution would bind, and would be construed and applied by, federal judges.

But this is all quite circular. Why is the power to declare federal statutes unconstitutional conceded to state courts? In order to enable one to lodge it in the federal courts also, and for no other reason. We have seen the need for judicial authority to construe federal statutes and treaties, and the reasons for subjecting state courts to federal appellate jurisdiction when they do so. We have also seen, however, that there is no similar exigency dictating similar judicial authority and similar appellate jurisdiction when the validity of a federal statute under the Constitution is in question, because neither state nor federal courts need to decide that for themselves in the first instance; they can take it as settled for them by the federal legislature and President. The ends of uniformity and of the vindication of federal authority are served in this fashion, without recourse to any power in the federal judiciary to lay down the meaning of the Constitution.

"Thus," the opinion in *Marbury* v. *Madison* concludes, "the particular phraseology of the Constitution of the United States confirms and strengthens the principle supposed to be essential to all written constitutions, that a law repugnant to the constitution is void," and that it is for the federal courts to declare it so. I have attempted to show that the principle must indeed be "supposed," and that the "phraseology of the Constitution" itself neither supports nor disavows it. I have suggested that it is of value to be aware that this is so, both for the sake of the security of the principle against attack and, as we shall see, for the sake of a true understanding of the nature and reach of the principle. Of course, the document must be read as a whole, and any particular phraseology is informed by the purpose of the whole. But I have tried to show that the purpose around which Marshall organized his argument does not necessarily emerge from the text.

Our discussion has centered on the claim actually staked out in *Marbury* v. *Madison*—that is, that a federal court has the power to strike down a duly enacted federal statute on the ground that it is repugnant to the Constitution. Of necessity, I have dealt also with the power, if any, of state judges to do the same. Marshall elsewhere established as well the separate, though of course closely connected, power of the federal courts to strike down state statutes and other actions for repugnancy to the federal Constitution. The bare text of Article III and of the Supremacy Clause is again equivocal. The Supremacy Clause, addressing itself to state judges alone, does put them on a different plane than state legislators and other officials. Yet it says nothing of federal judges, and hence it would not foreclose a system in which the sole reliance for the integrity and supremacy of the federal Constitution as against contravening state enactments would be on the conscientious performance of duty by state judges, subject to no other control. There is surely, however, a strong interest, to which we have alluded in connection with federal statute and treaty law, in the uniform construction and application of the Constitution as against inconsistent state law throughout the country. This is an interest fairly to be imputed to states which formed a federal union, and it is an interest that can be vindicated only by a federal institution. Congress can and in fact does from time to time perform this function, both as to statute and as to constitutional law; but, if for no other reason than that the instances in which performance of this function is necessary are extremely numerous, it is obviously sensible to lodge the function as well, and indeed chiefly, in the federal judiciary. This is not compelled by the language of the Constitution; it is implied from desirable ends that are attributed to the entire scheme. But most assuredly there is nothing in the language that forbids it. And Congress has so provided—consistently, from the first Judiciary Act of the first Congress onward—and it has done so unambiguously.

Judiciary acts have, from the beginning, also given the Supreme Court jurisdiction to review state court cases in which is drawn in question the validity of a treaty or statute of the United States, presumably under the federal Constitution. If that was a grant to the Supreme Court of final authority to construe the Constitution as against acts of Congress, why, then, well and good. Nothing in the text prevents such a gesture of congressional abnegation, although in that event, what Congress can give away, Congress can, at least in theory, take back. But it is question-begging so to understand this provision of the first Judiciary Act. Reading no presuppositions into it, one may as easily conclude that the Supreme Court was meant only to enforce against state courts a rule that duly enacted federal statutes are constitutional by virtue of their due enactment. There is no similar ambiguity, however, in the first Judiciary Act's grant to the Supreme Court of jurisdiction to review cases which draw in question the validity of a statute of, or an authority exercised under, any state, on the ground of its being repugnant to the Constitution, treaties, or laws of the United States. This provision would be senseless unless it was intended to authorize the Court, in these circumstances, to construe and apply the federal Constitution as well as federal statute and treaty law. Only thus could this provision serve the interest of uniformity and of the superiority of federal power—and what other purpose could it have? As we have seen, the Supremacy Clause itself does not compel, although it permits and no doubt invites, this arrangement. This being so, Congress could change it all tomorrow. And perhaps it could, if textual considerations were all that governed the matter, just as it could change the course of the Mississippi River, if all we had to indicate the location of its bed were some general description by a traveler of a body of water traversing the middle of the country from north to south.

The Moral Approval of the Lines:[7] *History*

The analogy to the Mississippi may be a trifle fetched; yet, I am prepared to defend it as we come to examine foundations for the doctrine of judicial review other than textual exegesis. *Marbury* v. *Madison,* relating to the power to hold federal statutes unconstitutional, and *Martin* v. *Hunter's Lessee*[8] and *Cohens* v. *Virginia,*[9] which assumed the power of judicial review of state actions, were decided, respectively, in 1803, 1816, and 1821. They met with controversy, to be sure, which has also recurred sporadically since. But their doctrines have held sway for roughly a century and a half. So long have they been among the realities of our national existence. Settled expectations have formed around them. The life of a nation that now encompasses 185 million people spread over a continent and more depends upon them in a hundred different aspects of its organization and coherence. It is late for radical changes. Perhaps *Marbury* v. *Madison* is a historical accident attributable to the political configuration of the earliest years, to Marshall's political antecedents, and to the force and statesmanlike deviousness of his personality. It was a half century before the power to strike down an act of Congress was again exercised, and at that time, in the *Dred Scott Case* of exceedingly bad odor, it was asserted in a fashion that would have assured its evanescence rather than permanence. But *Marbury* v. *Madison* did occur, and if it was an accident, it was not the first to play an important role in the permanent shaping of a government. One of the reasons that the "accident" has endured is that Marshall's own view of the scope of legislative power had grandeur. He undertook to expound the Constitution with finality, but it was Marshall himself who enjoined his posterity never to forget "that it is a *constitution* we are expounding," a living charter, embodying implied as well as expressed powers, "adapted to the various *crises* of human affairs," open to change, capable of growth. This was the Marshall of *McCulloch* v. *Maryland*,[10] decided in 1819. If assumption of the power was accident, the vision and wisdom with which it was exercised in the early years cannot have been. And if it was accident, it had nevertheless been somewhat arranged; if *Marbury* v. *Madison* was *ex tempore*, it had nonetheless been well prepared. For, although the Framers of the Constitution had failed to be explicit about the function of judicial review, the evidence of their deliberations demonstrates that they foresaw—indeed, invited—it.

This has frequently been denied, whenever the impulse to radical change has come upon people. And *Marbury* v. *Madison* has been attacked, not merely for its apparent frailties, but as an act of "usurpation." Yet, as Professor Felix Frankfurter wrote in 1924: "Lack of historical scholarship, combined with fierce prepossessions, can alone account for the persistence of this talk. One would suppose that, at least, after the publication of Beard, *The Supreme Court and the Constitution*, there would be an end to this empty controversy."[11] Beard wrote in 1912; Farrand published *The Records of the Federal Convention* in 1911 and *The Framing of the Constitution* in 1913. There have been some further accessions to our knowledge since, to be sure, and the books of history are never closed. Nor are historical hypotheses provable with mathematical precision. But it is as clear as such matters can be that the Framers of the Constitution specifically, if tacitly, expected that the federal courts would assume a power—of whatever exact dimensions —to pass on the constitutionality of actions of the Congress and the President, as well as of the several states. Moreover, not even a colorable showing of decisive historical evidence to the contrary can be made. Nor can it be maintained that the language of the Constitution is compellingly the other way. At worst it may be said that the intentions of the Framers cannot be ascertained with finality; that there were some who thought this and some that, and that it will never be entirely clear just exactly where the collective judgment—which alone is decisive—came to rest. In any debate over the force of the tradition, such is the most that can be said against the claims of judicial review.

Continuity with the past, said Holmes, is not a duty; it is merely a necessity. But Holmes also told us that it is "revolting to have no better reason for a rule of law than that so it was laid down in the time of Henry IV. It is still more revolting if the grounds upon which it was laid down have vanished long since, and the rule simply persists from blind imitation of the past."[12] Judicial review is a present instrument of government. It represents a choice that men have made, and ultimately we must justify it as a choice in our own time. What are the elements of choice?

The Counter-Majoritarian Difficulty

The root difficulty is that judicial review is a counter-majoritarian force in our system. There are various ways of sliding over this ineluctable reality. Marshall did so when he spoke of enforcing, in behalf of "the people," the limits that they have ordained for the institutions of a limited government. And it has been done ever since in much the same fashion by all too many commentators. Marshall himself followed Hamilton, who in the 78th *Federalist* denied that judicial review implied a superiority of the judicial over the legislative power—denied, in other words, that judicial review constituted control by an unrepresentative minority of an elected majority. "It only supposes," Hamilton went on, "that the power of the people is superior to both; and that where the will of the legislature, declared in its statutes, stands in opposition to that of the people, declared in the Constitution, the judges ought to be governed by the latter rather than the former." But the word "people" so used is an abstraction. Not necessarily a meaningless or a pernicious one by any means; always charged with emotion, but nonrepresentational—an abstraction obscuring the reality that when the Supreme Court declares unconstitutional a legislative act or the action of an elected executive, it thwarts the will of representatives of the actual people of the here and now; it exercises control, not in behalf of the prevailing majority, but against it. That, without mystic overtones, is what actually happens. It is an altogether different kettle of fish, and it is the reason the charge can be made that judicial review is undemocratic.

Most assuredly, no democracy operates by taking continuous nose counts on the broad range of daily governmental activities. Representative democracies—that is to say, all working democracies—function by electing certain men for certain periods of time, then passing judgment periodically on their conduct of public office. It is a matter of a laying on of hands, followed in time by a process of holding to account—all through the exercise of the franchise. The elected officials, however, are expected to delegate some of their tasks to men of their own appointment, who are not directly accountable at the polls. The whole operates under public scrutiny and criticism—but not at all times or in all parts. What we mean by democracy, therefore, is much more sophisticated and complex than the making of decisions in town meeting by a show of hands. It is true also that even decisions that have been submitted to the electoral process in some fashion are not continually resubmitted, and they are certainly not continually unmade. Once run through the process, once rendered by "the people" (using the term now in its mystic sense, because the reference is to the people in the past), myriad decisions remain to govern the present and the future despite what may well be fluctuating majorities against them at any given time. A high value is put on stability, and that is also a counter-majoritarian factor. Nevertheless, although democracy does not mean constant reconsideration of decisions once made, it does mean that a representative majority has the power to accomplish a reversal. This power is of the essence, and no less so because it is often merely held in reserve.

I am aware that this timid assault on the complexities of the American democratic system has yet left us with a highly simplistic statement, and I shall briefly rehearse some of the reasons. But nothing in the further complexities and perplexities of the system, which modern political science has explored with admirable and ingenious industry, and some of which it has tended to multiply with a fertility that passes the mere zeal of the discoverer—nothing in these complexities can alter the essential reality that judicial review is a deviant institution in the American democracy.

It is true, of course, that the process of reflecting the will of a popular majority in the legislature is deflected by various inequalities of representation and by all sorts of institutional habits and characteristics, which perhaps tend most often in favor of inertia. Yet it must be remembered that statutes are the product of the legislature and the executive acting in concert, and that the executive represents a very different constituency and thus tends to cure inequities of over- and underrepresentation. Reflecting a balance of forces in society for purposes of stable and effective government is more intricate and less certain than merely assuring each citizen his equal vote. Moreover, impurities and imperfections, if such they be, in one part of the system are no argument for total departure from the desired norm in another part. A much more important complicating factor—first adumbrated by Madison in the 10th *Federalist* and lately emphasized by Professor David B. Truman and others[13]—is the proliferation and power of what Madison foresaw as "faction," what Mr. Truman calls "groups," and what in popular parlance has always been deprecated as the "interests" or the "pressure groups."

No doubt groups operate forcefully on the electoral process, and no doubt they seek and gain access to and an effective share in the legislative and executive decisional process. Perhaps they constitute also, in some measure, an impurity or imperfection. But no one has claimed that they have been able to capture the governmental process except by combining in some fashion, and thus capturing or constituting (are not the two verbs synonymous?) a majority. They often tend themselves to be majoritarian in composition and to be subject to broader majoritarian influences. And the price of what they sell or buy in the legislature is determined in the biennial or quadrennial electoral marketplace. It may be, as Professor Robert A. Dahl has written, that elections themselves, and the political competition that renders them meaningful, "do not make for government by majorities in any very significant way," for they do not establish a great many policy preferences.

However, "they are a crucial device for controlling leaders." And if the control is exercised by "groups of various types and sizes, all seeking in various ways to advance their goals," so that we have "minorities rule" rather than majority rule, it remains true nevertheless that only those minorities rule which can command the votes of a majority of individuals in the legislature who can command the votes of a majority of individuals in the electorate. In one fashion or another, both in the legislative process and at elections, the minorities must coalesce into a majority. Although, as Mr. Dahl says, "it is fashionable in some quarters to suggest that everything believed about democratic politics prior to World War I, and perhaps World War II, was nonsense," he makes no bones about his own belief that "the radical democrats who, unlike Madison, insist upon the decisive importance of the election process in the whole grand strategy of democracy are essentially correct."[14]

The insights of Professor Truman and other writers into the role that groups play in our society and our politics have a bearing on judicial review. They indicate that there are other means than the electoral process, though subordinate and subsidiary ones, of making institutions of government responsive to the needs and wishes of the governed. Hence one may infer that judicial review, although not responsible, may have ways of being responsive. But nothing can finally depreciate the central function that is assigned in democratic theory and practice to the electoral process; nor can it be denied that the policy-making power of representative institutions, born of the electoral process, is the distinguishing characteristic of the system. Judicial review works counter to this characteristic.

It therefore does not follow from the complex nature of a democratic system that, because admirals and generals and the members, say, of the Federal Reserve Board or of this or that administrative agency are not electorally responsible, judges who exercise the power of judicial review need not be responsible either, and in neither case is there a serious conflict with democratic theory.[15] For admirals and generals and the like are most often responsible to officials who are themselves elected and through whom the line runs directly to a majority. What is more significant, the policies they make are or should be interstitial or technical only and are reversible by legislative majorities. Thus, so long as there has been a meaningful delegation by the legislature to administrators, which is kept within proper bounds, the essential majority power is there, and it is felt to be there—a fact of great consequence. Nor will it do to liken judicial review to the general lawmaking function of judges. In the latter aspect, judges are indeed something like administrative officials, for their decisions are also reversible by any legislative majority—and not infrequently they are reversed. Judicial review, however, is the power to apply and construe the Constitution, in matters of the greatest moment, against the wishes of a legislative majority, which is, in turn, powerless to affect the judicial decision.

"For myself," said the late Judge Learned Hand,

it would be most irksome to be ruled by a bevy of Platonic Guardians, even if I knew how to choose them, which I assuredly do not. If they were in charge, I should miss the stimulus of living in a society where I have, at least theoretically, some part in the direction of public affairs. Of course I know how illusory would be the belief that my vote determined anything; but nevertheless when I go to the polls I have a satisfaction in the sense that we are all engaged in a common venture. If you retort that a sheep in the flock may feel something like it; I reply, following Saint Francis, "My brother, the Sheep."[16]

This suggests not only the democratic value that inheres in obtaining the broad judgment of a majority of the people in the community and thus tending to produce better decisions. Judge Hand, if anything, rather deprecated the notion that the decisions will be better, or are affected at all. Some might think that he deprecated it beyond what is either just or realistic when he said that the belief that his vote determined anything was illusory. Hardly altogether. But the strong emphasis is on the related idea that coherent, stable—and *morally supportable*—government is possible only on the basis of consent, and that the secret of consent is the sense of common venture fostered by institutions that reflect and represent us and that we can call to account.

It has been suggested[17] that the Congress, the President, the states, and the people (in the sense of current majorities) have from the beginning and in each generation acquiesced in, and thus consented to, the exercise of judicial review by the Supreme Court. In the first place, it is said that the Amending Clause of the Constitution has been employed to reverse the work of the Court only twice, perhaps three times; and it has never been used to take away or diminish the Court's power. But the Amending Clause itself incorporates an extreme minority veto. The argument then proceeds to draw on the first Judiciary Act, whose provisions regarding the jurisdiction of the federal courts have been continued in effect to this day. Yet we have seen that the Judiciary Act can be read as a grant of the power to declare federal statutes unconstitutional only on the basis of a previously and independently reached conclusion that such a power must exist. And even if the Judiciary Act did grant this power, as it surely granted the power to declare state actions unconstitutional, it amounted to an expression of the opinion of the first Congress that the Constitution implies judicial review. It is, in fact, extremely likely that the first Congress thought so. That is important; but it merely adds to the historical evidence on the point, which, as we have seen, is in any event quite strong. Future Congresses and future generations can only be said to have acquiesced in the belief of the first Congress that the Constitution implies this power. And they can be said to have become resigned to what follows, which is that the power can be taken away only by constitutional amendment. That is a very far cry from consent to the power on its merits, as a power freely continued by the decision or acquiescence of a majority in each generation. The argument advances not a step toward justification of the power on other than historical grounds.

A further, crucial difficulty must also be faced. Besides being a counter-majoritarian check on the legislature and the executive, judicial review may, in a larger sense, have a tendency over time seriously to weaken the democratic process. Judicial review expresses, of course, a form of distrust of the legislature. "The legislatures," wrote James Bradley Thayer at the turn of the century,

are growing accustomed to this distrust and more and more readily inclined to justify it, and to shed the considerations of constitutional restraints,—certainly as concerning the exact extent of these restrictions,—turning that subject over to the courts; and what is worse, they insensibly fall into a habit of assuming that whatever they could constitutionally do they may do,—as if honor and fair dealing and common honesty were not relevant to their inquiries. The people, all this while, become careless as to whom they send to the legislature; too often they cheerfully vote for men whom they would not trust with an important private affair, and when these unfit persons are found to pass foolish and bad laws, and the courts step in and disregard them, the people are glad that these few wiser gentlemen on the bench are so ready to protect them against their more immediate representatives. . . . [I]t should be remembered that the exercise of it [the power of judicial review], even when unavoidable, is always attended with a serious evil, namely, that the correction of legislative mistakes comes from the outside, and the people thus lose the political experience, and the moral education and stimulus that comes from fighting the question out in the ordinary way, and correcting their own errors. The tendency of a common and easy resort to this great function, now lamentably too common, is to dwarf the political capacity of the people, and to deaden its sense of moral responsibility. It is no light thing to do that.[18]

To this day, in how many hundreds of occasions does Congress enact a measure that it deems expedient, having essayed consideration of its constitutionality (that is to say, of its acceptability on principle), only to abandon the attempt in the declared confidence that the Court will correct errors of principle, if any? It may well be, as has been suggested,[19] that any lowering of the level of legislative performance is attributable to many factors other than judicial review. Yet there is no doubt that what Thayer observed remains observable. It seemed rather a puzzle, for example, to a scholar who recently compared British and American practices of legislative investigation. Professor Herman Finer wrote, with what might have seemed to Thayer charming ingenuousness:

Is it not a truly extraordinary phenomenon that in the United States, where Congress is not a sovereign body, but subordinate to a constitution, there appear to be less restraints upon the arbitrary behavior of members in their . . . rough handling of the civil rights of the citizen during investigations. . . ? Though Parliament is sovereign and can legally do anything it likes, its practices are kinder, more restrained, and less invasive of the rights of those who come under its investigative attention. The student is forced to pause and reflect upon this remarkable reversal of demeanor and status.[20]

Finally, another, though related, contention has been put forward. It is that judicial review runs so fundamentally counter to democratic theory that in a society which in all other respects rests on that theory, judicial review cannot ultimately be effective. We pay the price of a grave inner contradiction in the basic principle of our government, which is an inconvenience and a dangerous one; and in the end to no good purpose, for when the great test comes, judicial review will be unequal to it. The most arresting expression of this thought is in a famous passage from a speech of Judge Learned Hand, a passage, Dean Eugene V. Rostow has written, "of Browningesque passion and obscurity," voicing a "gloomy and apocalyptic view."[21] Absent the institution of judicial review, Judge Hand said:

I do not think that anyone can say what will be left of those [fundamental principles of equity and fair play which our constitutions enshrine]; I do not know whether they will serve only as counsels; but this much I think I do know—that a society so riven that the spirit of moderation is gone, no court *can* save; that a society where that spirit flourishes, no court *need* save; that in a society which evades its responsibility by thrusting upon the courts the nurture of that spirit, that spirit in the end will perish.[22]

Over a century before Judge Hand spoke, Judge Gibson of Pennsylvania, in his day perhaps the ablest opponent of the establishment of judicial review, wrote: "Once let public opinion be so corrupt as to sanction every misconstruction of the Constitution and abuse of power which the temptation of the moment may dictate, and the party which may happen to be predominant will laugh at the puny efforts of a dependent power to arrest it in its course."[23] And Thayer also believed that "under no system can the power of courts go far to save a people from ruin; our chief protection lies elsewhere."[24]

The Moral Approval of the Lines:[25] *Principle*

Such, in outline, are the chief doubts that must be met if the doctrine of judicial review is to be justified on principle. Of course, these doubts will apply with lesser or greater force to various forms of the exercise of the power. For the moment the discussion is at wholesale, and we are seeking a justification on principle, quite aside from supports in history and the continuity of practice. The search must be for a function which might (indeed, must) involve the making of policy, yet which differs from the legislative and executive functions; which is peculiarly suited to the capabilities of the courts; which will not likely be performed elsewhere if the courts do not assume it; which can be so exercised as to be acceptable in a society that generally shares Judge Hand's satisfaction in a "sense of common venture"; which will be effective when needed; and whose discharge by the courts will not lower the quality of the other departments' performance by denuding them of the dignity and burden of their own responsibility. It will not be possible fully to meet all that is said against judicial review. Such is not the way with questions of government. We can only fill the other side of the scales with countervailing judgments on the real needs and the actual workings of our society and, of course, with our own portions of faith and hope. Then we may estimate how far the needle has moved.

The point of departure is a truism; perhaps it even rises to the unassailability of a platitude. It is that many actions of government have two aspects: their immediate, necessarily intended, practical effects, and their perhaps unintended or unappreciated bearing on values we hold to have more general and permanent interest. It is a premise we deduce not merely from the fact of a written constitution but from the history of the race, and ultimately as a moral judgment of the good society, that government should serve not only what we conceive from time to time to be our immediate material needs but also certain enduring values. This in part is what is meant by government under law. But such values do not present themselves ready-made. They have a past always, to be sure, but they must be continually derived, enunciated, and seen in relevant application. And it remains to ask which institution of our government—if any single one in particular—should be the pronouncer and guardian of such values.

Men in all walks of public life are able occasionally to perceive this second aspect of public questions. Sometimes they are also able to base their decisions on it; that is one of the things we like to call acting on principle. Often they do not do so, however, particularly when they sit in legislative assemblies. There, when the pressure for immediate results is strong enough and emotions ride high enough, men will ordinarily prefer to act on expediency rather than take the long view. Possibly legislators—everything else being equal—are as capable as other men of following the path of principle, where the path is clear or at any rate discernible. Our system, however, like all secular systems, calls for the evolution of principle in novel circumstances, rather than only for its mechanical application. Not merely respect for the rule of established principles but the creative establishment and renewal of a coherent body of principled rules—that is what our legislatures have proven themselves ill equipped to give us.

Initially, great reliance for principled decision was placed in the Senators and the President, who have more extended terms of office and were meant to be elected only indirectly. Yet the Senate and the President were conceived of as less closely tied to, not as divorced from, electoral responsibility and the political marketplace. And so even then the need might have been felt for an institution which stands altogether aside from the current clash of interests, and which, insofar as is humanly possible, is concerned only with principle. We cannot know whether, as Thayer believed, our legislatures are what they are because we have judicial review, or whether we have judicial review and consider it necessary because legislatures are what they are. Yet it is arguable also that the partial separation of the legislative and judicial functions—and it is not meant to be absolute—is beneficial in any event, because it makes it possible for the desires of various groups and interests concerning immediate results to be heard clearly and unrestrainedly in one place. It may be thought fitting that somewhere in government, at some stage in the process of law-making, such felt needs should find unambiguous expression. Moreover, and more importantly, courts have certain capacities for dealing with matters of principle that legislatures and executives do not possess. Judges have, or should have, the leisure, the training, and the insulation to follow the ways of the scholar in pursuing the ends of government. This is crucial in sorting out the enduring values of a society, and it is not something that institutions can do well occasionally, while operating for the most part with a different set of gears. It calls for a habit of mind, and for undeviating institutional customs. Another advantage that courts have is that questions of principle never carry the same aspect for them as they did for the legislature or the executive. Statutes, after all, deal typically with abstract or dimly foreseen problems. The courts are concerned with the flesh and blood of an actual case. This tends to modify, perhaps to lengthen, everyone's view. It also provides an extremely salutary proving ground for all abstractions; it is conducive, in a phrase of Holmes, to thinking things, not words, and thus to the evolution of principle by a process that tests as it creates.

Their insulation and the marvelous mystery of time give courts the capacity to appeal to men's better natures, to call forth their aspirations, which may have been forgotten in the moment's hue and cry. This is what Justice Stone called the opportunity for "the sober second thought."[26] Hence it is that the courts, although they may somewhat dampen the people's and the legislatures' efforts to educate themselves, are also a great and highly effective educational institution. Judge Gibson, in the very opinion mentioned earlier (p. 23), highly critical as he was, took account of this. "In the business of government," he wrote, "a recurrence to first principles answers the end of an observation at sea with a view to correct the dead reckoning; and, for this purpose, a written constitution is an instrument of inestimable value. It is of inestimable value also, in rendering its principles familiar to the mass of the people. . . ."[27] The educational institution that both takes the observation to correct the dead reckoning and makes it known is the voice of the Constitution: the Supreme Court exercising judicial review. The Justices, in Dean Rostow's phrase, "are inevitably teachers in a vital national seminar."[28] No other branch of the American government is nearly so well equipped to conduct one. And such a seminar can do a great deal to keep our society from becoming so riven that no court will be able to save it. Of course, we have never quite been that society in which the spirit of moderation is so richly in flower that no court need save it.

Thus, as Professor Henry M. Hart, Jr., has written, and as surely most of the profession and of informed laity believe; for if not this, what and why?—thus the Court appears "predestined in the long run, not only by the thrilling tradition of Anglo-American law but also by the hard facts of its position in the structure of American institutions, to be a voice of reason, charged with the creative function of discerning afresh and of articulating and developing impersonal and durable principles. . . ."[29] This line of thought may perhaps blunt, if it does not meet, the force of all the arguments on the other side. No doubt full consistency with democratic theory has not been established. The heart of the democratic faith is government by the consent of the governed. The further premise is not incompatible that the good society not only will want to satisfy the immediate needs of the greatest number but also will strive to support and maintain enduring general values. I have followed the view that the elected institutions are ill fitted, or not so well fitted as the courts, to perform the latter task. This rests on the assumption that the people themselves, by direct action at the ballot box, are surely incapable of sustaining a working system of general values specifically applied. But that much we assume throughout, being a representative, deliberative democracy. Matters of expediency are not generally submitted to direct referendum. Nor should matters of principle, which require even more intensive deliberation, be so submitted. Reference of specific policies to the people for initial decision is, with few exceptions, the fallacy of the misplaced mystics, or the way of those who would use the forms of democracy to undemocratic ends. It is not the way in which working democracies live. But democracies do live by the idea, central to the process of gaining the consent of the governed, that the majority has the ultimate power to displace the decision-makers and to reject any part of their policy. With that idea, judicial review must achieve some measure of consonance.

Democratic government under law—the slogan pulls in two opposed directions, but that does not keep it from being applicable to an operative polity. If it carries the elements of explosion, it doesn't contain a critical mass of them. Yet if the critical mass is not to be reached, there must be an accommodation, a degree of concord between the diverging elements. Having been checked, should the people persist; having been educated, should the people insist, must they not win over every fundamental principle save one—which is the principle that they must win? Are we sufficiently certain of the permanent validity of any other principle to be ready to impose it against a consistent and determined majority, and could we do so for long? Have not the people the right of peaceable revolution, as assuredly, over time, they possess the capacity for a bloody one?

The premise of democracy is egalitarian, and, as Professor Herbert J. Muller has written, every bright sophomore knows how to punch holes in it. Yet, as Mr. Muller goes on to say, there is "no universal standard of superiority," there are no sure scales in which to weigh all the relevant virtues and capacities of men, and many a little man may rightly claim to be a better citizen than the expert or the genius. Moreover, and most significantly, "all men are in fact equal in respect of their common structure and their common destiny." Hence, to repeat the insight of Judge Hand, government must be their common venture. Who will think it moral ultimately to direct the lives of men against the will of the greater number of them? Or wise? "Man's historical experience should sober the revolutionaries who know the certain solution to our problems, and sober as well the traditionalists whose solution is a return to the ancient faiths, which have always failed in the past."[30]

To bring judicial review into concord with such presuppositions requires a closer analysis of the actual operation of the process in various circumstances. The preliminary suggestions may be advanced that the rule of principle imposed by the Court is seldom rigid, that the Court has ways of persuading before it attempts to coerce, and that, over time, sustained opinion running counter to the Court's constitutional law can achieve its nullification, directly or by desuetude. It may further be that if the process is properly carried out, an aspect of the current—not only the timeless, mystic—popular will finds expression in constitutional adjudication. The result may be a tolerable accommodation with the theory and practice of democracy.

The Mystic Function

This inquiry into a general justification of judicial review cannot end without taking account of a most suggestive and perceptive argument recently advanced by Professor Charles L. Black, Jr.[31] It begins by emphasizing that the Court performs not only a checking function but also a legitimating one, as Mr. Black well calls it. Judicial review means not only that the Court may strike down a legislative action as unconstitutional but also that it may validate it as within constitutionally granted powers and as not violating constitutional limitations. Mr. Black contends, further, that the legitimating function would be impossible of performance if the checking function did not exist as well: what is the good of a declaration of validity from an institution which is by hypothesis required to validate everything that is brought before it? This is plainly so, though it is oddly stated. The picture is accurate, but it is stood on its head. The truth is that the legitimating function is an inescapable, even if unintended, by-product of the checking power. But what follows? What is the nature of this legitimating function, and what the need for it?

With a relish one can readily share, Mr. Black cites the story of the French intellectual who, upon arrival in New York harbor, exclaims: "It is wonderful to breathe the sweet air of legitimacy!" He contends essentially that what filled the Frenchman's lungs, what smelled to him so different from the succession of short-lived empires and republics endemic to his homeland, was the sweet odor of the Supreme Court of the United States. But I think it much simpler and nearer the reality of both the American and the French experience to begin with the proposition that legitimacy comes to a regime that is felt to be good and to have proven itself as such to generations past as well as in the present. Such a government must be principled as well as responsible; but it must be felt to be the one without having ceased to be the other, and unless it is responsible it cannot in fact be stable, and is not in my view morally supportable. Quite possibly, there have been governments that were electorally responsible and yet failed to attain stability.

But that is not to say that they would have attained it by rendering themselves less responsible—that is, by divorcing the keepers
of their principles from the electoral process. Legitimacy, being
the stability of a good government over time, is the fruit of consent
to specific actions or to the authority to act; the consent to the
exercise of authority, whether or not approved in each instance,
of as unified a population as possible, but most importantly, of a
present majority.

Very probably, the stability of the American Republic is due in
large part, as Professor Louis Hartz has eloquently argued, to the
remarkable Lockeian consensus of a society that has never known
a feudal regime; to a "moral unity" that was seriously broken only
once, over the extension of slavery. This unity makes possible a
society that accepts its principles from on high, without fighting
about them. But the Lockeian consensus is also a limitation on the
sort of principles that will be accepted. It is putting the cart before
the horse to attribute the American sense of legitimacy to the
institution of judicial review. The latter is more nearly the fruit
of the former, although the "moral unity" must be made manifest,
it must be renewed and sharpened and brought to bear—and this
is an office that judicial review can discharge.[32]

No doubt it is in the interest of the majority to obtain the
acquiescence of the minority as often and in as great a degree as
possible. And no doubt the Court can help bring about acquiescence by assuring those who have lost a political fight that merely
momentary interest, not fundamental principle, was in play. Yet
is it reasonable to assume that the majority would wish to see itself
checked from time to time just to have an institution which, when
it chooses to go along with the majority's will, is capable of helping
to assuage the defeated minority? That is too much of an indirection. The checking power must find its own justification, particularly in a system which, in a number of important ways, (e.g., the
Senate's reflection of the federal structure, practices of legislative
apportionment), offers prodigious political safeguards to the
minority.

Thus the legitimating function of judicial review cannot be
accepted as an independent justification for it. Yet it exists. Not
only is the Supreme Court capable of generating consent for hotly

controverted legislative or executive measures; it has the subtler power of adding a certain impetus to measures that the majority enacts rather tentatively. There are times when the majority might, because of strong minority feelings, be inclined in the end to deny itself, but when it comes to embrace a measure more firmly, and the minority comes to accept it, because the Court—intending perhaps no such consequence—has declared it consistent with constitutional principle. This tendency touches on Thayer's anxiety that judicial review will "dwarf the political capacity of the people" and "deaden its sense of moral responsibility." We shall return to it as a consideration that should cause the Court to stay its hand from time to time.

But the Supreme Court as a legitimating force in society also casts a less palpable yet larger spell. With us the symbol of nationhood, of continuity, of unity and common purpose, is, of course, the Constitution, without particular reference to what exactly it means in this or that application. The utility of such a symbol is a commonplace. Britain—the United Kingdom, and perhaps even the Commonwealth—is the most potent historical demonstration of the efficaciousness of a symbol, made concrete in the person of the Crown. The President in our system serves the function somewhat, but only very marginally, because the personification of unity must be above the political battle, and no President can fulfill his office while remaining above the battle. The effective Presidents have of necessity been men of power, and so it has in large part been left to the Supreme Court to concretize the symbol of the Constitution. Keeping in mind that this is offered as an observation, not as justification, it is surely true that the Court has been able to play the role partly—but only partly—by virtue of its power of judicial review.

The Court is seen as a continuum. It is never, like other institutions, renewed at a single stroke. No one or two changes on the Court, not even if they include the advent of a new Chief Justice, are apt to be as immediately momentous as a turnover in the presidency. To the extent that they are instruments of decisive change, Justices are time bombs, not warheads that explode on impact. There are exceptions, to be sure. In 1870, President Grant made two appointments that promptly resulted in the reversal of a quite crucial recent decision concerning the monetary powers of the federal government.[33] And it may seem that strong new doctrine became ascendant soon after the first of President Roosevelt's appointees, Mr. Justice Black, came on the Bench in 1937. But on the whole, the movements of the Court are not sudden and not suddenly affected by new appointments. Continuity is a chief concern of the Court, as it is the main reason for the Court's place in the hearts of its countrymen.

No doubt, the Court's symbolic—or, if you will, mystic—function would not have been possible, would not have reached the stage at which we now see it, if the Court did not exercise the power of judicial review. It could scarcely personify the Constitution unless it had the authority finally to speak of it. But as the symbol manifests itself today, it seems not always to depend on judicial review. It seems at times to have as much to do with the life tenure of the Court's members and with the fact of the long government service of some of them, not only on the Court; in short, with the total impression of continuity personified. Here the human chain goes back unbroken in a small, intimate group to the earliest beginnings. Take two recent retirements. Mr. Justice Minton, who left in October 1956, was a fire-eating New Deal Senator, and when he retired from the Court men no doubt remembered his stance in the 'thirties and thought, perhaps a little self-deprecatingly, of the emotions it had aroused. Mr. Justice Reed, who retired early in 1957, had, some twenty years earlier, when he was Solicitor General, argued a number of celebrated New Deal cases. His was the second of President Franklin Roosevelt's appointments, and he sat with Hughes and Brandeis and McReynolds. When McReynolds went, in 1941, a remembrance of the Wilson era and of trust-busting in the early 1900's went with him. Justice Van Devanter, a contemporary of McReynolds who retired in 1937, had been appointed by Taft, had held office under McKinley, and had sat with appointees of Cleveland and of Hayes. And so on back.

Senior members of the Court are witnesses to the reality and validity of our present—distracted, improbable, illegitimate as it often appears—because in their persons they assure us of its link to the past which they also witnessed and in which they were themselves once the harbingers of something outrageously new. This is true not only of those who are constructive and creative; it is true of Justices who oppose all that is not as they knew it. Say what they will, their very existence among us reassures us. When the great Holmes, who was wounded at Ball's Bluff and at Antietam, retired in 1932, being past ninety, the emotional public response was not due wholly to his undoubted greatness. It was also that his years, his years alone, fulfilled one of the functions of the Supreme Court.

*   *   *

The foregoing discussion of the origin and justification of judicial review has dealt for the most part indiscriminately with the power of the federal courts to strike down federal legislation and the power of those courts to pass on actions of the states. There are, of course, differences. Many judges and commentators who have questioned the power of judicial review of federal legislation have freely conceded the same power when exercised with respect to state actions. It is vital, as we have seen, that some federal agency have power authoritatively to declare and apply federal law to the member states of the federation. Clearly, for the sake of full effectiveness, a substantial portion of this power must be exercised by a judicial body. Yet it remains true that when the Court invalidates the action of a state legislature, it is acting against the majority will within the given jurisdiction; what is more, it also promises to foreclose majority action on the matter in issue throughout the country. The Court represents the national will against local particularism; but it does not represent it, as the Congress does, through electoral responsibility. The need to effectuate the superiority of federal over state law is not a sufficient justification for judicial review of state actions in those instances in which the federal law in question is constitutional and hence judge-made. In this respect also, therefore, the function must be supported by the other reasons we have surveyed. This is not to say, however, that there will not be instances when it seems justifiable to exercise judicial review more vigorously against the states than against the federal legislature or executive, and instances calling for less vigor as well.

CHAPTER 2

The Premise of Distrust
and Rules of Limitation

In treating of its establishment and justification, I have spoken of judicial review in one sense as if we knew no more about it than what was vouchsafed us in *Marbury* v. *Madison*. That is, I have dealt with it at large, as the power to strike down on constitutional grounds both federal and state legislation and executive action. This is, of course, a very gross statement of the matter. It is an attempt to view the function as a whole without examining the process. And it is absurd, except as one may find it convenient for analytical purposes. I did find it convenient to consider arguments that would deny the power of judicial review, whatever the nature and range of the process by which it is exercised; and to counter with the statement of a justification in general terms, which might then serve as a guide in a consideration of the proper nature and range of the process. The artificiality of this approach will not have disguised the fact that it is one and the same inquiry to seek a justification for judicial review and an appreciation of the proper quality and reach of the process; the answers to the two halves of the inquiry determine each other. Nor will it have been missed that the establishment which took place in *Marbury* v. *Madison* and the other early cases opened more problems than it settled or than are settled yet.

I propose in this and the following chapter to view the process with greater particularity, through a highly selective treatment of certain commentators and schools of thought. I shall be dealing, first, with writers who approach the process from a premise of distrust or, at any rate, reluctance to give it the freest rein; and, secondly, with the school that comes to judicial review with greater certitude about its broad usefulness and hence with a more hospitable attitude toward its vigorous exercise. Perhaps it is rude and unjust to construct such a line-up. In that event, the organization of these two chapters will prove to be arbitrary, but the rest of the injustice should wash out in the discussion.

The Rule of the Clear Mistake

One of the earliest scholarly treatments of the process of judicial review is James Bradley Thayer's "The Origin and Scope of the American Doctrine of Constitutional Law,"[1] published in 1893. This paper is a singularly important piece of American legal scholarship, if for no other reason than that Holmes and Brandeis, among modern judges, carried its influence with them to the Bench, as more recently did Mr. Justice Frankfurter.

The power of review, says Thayer, must be conceived of strictly "as a judicial one," quite unlike, and distinct from, the functions of the political branches of government. In discharging their limited office, the courts must be astute not to trench upon the proper powers of the other departments of government, nor to confine their discretion. Full and free play must be allowed to "that wide margin of considerations which address themselves only to the practical judgment of a legislative body." Moreover, every action of the other departments embodies an implicit decision on their part that it was within their constitutional power to act as they did. The judiciary must accord the utmost respect to this determination, even though it be a tacit one.

This meant for Thayer—and he attempted to prove that it had generally meant to the courts—that a statute could be struck down as unconstitutional only "when those who have the right to make laws have not merely made a mistake, but have made a very clear one,—so clear that it is not open to rational question." After all, the Constitution is not a legal document of the nature of a deed of title or the like, to be read closely and construed with technical finality, but a complex charter of government, looking to unforeseeable future exigencies. Most frequently, reasonable men will differ about its proper construction. The Constitution leaves open "a range of choice and judgment," so that "whatever choice is rational is constitutional." The Court, exercising the power of judicial review, is to be "the ultimate arbiter of what is rational and permissible," but is to have no further concern with policy choices.

What is the upshot of Thayer's teaching? He takes us, as did the Marshall of *McCulloch* v. *Maryland* (1819) himself, beneath the bland proposition advanced in *Marbury* v. *Madison,* and insists that in the vast majority of cases, judicial review is not simply a matter of measuring a statute against crisply defined constitutional provisions but, rather, a policy-making process, in which judges engage after the legislators have, for their part, made a choice. But, like Marshall, Thayer assumed that judicial policy choices are to be made with reference to the written Constitution, and that the chief method to be employed is construction of the document. He was aware, however, that construction involves hospitality to large purposes, not merely textual exegesis. The latter alone would be unavailing. Such is the nature of this document. Like Marshall, like Hamilton—and like Jefferson when the need arose, though only then—Thayer was a loose rather than a strict constructionist. And like Marshall, excepting only in *Marbury* v. *Madison,* he took the consequences, which generally entail narrowing the scope of the Court's power to negative legislative and executive choices.

There are some constitutional provisions, to be sure, of which no latitudinarian construction is possible. Most of these are housekeeping provisions, such as the ones prescribing terms of office and the like, which must in the nature of things be quite definite. They do not each separately pronounce any great principle, although there is embedded in their totality something of the essence of the democratic political system. For the rest, there are perhaps a few commands that approach in precision that of the Seventh Amendment concerning trial by jury "where the value in controversy shall exceed twenty dollars." But there is nothing else quite so exact, and the major heads of power and of limitation only mark, as Marshall said, "the great outlines." "Commerce," "Money," "War," "Taxes," and "Freedom of Speech," "Due Process of Law," "Equal Protection of the Laws"—such are some of the majestic concepts suited to a Constitution that was intended, in Marshall's words, "to endure for ages to come." Obviously, men may in full and equal reason and good faith hold differing views about the proper meaning and specific application of provisions such as these. And Thayer, following Marshall in *McCulloch* v. *Maryland*, laid it down that the Court might nullify a statute only if it could not rationally be said to proceed from a plausible construction of the Constitution; even though on a free vote, so to speak, the Court itself would have adopted a construction contrary to that which is implicit in the statute. If the legislature is to be held to have made a mistake, it must be "a very clear one." Thus, in the *McCulloch* case, Marshall upheld the power of Congress to incorporate the Bank of the United States, although the Constitution is thoroughly inconclusive on the point. But Congress thought it had the power, and the President agreed. "It would require no ordinary share of intrepidity," said Marshall, speaking as a man who had no ordinary share, "to assert that [the measure] was a bold and plain usurpation, to which the constitution gave no countenance."

"Taken seriously," Felix S. Cohen wrote in a later day, "this conception [that what is rational is constitutional] makes of our courts lunacy commissions sitting in judgment upon the mental capacity of legislators and, occasionally, of judicial brethren."[2] That is cleverly put, but the principle of the constitutional rationality of legislation is nevertheless meaningful, and it is by no means trivial in either the number or the importance of the instances in which it can come into play. "This leaves to our courts," said Thayer, "a great and stately jurisdiction." Cohen himself felt constrained to point out that "some such conception" served as the major premise of Brandeis' famous brief in *Muller* v. *Oregon*,[3] on which the constitutionality of legislation limiting hours of labor for women was sustained. The principle continues to possess dignity and utility. It is crucial to any accommodation between judicial review and the democratic faith. But it is not addressed —except by the unwarranted inference that it is simply meant to preclude their submission to judicial review—to all the problems faced by the process as it has operated in our day. Not nearly. That is the difficulty—not that the principle is fatuous.

In determining whether a legislative or an executive choice of policy is rational and hence constitutional, the Court is confronted, strictly speaking, with three inquiries; or perhaps it is more accurate to say, with three thirds of one problem. The Constitution sets up two systems of limited government consisting of institutions that are meant to be circumscribed by more particular limitations within the general one. Thus the first question must be whether the subject matter to which the executive or legislature, state or federal, has addressed itself can be related to the sphere of action assigned to it; this is to say, whether the subject matter can be brought within Marshall's "great outlines": "Commerce," "War," etc. But constitutional grants of power embody and imply—such, following Marshall, is the Thayerian hypothesis—broad and over-lapping purposes, and it is unlikely, therefore, that a head of power will not be found to fit, either in what is enumerated for the federal government or in what is reserved and not forbidden to the states. Yet this is a first and somewhat formal step in analysis only, for purposes *are* implicit in all powers conferred on limited branches of government—broad and far-reaching purposes, but each one in itself not without limit. There follows, therefore, a closely related and more difficult third of the problem, which is whether a given legislative or executive action is rationally suited to carry out the purposes of a constitutional head of power. Congress establishes a Bank of the United States, in which it deposits federal monies. It is not difficult, as a formal matter, to relate this action to the granted power to levy taxes, or to the power to raise armies. As to the latter, it may be said that Congress needed to make provision for paying its troops in the various places where they are stationed. But there remained the somewhat different question in the *McCulloch* case whether establishment of a national bank was a rationally suitable means for effectuating this purpose. It was not the only possible means; nor, however, was it disingenuous, as, for example, going on to forbid competition by private or state banks might have been. On the other hand, author-izing the national bank to act as trustee, executor of estates, and the like and thus to maintain itself as a viable institution in com-petition with state banks would be this side of disingenuousness. Such a "process of filiation of necessities," Jefferson feared, was "the House that Jack Built," one thing leading to another without end.[4] Yet the connection can become so remote as to cease to be rational, the more readily if the legislature itself states and is held to a relatively limited purpose within the broader constitutional one, or when the permissible constitutional purpose is eroded by collision with a principle drawn from one of the prohibitions that the Bill of Rights suggests.[5] This brings us to another, equally intertwined, third of the problem.

When the head of granted power is seen in relation to one of those limitations, chiefly intended to safeguard individual rights, which cut across all functions of government, does the choice of means represented by the action under examination constitute a rational accommodation between affirmative power and negative safeguard? Here is where Thayer's rule tends to break down. For it may not signify a great deal to conclude that such an accommodation is rational. The real question may be whether it is good. Hence the answer may depend on the assignment of preponderant weight to one or another value. This is a process in which reason is an indispensable aid, but which it cannot carry through unaided. To the extent that the necessary choice of values is implicit in the constitutional language or in the tradition for which that language is shorthand, and is assumed to be acceptable on that basis, rational analysis may serve as an adequate tool. But as time passes, fewer and fewer relevantly decisive choices are to be divined out of the tradition of our founding. Our problems have grown radically different from those known to the Framers, and we have had to make value choices that are effectively new, while maintaining continuity with tradition. Anything that might still properly be called "construction" of the written Constitution has come to suffice less and less. And so it has not always been possible to be satisfied that what is rational is constitutional. This is very far from conceding, however, the present fatuousness of the principle that what is irrational is unconstitutional.

It does not take a lunatic legislature to enact measures that are irrational. It only takes a legislature more than normally whipped up, very intent on the expedient purpose of the moment, acting under severe pressure, rushed, tired, lazy, mistaken, or, forsooth, ignorant. Certainly this is not a daily phenomenon, and certainly, therefore, the rule of the clear mistake will usually produce, as it did in *McCulloch* v. *Maryland* itself, decisions upholding the constitutionality of legislative actions. It is meant to do so. Not because it proceeds from the illusion that weighty legislative deliberation is always devoted to constitutional niceties. If that were the reality, we would have much less justification for judicial review than we have. Thayer had no such illusion. He observed that the vigorous exercise of judicial review discourages consideration of constitutional problems in the legislature. A limitation of the function of review might contribute, he thought, to sounder and more principled deliberations in lawmaking. That is very far from harboring illusions about present practice. Nor is it the sole or the chief basis for the rule of the clear mistake. Short of employing its ultimate power, the court has the means, as we shall see, of directing legislative attention to questions of principle. And there is something to be said on the other hand, as I have remarked, for the relatively unencumbered operation, at some stage in the formation of policy, of a process that registers a balance of wills and of interests and little else. The rule of the clear mistake aims at accommodation with the theory of representative democracy. It proceeds from the realization, in the words of Mr. Justice Frankfurter, that courts "are not representative bodies. They are not designed to be a good reflex of a democratic society."[6] Therefore the rule is meant to limit the area of judicial policy-making, keeping the judicial function distinct from the legislative and thus capable of being justified. It is a conceptual tool for distilling out of a typical public issue one element of principle, as distinguished from a number of allowable choices that may be made on grounds of expediency. But the rule does not lead by indirection to a total abdication of the power of judicial review.

I take as one fairly recent example a decision of some consequence: *Wieman* v. *Updegraff*, handed down in 1952.[7] The state of Oklahoma, exercising its power over the public service, set out "to make loyalty a qualification to hold public office or be employed by the State." In pursuance of this purpose, the state required its employees to swear that in the five years immediately preceding the taking of the oath they had not been members of any group whatever that had been listed by the Attorney General of the United States as a Communist-front or subversive organization.

Failure to take the oath resulted in automatic dismissal. But obviously, as the Supreme Court pointed out, membership in one of these organizations might have been innocent. A man might have joined a proscribed organization without being aware of its true nature, which, after all, it is the purpose of a "front organization" to disguise. The group itself might have been innocent at the time of affiliation and have come to have an illegitimate purpose later, perhaps after the person in question had left it. Or, conversely, it might have cleansed itself by the time of his affiliation, having previously been dedicated to subversive activity. The required oath did not take account of these discriminations; the sanction of dismissal followed, without recourse, upon failure to swear. And so the Court struck down the oath requirement as arbitrary. It was irrational to consider that the end of a loyal public service would be served by dismissing people who had innocently belonged to organizations that might themselves have been totally innocent at the time of membership. This was simply absurd— lunatic, if one feels the need for a stronger word—but in fact the product of excessive and indiscriminate legislative zeal, and of poor analysis.

The relevant distinction is not between rationality and lunacy but between rationality and will, or, perhaps it is meaningful to say, between rationality and uncontrolled emotion. It is not lunatic to take the position that the public service must be kept clear of any taint of disloyalty, and that to exclude from it even possibly innocent persons is to take absolutely no chances. That is a sane and a zealous attitude. But it is not rational; it is not even thoughtful. It is governed by a heightened emotion—anxiety, in this case —and it will not pass the test of a calm judgment resting on allowable inferences drawn from common human experience. Such a judgment will vary with what is known of relevant human experience. It must be an informed judgment, and it may change as it becomes better informed. But it will discriminate between arbitrary guesses and calculations of probability. In any event, this is the Court's independent judgment to make, and unless one takes a cynical view of the human capacity to reason, it is a possible judgment and one that will answer to descriptions of "correct" or "erroneous."

It is evident, however, that this disposition of *Wieman* v. *Upde-*

graff left untouched another problem implicit in the case: namely, whether under any circumstances it is permissible for a state to make "loyalty" a standard of public employment. It should be evident also that Thayer's rule cannot yield all the answer to this question that we may want. If the state had required its employees to have blond hair, we should apply the rule of the clear mistake and make an end of the matter. Such a standard is absurd. Similarly, we should uphold as rational and as raising no other difficulties a requirement that applicants for state employment be able to read and write. But the criterion of loyalty calls for a judgment weighing the value of freedom of speech, opinion, and association against the need of the state to assure itself of the allegiance of its agents. Reasonable men may and will differ. The Supreme Court has in other cases struck the balance in favor of the state's need to protect itself. But reason alone will not produce such a judgment.

A striking demonstration—to take another example—of how and why the limits of Thayer's rule are reached may be found in an opinion of Mr. Justice Harlan in the recent Connecticut birth-control case.[8] A Connecticut statute makes it a crime for married couples as well as others to use contraceptives. Although he could find no explicit constitutional language on the point, Justice Harlan, speaking for himself in dissent, concluded that as applied to a married couple the statute was "an intolerable and unjustifiable invasion of privacy in the conduct of the most intimate concerns of an individual's personal life." Obviously, the Connecticut statute is the expression of a moral judgment which, as Justice Harlan noted, cannot be said to be correct or incorrect. Certainly it cannot be deemed irrational. It falls, so far as reason can judge it, within the generally permissible area of state supervision of the morals of the citizenry. But, again obviously, it regulates the manner in which persons lawfully married practice the marital intimacy. Assigning the highest of values to conjugal privacy, Justice Harlan decided that the state should be foreclosed from such direct regulation enforced by means of criminal sanctions. Under these circumstances, he added, "it will not do to urge in justification . . . [of the statute] simply that [it] is rationally related to the effectuation of a proper state purpose. A closer scrutiny and stronger justification than that are required." An additional judgment to the one opened up by the rule of the clear mistake is called for.

Thayer did not say that courts ought not to make such judgments, nor how they should make them. He simply did not speak to this problem. He addressed himself only to situations in which the underlying value judgment was as clear—to him at least—as it would be to us in the case of literacy as a standard of public employment. He derived the clarity of his implicit value judgments from the roomy view of the major constitutional heads of power that he shared with Marshall; and, one may suppose, from the secure, well-ordered, economical, modestly relativistic—and rarely tested—system of values of a nineteenth-century gentleman. In cases such as he had chiefly in mind, rationality was thus the only possible issue open to judicial review. For no one has yet offered a coherent justification of a process of judicial review that freely and avowedly takes onto itself the final decision of those matters of expediency and prudence which are thrashed out in the legislative give and take. Thayer's rule of the clear mistake should, therefore, be expanded to read as follows: What is rational, and rests on an unquestioned, shared choice of values, is constitutional.

It will be profitable briefly to examine the workings of Thayer's rule in his own hands. In 1887, Thayer published a celebrated article[9] in which he considered "whether Congress has the power to make paper a good tender in payment of debts," carefully distinguishing the "very different" question "whether under any given circumstances it is wise or right that Congress should use" the power. He found that the question of power had been left open by the text and history of the relevant constiutional provisions. As a confirmed loose constructionist, he therefore believed that Congress was free to infer the power. He took only some five pages to notice the argument that the legislation making paper money legal tender violated "the spirit of the Constitution . . . because it is unjust." This was an argument of "very slight importance. I do not mean that it is of slight importance to do an unjust thing; that is never a matter of small importance." He meant only that this argument was slight. He quoted with approval an unsigned note by Holmes, then a member of the Boston bar, saying that the question of "justice" here was after all only "a point of political economy." For his own part, Thayer concluded that the statute worked "no direct and inevitable injury" to creditors, at least no such injury as had not been caused them by past legislation. And so there was on this "slight" point nothing for judicial review to review—although Chief Justice Chase and others had thought the contrary.[10]

In February 1899, Thayer published an address on "Our New Possessions."[11] The United States, he argued, had the implied power to acquire colonies. He had opposed the acquisition, and he advocated a constitutional amendment to foreclose the possibility of statehood for Hawaii. But he could not doubt the power, and he set forth his spacious view in a passage that deserves more fame than has come to it:

That it was unconstitutional to buy Louisiana and Florida; . . . that it was unconstitutional to charter a bank, to issue paper money, to make it legal tender, to enact a protective tariff,—that these and a hundred other things were a violation of the Constitution has been solemnly and passionately asserted by statesmen and lawyers. . . . The trouble has been, then and now, that men imputed to our fundamental law their own too narrow construction of it . . . and sought thus, when the question was one of mere power, to restrict its great liberty . . . [The Constitution] is forever dwarfing its commentators, both statesmen and judges, by disclosing its own greatness. . . . Petty judicial interpretations have always been, are now, and always will be, a very serious danger to the country.

But men contended that it was "un-American" and contrary to the "spirit of the Constitution" for the United States to govern "vassal states and subject peoples." Thayer thought not. He was generously concerned with Indian rights, but he was also of the opinion that "the entire recent history of England and of the United States shows that a wise and free colonial administration, as regards the people who are governed, is one of the most admirable contrivances for the improvement of the human race and their advancement in happiness and self-government, that has ever been vouchsafed to man." He thought it "childish literalness" to consider that "all men, however savage and however unfit to govern themselves, were oppressed when other people governed them." Hence the issue of colonial acquisition—though not necessarily of what in detail constitutes "wise and free colonial administration"—"was one of mere power."

Thus Thayer stopped short of asking what value judgments courts may make in the exercise of judicial review, and how. What he did say about the proper nature of the process is neither invalid nor obsolescent. It is—for the questions of our day and for the temper of our time—simply not enough.

More recent discussions of the process of judicial review must be seen against the background of the history of the Court since the turn of the century. It should occasion no surprise that there has been considerable change over the years in the substance of the problems coming to the Court, and that hence the process has tended to appear in different aspects; different features of it are highlighted for different generations. In its earliest years the Court was occupied with staking out its claim to the power of judicial review. Subsequently, it struggled with the problem of protecting a common national market against particularistic economic actions of the states. Just before the Civil War, the Court committed the *Dred Scott Case*, and that, as Fouché might have said, was "more than a crime; it was a blunder." There followed, through a war which, like all wars, was very hard on judges, the most ineffectual period in the Court's history. But the Court survived it and launched itself upon a task of qualified but nonetheless vigorous protection of the business community against government. It is this development of which Thayer deplored the excesses. The dominant value was laissez faire. For a season it was quite widely shared, and the Court enjoyed immense prestige. Serving this value in the most uncompromising fashion, at a time when it was well past its heyday, five Justices, in a series of spectacular cases in the 1920's and 1930's, went to unprecedented lengths to thwart the majority will. The consequence was very nearly the end of the story. But the Court, lying down to bleed a while, rose to fight again. It has entered in the present generation upon another period of vigorous activity. The central problems now concern civil liberties.

In the 'twenties and 'thirties, the reaction, both scholarly and popular, was violent. The influential and ultimately decisive criticism of the Court in this period followed the Thayer tradition and asserted Thayer's principle. Given the critics' scheme of values, the rule that what is rational is constitutional was quite sufficient to resolve—and to resolve differently than did the Court—most of the problems that were current. Reaction has been nearly as violent in our day. In vulgarity, as Paul A. Freund has said, it has reached remarkable heights of "ignorant and disgraceful billingsgate." But now as before there are two separate debates going on about the Supreme Court. One, the shouting match of the segregationists and security-mongers, is deafening, interminable, and, since it turns wholly on immediate controversies, timely. The other, which alone is worthy of attention, is muted, constant, and timeless.

The Rule of the Successful Operation of the Venture at Hand

The most radical recent critique was delivered by the late Judge Learned Hand in his 1958 Holmes Lectures at the Harvard Law School.[12] Judge Hand was not satisfied with the justification for the doctrine of judicial review offered in *Marbury* v. *Madison*. He was also unwilling to rest on the historical evidence. He would say merely that "there were other reasons, not only proper but essential, for inferring such a power in the Constitution"; reasons, "though not expressed," which made judicial review "essential to prevent the failure of the venture at hand." These are that in a government of divided functions, someone must "keep the states, Congress, and the President within their prescribed powers." The Court is and remains the institution best suited to this task, and the alternatives to entrusting the task to it were and remain prohibitive. The real alternative would have been to let the power gravitate to Congress, and the result of that would in turn have been the effective defeat of the separation of powers that the Constitution purported to impose. Congress would have become omnipotent, the executive would have been made subject to it, and the states would have been at its mercy. It may be noted in passing that these reasons for inferring the power of judicial review are not so unlike the argument in *Marbury* v. *Madison* as Judge Hand intended them to be, and are in fact rather similarly vulnerable.

If such reasons, exigent though they may be, constitute the sole justification for lodging in the Court the power of judicial review, certain strictures on that power necessarily follow. The Court must, before each exercise of the power, ask itself "how importunately the occasion demands" the exercise, and often must refrain because the demand is not importunate enough, and because a power engrafted on the basic charter only out of recognition of a necessity "to prevent the failure of the undertaking" is by hypothesis to be used reluctantly and sparingly. What is more important, the Court must take care to confine its function strictly "to the need that evoked it; that is, it was and always has been necessary to distinguish between the frontiers of another department's authority and the propriety of its choices within those frontiers." The latter is none of the Court's business.

Having drawn these conclusions, Judge Hand proceeded to examine the function of the Court in applying the Bill of Rights: the first eight amendments to the Constitution and the Due Process and Equal Protection Clauses of the Fourteenth. These provisions, Judge Hand conceded, establish limitations upon the legislative and executive branches of the government, and, indeed, upon the judicial branch itself. But they do not constitute such frontiers, marking the separation of powers among the several departments, as Judge Hand would have the Court police. For it is exceedingly hard to assign any meaning to these clauses definite enough to make of them "guides on concrete occasions." It is true, as Judge Hand of course recognized, that scarcely any provision of the Constitution is clear enough to apply itself. But, he maintained, some of the "frontier" provisions have fixed historical meaning, while the Bill of Rights is so much less clear than anything else that the difference, though technically one of degree, has the significance of a difference in kind. The Bill of Rights prescribes "no more than that temper of detachment, impartiality, and an absence of self-directed bias that is the whole content of justice." Therefore, if the Court is to apply the Bill of Rights as a limitation upon the legislative and executive authority in, let us say, a free-speech case, it must test the justice of the arrangement which the legislature and the executive have decreed. For every such arrangement involves a balancing of values and a prophecy that the balance struck will be beneficial. But to apply this test was, for Judge Hand, necessarily to duplicate the work of the legislature and the executive themselves; it was to pass on the propriety of choices, to act as a "third legislative chamber," rather than simply to draw boundaries and define frontiers. Therefore it was inadmissible.

I cannot frame any definition that will explain when the Court will assume the role of the third legislative chamber and when it will limit its authority to keeping Congress and the states within their accredited authority. Nevertheless, I am quite clear that it has not abdicated its former function, as to which I hope that it may be regarded as permissible for me to say that I have never been able to understand on what basis it does or can rest except as a *coup de main*.

Quite evidently, Judge Hand's prescription of judicial restraint is very strong medicine. Indeed, it is the therapy of nearly total abstinence. Most students of the Court would not wish to administer it, and plainly the patient himself rejects it. Two things are to be remarked. First, Judge Hand's conclusions depend on a reading of history which, as we have seen, is far from being the prevalent one. Secondly, Judge Hand took no account at all of any presumption in favor of existing practice. There is a great deal to be said, as we have earlier noted, for a theory that is able to accommodate (rather than feeling constrained to relegate to the category of a *coup de main*) more of what the Court has done in fact than Judge Hand was able to accept. This would be an insufficient argument if a roomier justification for the practice of judicial review were not supportable in principle—roomier, that is, than Judge Hand's rigorously constricted one. Such a justification is possible, however, because it need not be accepted that, when it makes value choices under the broad provisions of the Bill of Rights, the Supreme Court merely duplicates the work of the legislature. The functions can be differentiated up to a point by means of Thayer's rule, which forms part of the content of Due Process, and more generally along the lines sketched in Chapter 1. Judge

Hand did not embark upon any detailed discussion of the process of judicial review, even as related to the frontier-policing job that he conceded to it. He remarked that in this job, history is a great aid. Beyond that, his diagnosis was lameness, and his cure amputation.

The Rule of the Neutral Principles

Another recent fundamental critique, Professor Herbert Wechsler's 1959 Holmes Lecture,[13] was delivered from the same rostrum as Judge Hand's. Mr. Wechsler does not accept Judge Hand's severe restriction and sole justification of judicial review. Like most commentators, he sees in the history of the framing of the Constitution an invitation to establish more sweeping powers. What is more remarkable, he believes that the existing power of the Supreme Court "is grounded in the language of the Constitution and is not a mere interpolation."*

It naturally follows for Mr. Wechsler that he must go beyond the point at which Judge Hand elected to stop and find a justification for the rest of the practice of judicial review, which Judge Hand simply deplored, and also an understanding of the proper nature of the process. It follows also, since he deals with the problems of our day, that Mr. Wechsler must go beyond Thayer. He offers this formulation: "I put it to you that the main constituent of the judicial process is precisely that it must be genuinely principled, resting with respect to every step that is involved in reaching judgment on analysis and reasons quite transcending the immediate result that is achieved." A choice of competing values is reflected in legislative and executive action, and it is this choice that the Court must consider in light of its own value judgment; but what is crucial "is not the nature of the question, but the nature of the answer that may validly be given by the courts." For the courts, the answer may not proceed from expediency. And so

---

* I have dealt in the previous chapter with the textual argument, proceeding from the Supremacy Clause, in which Mr. Wechsler places chief reliance, and I shall treat in a later chapter of certain conclusions that he draws regarding the jurisdiction of the Court and the Court's obligation to exercise it in full.

Mr. Wechsler finds his middle ground between "the third legislative chamber" that Judge Hand feared and the abandonment of
the greater part of the function of judicial review; that middle
ground is a process "that embodies what are surely the main quali-
ties of law, its generality and its neutrality." This, he tells us, is
what Mr. Justice Jackson must have had in mind when he referred
to "a rule of law,"[14] and this is what Mr. Justice Frankfurter meant
when he called upon judges for "allegiance to nothing except the
effort, amid tangled words and limited insights, to find the path
through precedent, through policy, through history, to the best
judgment that fallible creatures can reach in that most difficult of
all tasks: the achievement of justice between man and man, between man and state, through reason called law."[15]

Mr. Wechsler's point of departure is something like the general
justification of judicial review that I tried to formulate in the previous chapter. This is, by and large, the commonly accepted
view among students of the subject. From it Mr. Wechsler goes forward to tell us something more of the process. He insists that it must
be disinterested. That is, first and most obviously, the judges must
stand aside from the party politics of the day. Secondly, they must
be free from the deflecting pressures of the ego. Thirdly, and most
importantly, the values the Court vindicates must have a content
greater than any single concern of the moment. The function of
judicial review arises in the limiting context of cases, to be sure;
but while the Court should not surmount the limitation, it must
rise above the case.

Mr. Wechsler, however, does not use the term "disinterestedness." His word is "neutrality." He has since conceded that it may
have certain enigmatic overtones. But—"this is an enigmatic subject."[16] One rule of decision that would surely qualify as sufficiently neutral is Thayer's principle of the clear mistake. But Mr.
Wechsler is the first to admit that more is needed. He most certainly does not

deny that constitutional provisions are directed to protecting certain
values or that the principled development of a particular provision is
concerned with the value or the values thus involved. The demand of
neutrality is that a value and its measure be determined by a general
analysis that gives no weight to accidents of application, finding a scope

that is acceptable whatever interest, group, or person may assert the claim. So, too, when there is conflict among values having constitutional protection, calling for their ordering or their accommodation, I argue that the principle of resolution must be neutral in a comparable sense (both in the definition of the individual competing values and in the approach that it entails to value competition).[17]

In the statement and in many applications, this is not at all enigmatic. Like Thayer's rule, it is also neither trivial nor fatuous. Indeed, like Thayer's rule, it is an indispensable elaboration of any general justification of judicial review as a process for the injection into representative government of a system of enduring basic values. One recent case in which the rule of the neutral principles failed of vindication may serve to illustrate its continued utility and importance. *Shelton* v. *Tucker*[18] presented yet another aspect of the problem of standards for public employment, to which the Court, in *Wieman* v. *Updegraff*, had earlier applied Thayer's rule of the clear mistake. In this instance, a 1958 Arkansas statute provided that no person could be employed as a teacher in a public school or college of the state until he had submitted an affidavit listing all organizations to which he currently belonged or made payments of dues or other regular contributions. Teachers in Arkansas are hired on a year-to-year basis, there being no civil-service tenure, and thus the statute in effect required all teachers employed by the state to file the affidavit within at most one year and terminated the employment of those who failed to do so. The statute was put in question by the suit of a teacher who declined to make the affidavit and was consequently not rehired. The evidence showed that "he was not a member of the Communist Party or of any organization advocating the overthrow of the government by force, and that he was a member of the National Association for the Advancement of Colored People." The Supreme Court, dividing five to four, held the statute unconstitutional.

It was clear, the Court said, that a state should have power "to investigate the competence and fitness of those whom it hires to teach in its schools," and in general—applying Thayer's rule— there was sufficient rational connection between that permissible purpose and an inquiry into a teacher's out-of-school associations. On the other hand, it was clear also that the duty to disclose such associations would have a tendency to impair the average teacher's indulgence of the spontaneous urge to join, especially where employment was renewable at such short periods as in Arkansas and where there was no guarantee that the information obtained by the state would be kept confidential. Public exposure, of course, would work a further inhibition upon the freedom to join unpopular groups. Moreover, these inhibitions are particularly harmful in the case of teachers, in whose freedom of intellectual inquiry society has a great stake. Yet the Court did not hold that the state should be forbidden to make its inquiries into associations under these conditions or that it should be foreclosed from inquiring into particularly unpopular associations or into certain classes of them, such as religious or political. Rather, the Court implicitly rested on the premise of previous decisions that the state's interest in the fitness of its employees generally outweighs the desirability of sustaining an atmosphere of freedom of private association.

On what ground, then, did the Court strike down the statute? It said that the question was not whether Arkansas could ask certain of its teachers about all their organizational associations; nor whether the state could ask all of its teachers about certain associations; nor whether teachers could be asked how many associations they had or how much time they spent on them. The decisive point was the broad scope of the disclosures Arkansas required of all teachers. Many of the associations of which disclosure was required "could have no possible bearing upon the teacher's occupational competence or fitness." But we were not told which. If this were so, then it was not true, as the Court had just said, that Arkansas could "ask certain of its teachers about all their organizational relationships." Moreover, it could scarcely be that Arkansas had a permissible interest in finding out how many organizations its teachers belonged to and how much time they spent in organizational activity but might not verify that information by inquiring into the names of the organizations that a teacher had joined.

The Court, however, reasoned by analogy to certain earlier cases in which it had struck down ordinances prohibiting the distribution of literature in public places without a license. These ordinances had fallen because the state's interest in good order and in the prevention of fraud, littering of the streets, and like inconveniences was held not to justify the broad restrictions on freedom of speech that were actually imposed. In other words, in those cases, the Court had weighed the rather limited purpose the state was allowed to pursue against the total effect of the action taken and had found that the ordinances were broader than their purpose immediately required and that, since in their breadth they affected other important values, they should be struck down, leaving to the state the alternative of enacting a narrower measure to achieve its allowable end. The analogy to the present case would have been apt had the Court been able to hold that Arkansas had only a limited interest in informing itself of the extracurricular activities of its teachers and that the broad statute in question went beyond that limited interest. But the Court did not so hold. It affirmed as permissible on principle the state's interest in investigating the full range of its teachers' outside activities. Then it superimposed the holding that the inquiry made by the present statute was nevertheless too broad. The Court did not say in what respect, and it did not take back one whit of its previous concessions as to the range of the permissible state interest. Such a decision lacks neutral principle because it lacks intellectual coherence.

The decisive factor in the Court's judgment may have been the more-than-tenable surmise that Arkansas would dismiss teachers whom it had found to be members of the NAACP, and that dismissals would actually rest on such membership even though other, spurious grounds would be formally assigned. Despite the Court's assumption that the state may inquire into a teacher's commitments and use of his free time and may require him to disclose the totality of his affiliations, including one with the NAACP, a dismissal for NAACP membership would lack rationality, at least in the absence of a showing of some particular interference with the teacher's professional effectiveness. For in light of the "conventional wisdom" of the day—which must qualify as rational, although experience may have disproved it two decades hence— inferences as to loyalty and even as to an individual's intellectual integrity and freedom may be drawn, say, from Communist Party membership. But little beyond a peaceable dedication to the ideal of equality of the races can be inferred from adherence to the

NAACP, and such an inference without more is not relevant to any purpose the state is permitted to pursue. This problem, however, was not present in the case and might never arise. The plaintiff here had failed to file his affidavit and had been dismissed for that reason. Hence there was no call as yet to decide questions of dismissal for NAACP membership, or dismissal at will, without any procedural safeguards, and the Court in fact did not deal with such questions.

"Of course," as Justice Harlan said in dissent, "this decision has a natural tendency to enlist support, involving as it does an unusual statute that touches constitutional rights whose protection in the context of the racial situation in various parts of the country demands the unremitting vigilance of the courts." But it is evident on the face of the opinion that the Court was unable to evolve a principle on which to dispose of this case.

To tell the legislature of Arkansas that it must act rationally; to have told it, if such a principle were tenable, that it must employ as teachers all comers; to have told it that it may not permit the public disclosure of the private associations of its employees, although it may find out about them for itself; to have told it that certain associations (as, for example, family or religious ones) are so private that they may under no circumstances be inquired into; or to have made any or all of these injunctions applicable to teachers but not to the generality of public employees—a decision based on any of these, and perhaps other, principles, although some are less and some more tenable, might have been within the proper function of a Court empowered to enunciate and apply fundamental values. But to tell the legislature of Arkansas only that for inscrutable reasons a teacher named Shelton may not be fired, or that inquiries into membership in the NAACP, but not necessarily in any other organization, are not permitted—that is to revise, even if out of the most laudable of motives, a mere judgment of expediency; it is merely to disagree with the legislature on the thoroughness with which the fitness of Mr. Shelton should be inquired into, or on whether the NAACP is a worthier organization than the Elks or the Masons or the John Birch Society and should therefore be protected by special legislative exemptions.

There are other such examples, although, of course, not one or a dozen of them can be taken to characterize the present Court's discharge of its office. They do, however, demonstrate the utility of the principle of the neutral principles, the rule, in Justice Frankfurter's words, that the Court must not "sit like a kadi under a tree dispensing justice according to considerations of individual expediency."[19] The rule is a timely reminder that the inviting garden of what Cardozo, following Gény, called "judicial impressionism" is forbidden territory. The Justices must not benevolently constitute themselves "*les bons juges*" and do in each case what seems just for it alone. Rather, as Cardozo enjoined them to do, they must hold "fast to Kant's categorical imperative, 'Act on a maxim which thou canst will to be law universal.' " They must refuse "to sacrifice the larger and more universal good to the narrower and smaller. . . . We look beyond the particular to the universal, and shape our judgment in obedience to the fundamental interest of society. . . ."[20]

Yet it remains to ask the hardest questions. Which values, among adequately neutral and general ones, qualify as sufficiently important or fundamental or whathaveyou to be vindicated by the Court against other values affirmed by legislative acts? And how is the Court to evolve and apply them? I listed earlier a number of principles that the Court might have imposed on the Arkansas legislature; all, in my judgment, were neutral in the sense in which the actual decision in the *Shelton* case was not. Of course, each of these rested on a value judgment, and these value judgments, in turn, were not all equal. The question is, which might the Court properly have made, and which not? I have taken it for granted that Thayer's rule of the clear mistake embodies fundamental values: namely, an abhorrence of caprice and an attachment to the root ideas of federalism and of checks and balances, as they are irreducibly implicit in the constitutional scheme. But how are other values found and applied, and what weights are assigned to them when they come in conflict with competing values or interests? Our analysis of the rule of the neutral principles has yielded no answer to these questions.

It will not do to conclude, however, that Mr. Wechsler has nothing further to say about the kind of principles the Court may adopt. That, as Professor Louis H. Pollak has noted,[21] would be "to take

Professor Wechsler's vintage wine and water it down to grape juice"—though good, body-building grape juice. For Mr. Wechsler also offers some illustrations of the failure in application by the Court of his principle that decision must rest "on reasons with respect to all the issues in the case . . . that in their generality and neutrality transcend any immediate result that is involved." These illustrations turn the thrust of his thesis and present its enigmatic aspects. Among the decisions that provide for Mr. Wechsler "the hardest tests of my belief in principled adjudication" is the one that struck down segregation in public schools. Nobody could be more deeply sympathetic to the result than Mr. Wechsler. But he has grave doubts about the neutrality of the principle that was applied.

As Mr. Wechsler concedes, the *School Segregation Cases,* read in conjunction with certain brief orders that followed after them, have made clear that the principle in question is that racial segregation constitutes, *per se,* a denial of equality to the minority group against whom it is directed. That group, Mr. Wechsler adds, is the one "that is not dominant politically and, therefore, does not make the choice involved." Mr. Wechsler suggests several additional considerations. Does not the finding of a denial of equality depend on an estimate of the motive of the legislature? Or, alternatively, does it not make decisive the interpretation placed on the legislation by those who are affected by it? That is, is not segregation a denial of equality only because Negroes subjectively feel it to be such? After all, segregation by sex is not viewed as discriminating against females. For himself, Mr. Wechsler sees segregation statutes as regulations of the freedom to associate. They impair the freedom of whites and Negroes alike, and damage both. But the fact of the matter in the Southern states is that most whites do not wish to associate with Negroes. A legislature must make a choice between abridging Negro freedom to associate and abridging white freedom not to associate, "between denying the association to those individuals who wish it or imposing it on those who would avoid it." To order integration is simply to reverse such a legislative choice, not to avoid it or somehow make it unnecessary, for it cannot be avoided. "[I]s there a basis in neutral principles for holding that the Constitution demands that the claims for association should prevail?"

The reply question is this: What, on the score of generality and neutrality, is wrong with the principle that a legislative choice in favor of a freedom not to associate is forbidden, when the consequence of such a choice is to place one of the groups of which our society is constituted in a position of permanent, humiliating inferiority; when the consequence beyond that is to foster in the whites, by authority of the state, self-damaging and potentially violent feelings of racial superiority—feelings that, as Lincoln knew,[22] find easy transference from Negroes to other groups as their particular objects? It may be that this principle is wrong[23] or is on other grounds ill suited for pronouncement and application by the Court. But wherein is it lacking on the score of neutrality, in the terms in which so far we have analyzed that concept?

The point that the Court must necessarily rely on an estimate of legislative motive or of the subjective feelings of Negroes affected by segregation fails, in my judgment, entirely. Granted that it would be relatively novel, and in that degree *ad hoc,* as well as extremely difficult for the Court so to rely. But it is unnecessary. To determine that segregation establishes a relationship of the inferior to the superior race is to take objective notice of a fact of our national life and of experience elsewhere in the world, now and in other times, quite without reference to legislative motives and without reliance on subjective and perhaps idiosyncratic feelings. It is no different from a similarly experiential judgment that official inquiries into private associations inhibit the freedom to join, or that hearsay evidence, reported at second or third hand, has a tendency to become distorted. And so one is led to the surmise that if the judgment embodied in the *Segregation Cases* lacks neutrality for Mr. Wechsler, it must be because he understands the concept in some additional sense, beyond what we have so far assumed; it must be that there is some other standard he would impose on the process of judicial review.

More recently, Mr. Wechsler has shed further light on his position. If the Fourteenth Amendment is read to outlaw race or color as allowable legislative grounds of classification, the principle must be tested, he has said, not only by its effect on straight-out segregation, "but also by its impact upon measures that take race into account to equalize job opportunity or to reduce *de facto* segregation, as in New York City's schools." By its effect also, one might add, on such proposals as the benevolent quota in housing.[24] Mr. Wechsler carries this suggestion no further, but it is pregnant with an elaboration of the idea of neutrality which is of the very first importance.

Our point of departure, like Mr. Wechsler's, has been that judicial review is the principled process of enunciating and applying certain enduring values of our society. These values must, of course, have general significance and even-handed application. When values conflict—as they often will—the Court must proclaim one as overriding, or find an accommodation among them. The result is a principle, or a new value, if you will, or an amalgam of values, or a compromise of values; it must in any event also have general significance and even-handed application. For, again, the root idea is that the process is justified only if it injects into representative government something that is not already there; and that is principle, standards of action that derive their worth from a long view of society's spiritual as well as material needs and that command adherence whether or not the immediate outcome is expedient or agreeable. It follows, and I take it Mr. Wechsler suggests, that once the Court has arrived at a principle, it must apply that principle without compromise. Therefore, the Court should not rest judgment on a "principle" which may be incapable of uniform application. If, in order to be workable in our society as it actually exists, a rule of action must be modulated by pragmatic compromises, then that rule is not a principle; it is no more than a device of expediency. And it is for legislatures, not courts, to impose what are merely solutions of expediency. Courts must act on true principles, capable of unremitting application. When they cannot find such a principle, they are bound to declare the legislative choice valid. No other course is open to them.

This is an idea exquisitely poised on the brink of logomachy, but I think that it has substance and that it is crucial. A true principle may carry within itself its own flexibility, but—and this is the important thing—flexibility on its own terms. For example, one may lay it down that in all criminal proceedings the accused must have the assistance of counsel in order to ensure the protection of his rights. Or one may say, as the Court has in fact said, that the assistance of counsel is constitutionally required in all cases, except in relatively simple ones in the state courts, where the accused seems to have been able to cope for himself, so that his rights were in fact adequately protected. This is not a mere device of expediency; it is a principle with flexibility built in, within its own terms. But a "principle" that speech is not a fit subject for legislative regulation because it is a sacred and untrammeled right of Everyman, except that sometimes some laws may be allowed to restrict it—that would be no more than an invitation to judgments of expediency. So also must one view as a device of expediency a "principle" that race is a proscribed ground of legislative classification, except that it may be used sometimes.

Earlier we saw the rule of the neutral principles as foreclosing *ad hoc* constitutional judgments which express merely the judge's transient feeling of what is fair, convenient, or congenial in the particular circumstances of a litigation. The *Shelton* case was an apt illustration, because it was decided without reference to any standard that could be stated in terms one whit more general than its own result. A neutral principle, by contrast, is an intellectually coherent statement of the reason for a result which in like cases will produce a like result, whether or not it is immediately agreeable or expedient. Now the demand for neutral principles is carried further. It is that the Court rest judgment only on principles that will be capable of application across the board and without compromise, in all relevant cases in the foreseeable future: absolute application of absolute—even if sometimes flexible—principles. The flexibility, if any, must be built into the principle itself, in equally principled fashion. Thus a neutral principle is a rule of action that will be authoritatively enforced without adjustment or concession and without let-up. If it sometimes hurts, nothing is better proof of its validity. If it must sometimes fail of application, it won't do. Given the nature of a free society and the ultimate consensual basis of all its effective law, there can be but very few such principles.

But it may be argued that the exceptions to the principle of the

Segregation Cases which Mr. Wechsler foresees are themselves principled ones, quite like the exception to the right-to-counsel rule mentioned above. Benevolent quotas, for example, differ from segregation. They do not completely deny the Negro's freedom of association, with the inevitable consequence of keeping him in a situation of permanent inferiority. Rather, they take account of an ineluctable fact in his present situation—that whites will move out of a neighborhood in which the Negro population has risen above a certain percentage point—to the end that some integration may be obtainable now, and that in time, perhaps, the prejudices that result in segregation in any degree may be eradicated altogether. Aware of these facts, the state decrees, let us say, that 33.3% of units in a public housing project must be allocated to Negro tenants and the rest to whites. In other words, the present situation is that it is not within the power of the state to enforce genuine integration unless it is prepared to dictate where people must live and work. This might well be thought unwise, counterproductive, perhaps unenforceable, and wrong on yet additional grounds. Therefore, if it wishes to go beyond the ineffectual removal of legal bars to integration, the state or the federal government may have to legislate some degree of controlled segregation.

It is, of course, equally impossible for the state to impose completely genuine integration of the school population or of transportation and recreation facilities, for the same reason. We do not wish to force all whites to use only the public (integrated) schools and other facilities. To be sure, Mr. Wechsler is right when he assumes that a very considerable degree of unwanted association will be forced on the whites, because vast numbers of them have no practical alternative to using the public schools and other public facilities. This much restriction on the freedom not to associate necessarily inheres in the principle that decided the *Segregation Cases*, and it is a considerable one. But the alternatives—such as private schools—are not foreclosed. In the housing situation, however, it is not a minority, but the great majority of whites who have an alternative. The state finds that they will, under certain conditions, take it. To foreclose it would be to advance a radical step beyond the degree of restriction on the freedom not to associate that is implicit in the decision of the *Segregation Cases;* and, indeed, a radical step toward limiting other important freedoms as well. Hence the measure of controlled segregation I have described, the benevolent or benign quota, or *numerus clausus,* which may be thought to represent an effort to induce whites not to resort to alternative housing. Similarly, but without the need for benevolent quotas, the mere existence of a free, though integrated, public-school system or of cheap, though integrated, public transportation induces most whites not to resort to alternatives.

Yet it cannot be denied that in its objective operation, a benevolent quota is as invidious as straight-out segregation. The difference in immediate effect is that some Negroes will not be denied their freedom to associate. But most Negroes will be, and the others will be allowed to associate only on the basis of special arrangements that proclaim their apartness and hence inferiority. What may be hoped for from the benevolent quota is that association of the races—limited to begin with—will allay the fears and other irrationalities on which white prejudice is nurtured. Especially in the young. But only experience will show whether this hope can be sustained. And meanwhile, limited segregation may provide as much nourishment for prejudice as a complete prohibition against association of the races. Perhaps the Court would therefore hold the benevolent quota unconstitutional under the principle of the *Segregation Cases.* But should it? Must it do so before there has been significant experience with it? The issue could be posed all too soon. Some states have had administrative trial runs with the device, and one or two state courts have exhibited extreme hostility to it. What is perhaps more significant, private housing developers have shown great interest in the quota, and some have employed it. This, indeed, is how the idea originated. In one fashion or another, whether by aiding private developers or only because an attempt is made in a state court to enforce or break the quota, government becomes associated with it, and thus a test of its constitutionality may be precipitated. Will there be no way out for the Supreme Court under the principle of the *Segregation Cases?*

The Court might consider incorporating motive into its principle. But this raises a difficulty alluded to earlier. Motives are commonly quite inscrutable. Who is to say that the majority of a legis-

lature which enacts a statute segregating the schools is actuated
by a conscious desire to suppress and humiliate the Negro? Who
is to say that for many members more decent feelings are not decisive—the feeling, for example, that under existing circumstances
Negro children are better off and can be more effectively educated
in schools reserved exclusively for them, and that this is the most
hopeful road to the goal of equality of the races under law? One
need not approve the moral judgment that such a position subsumes or agree with the assessments and prophecies it imports to
recognize that sincere men may convince themselves that it represents the true motive for their action. As I have suggested, this
ought not affect the Court's own moral judgment or its objective
assessment of the consequences of segregation, from which that
judgment proceeds. In respect of benevolent quotas, we have assumed—the phrase itself plainly does—a different motive than is
generally imputed to segregationists. But it is not inconceivable
that a benevolent quota, like token integration, may be grounded in
a realistic racism, which desires to continue as much compulsory
segregation as the authorities can be brought to tolerate. Very
occasionally, the racist motive may be provable. For the most part,
it can only be surmised. And it is no more nor less a product of
unprovable surmise than the contrary, pure motive. The immediate effect of the quota, moreover, is the same no matter which
motive animates it.

When the law makes "purpose" decisive, as it often does, it
deals with a very different thing. In construing and applying a
statute, the Court may search the history of its enactment in order
to discover which one of a number of related policies—all permissible on principle—the legislature intended to effectuate. Acting
as the executor of the legislative will, that is, the Court may try
to divine the intended consequences of a statute so as to be able
faithfully to give rise to them. There is, unfortunately, much of
the fictive and the arbitrary in this process, but it is probably quite
unavoidable. In any event, no such inquiry is called for in our
example of the benevolent quota. In the general run of constitutional adjudications, "purpose" is considerably more of an arbitrary concept, having very definite uses. It is employed to attribute
to the authors of a measure the will to achieve the consequences

that the Court has found it to entail; or else to impute to them the desire to achieve an *a priori* end which, in the Court's judgment under the circumstances, is the only allowable one. Thus, in constitutional adjudication, "purpose" may be the name given to the Court's assessment of the effect of a statute or administrative action, which forms the basis of a principled judgment about it, or "purpose" may be a conclusion drawn from the Court's principled judgment. In either event, it is scarcely what the word might connote in other usages—namely, an intimation of subjective intent, to be sought for and received by the Court from elsewhere than its own independent judgment. The questions concerning benevolent quotas, therefore, must be whether their effect can be squared with the principle of the *Segregation Cases,* and, if not, whether a purpose conforming to some other, not inconsistent principle can be attributed to them. It is clear that the principle of the *Segregation Cases* cannot be made to fit. The benevolent quota, like segregation, is a classification by race. Is a principled modification of the principle possible?

That there should be no distinctions of race ordained by the state—that is a principle. That there should be no distinctions of race ordained by the state except when their consequence may be that the racial prejudices of the people are mitigated in the long run—that comes in the end only to this: that the state should try, in the ways best suited to prevailing conditions, to draw the races into a closer relationship. And this, in turn, is not a principled rule of behavior; it is the statement of a goal whose attainment will call for a great many prudential judgments, aimed at the goal, to be sure, but not proceeding immediately from principle. The question of which arrangement, based on the invidious criterion of race, is consistent with ultimate attainment of the goal will most often be answerable only by a doubtful and variable judgment of expediency. Not always; perhaps not at the extremes, and perhaps absolute segregation is such an extreme. But most often.

Tested against the great judicial event of the century, the general justification of judicial review which was outlined in the previous chapter, and which is also Mr. Wechsler's point of departure, may thus appear to fail. If judicial review is to remain a process of principled decision, it would seem that it must here either impose upon the country a rigidly doctrinaire rule of behavior which will appear almost ludicrous to anyone who has any sense of the actualities of the situation and of its different aspects in different states; or it must uphold the segregation of the races by law. Otherwise it meddles with insoluble questions, either of motive or of mere expediency.

I believe that Mr. Wechsler suggests something like such a conclusion, and the fact that he does so gives one much pause. If Mr. Wechsler is right, then the decision in the *Segregation Cases* leads straight to disaster, for the Court or for the country. The Court— if Mr. Wechsler is right—either has set out to be a third legislative chamber or is imposing on the country an absolute rule of absolute principle. Thus it is either totally at war with the theory and practice of democracy or, far from being a stabilizing influence, it is leading the country to ruin by intractable, doctrinaire stages of irrepressible conflict. Or both, for the absolute rule of principle is also at war with a democratic system. But Mr. Wechsler, I believe, is not right.

No society, certainly not a large and heterogeneous one, can fail in time to explode if it is deprived of the arts of compromise, if it knows no ways of muddling through. No good society can be unprincipled; and no viable society can be principle-ridden. But it is not true in our society that we are generally governed wholly by principle in some matters and indulge a rule of expediency exclusively in others. There is no such neat dividing line. There are exceptions, some of which are delineated, as we shall see, by the so-called doctrine of political questions. Most often, however, and as often as not in matters of the widest and deepest concern, such as the racial problem, both requirements exist most imperatively side by side: guiding principle and expedient compromise. The role of principle, when it cannot be the immutable governing rule, is to affect the tendency of policies of expediency. And it is a potent role.

Is it not clear that our nation would be severely damaged— inwardly, not merely in its external relations—if in the second half of the twentieth century it believed that segregation of the races was neither right nor wrong; if it were committed to no principle in the matter, one way or the other? But is it not equally clear—

as the example of the benevolent quota may show—that the problem of the association of the black and white races will not always
yield to principled resolution, that it must proceed through phases
of compromise and expedient muddling-through, or else fail of an
effective and peaceable outcome?

The Lincolnian Tension

The segregation crisis of the mid-twentieth century has its roots,
of course, in the slavery crisis of a hundred years before. And it
plays back faithfully an earlier tension between principle and expediency, which was reconciled in the person of Lincoln. The
manner of the reconciliation emerges with lucid force in a highly
original analysis of Lincoln's philosophy of politics, Professor
Harry V. Jaffa's *Crisis of the House Divided*. Only in the continuity of this reconciliation can the Supreme Court fulfill its
function.

The tradition of recent Lincoln scholarship, as represented by
the late James G. Randall, is quite hard on Lincoln as a principled
statesman. It is this tradition, itself revisionist, that Mr. Jaffa sets
out to revise. He disproves the contention that Lincoln had no
differences of principle with Stephen A. Douglas. Randall and
others have maintained that neither Lincoln nor Douglas was an
abolitionist, that neither proposed in practice to extend slavery
into Kansas and Nebraska, north of the line of the Missouri Compromise of 1820, and that the debate between them—about squatter sovereignty and the *Dred Scott Case* and all that—therefore
turned, in Randall's words, on "a talking point rather than a matter
for governmental action, a campaign appeal rather than a guide
for legislation." On the contrary, concludes Mr. Jaffa, principle
was the heart of the debate. Lincoln held "that free government
was, in principle, incompatible with chattel slavery. The sheet
anchor of American republicanism, he held, was that no man was
good enough to govern another without that other's consent. There
was no principle, Lincoln often argued, that might justify the
enslavement of Negroes that might not also, with equal force, be
used to enslave white men." Yet he was no abolitionist. He ac-

cepted the Missouri Compromise and the existence of slavery in the United States. What he could not accept was the *Dred Scott* decision, the declaration that, by the law of the Constitution and conformably to the aspirations of the Declaration of Independence, the Negro was a chattel. He would not accept that, and he made it the *casus belli,* for it was the point on which he impaled Douglas and around which he rallied free-soil opinion in the North.

How explain the course of Lincoln's conduct? What wisdom dictated the occasion for compromise and reconciled expediency to principle? And why was the stand on principle, inviting war, called for when it was?

While "the sheet anchor of American republicanism"—the principle, fixed by the Declaration of Independence, that all men, black or white, are equal in the right to own themselves—remained unrepudiated as such, Lincoln could tolerate compromises "arising from the fact that the blacks are already amongst us." "If all earthly power were given me," Lincoln said, "I should not know what to do, as to the existing institution." If he were to go ahead and do something, it would be by evolutionary steps. Sudden execution was impossible. And what to do and just how to do it— those were doubtful, prudential questions, though for himself Lincoln rather favored colonization in Liberia. Further, if the slaves were to be freed here, should they become socially and politically "our equals"? The feelings of "the great mass of white people" would not admit of this, and hence here also principle would have to yield to necessity. "Whether this feeling accords with justice and sound judgment, is not the sole question, if indeed, it is any part of it. A universal feeling, whether well or ill-founded, can not be safely disregarded."

Such was the existing compromise that Lincoln supported as being born of necessity. But it was supportable only while the principle was maintained—even if tacitly, and not as an inflexible rule of conduct; yet immutable, inexorable. Its maintenance was as necessary to the well-being of society as its perfect achievement was for the moment impossible. The "House Divided" speech was not a doctrinaire appeal for the uncompromising application of principle. Its argument was that the existing compromise with slavery was tolerable because it only recognized the present extent, it did not sanction the spread, of the institution; hence it placed it "where the public mind shall rest in the belief that it is in course of ultimate extinction."[25] Thus, subject to a tendency toward abolition, was slavery placed at the foundation of the Republic, when the states forbade the slave-trade and manumission was begun, in Virginia at least. In such a context did the Founding Fathers accept compromise of the principle they had proclaimed in the Declaration of Independence. What was now in danger was the tendency then set in motion.[26] The divided house that could not stand was not one where freedom and slavery attempted to coexist. It was the house of Douglas' squatter sovereignty, where the national government did not care whether slavery was voted up or down, the house where slavery could as well spread as disappear, because no moral consideration stood in the way, because no one had committed the nation to a moral principle. The fatal division was caused by diversity of goals, not of current practice. If the Missouri Compromise could be restored, said Lincoln in a famous passage, and of course the *Dred Scott* decision reversed,

and the whole slavery question replaced on the old ground of "toleration" by *necessity* where it exists, with unyielding hostility to the spread of it, on principle, I would, in consideration, gladly agree, that Judge Douglas should never be *out*, and I never *in*, an office, so long as we both or either, live.

Government of, by, and for the people was in Lincoln's thought required to be also principled government, with the counter-majoritarian restraints that this implies. This is why the idea of popular sovereignty—freeing the people to vote slavery up or down without reference to principle—was inadmissible, indeed, revolting. But principles were not hard and fast restraints derived from a non-democratic past. Rather, as Mr. Jaffa writes, they were evolved "from within the democratic ethos as perfections of that ethos." They were efficacious in guiding the tendency of public action. Their integrity was worth going to war for, although, if it was maintained, the most deep-cutting compromises were tolerable.

Here is the statement of the *casus belli*. It was not the existence of slavery, not the Fugitive Slave Law. It was the act repealing the Missouri Compromise (and all the more so, the *Dred Scott* decision), which repealed also the goal of eventual abolition and substituted a declared, explicit policy of "don't care."

This *declared* indifference but, as I must think, covert *real* zeal for the spread of slavery, I can not but hate. I hate it because of the monstrous injustice of slavery itself. I hate it because it deprives our republican example of its just influence in the world—enables the enemies of free institutions, with plausibility, to taunt us as hypocrites—causes the real friends of freedom to doubt our sincerity, and especially because it forces so many really good men amongst ourselves into an open war with the very fundamental principles of civil liberty—criticizing the Declaration of Independence, and insisting that there is no right principle of action but self-interest.[27]

Lincoln's thought, as Mr. Jaffa writes, "was the finely wrought consummation, of philosophic insight and a poetic gift, of a life devoted to the problem of 'the capability of a people to govern themselves.' "[28] The teaching of that life is that principled government by the consent of the governed often means the definition of principled goals, and the practice of the art of the possible in striving to attain them. The hard fact of an existing evil institution such as slavery and the hard practical difficulties that stood in the way of its sudden abolition justified myriad compromises short of abandoning the goal. The goal itself—the principle—made sense only as an absolute, and as such it was to be maintained. As such it had its vast educational value, as such it exerted its crucial influence on the tendency of prudential policy. But expedient compromises remained necessary also, chiefly because a radically principled solution would collide with widespread prejudices, which no government resting on consent could disregard, any more than it could sacrifice its goals to them.

Our democratic system of government exists in this Lincolnian tension between principle and expediency, and within it judicial review must play its role. Mr. Wechsler's dilemma is a false one. The constitutional function of the Court is to define values and proclaim principles. But this is not a function to be exercised with respect to some exceedingly few matters, while society is left wholly to its devices of expediency in dealing with the great number of its other concerns. Often, as with the segregation problem and slavery before it, we require principle and expediency at once. The rule of the neutral principles would excise the Court's function of declaring principled goals. More, it would require the Court to validate with overtones of principle most of what the political institutions do merely on grounds of expediency. Like Judge Hand, Mr. Wechsler appears rather to depreciate the calling of the judges as "teachers to the citizenry."[29]

Lincoln's thought, on the other hand, is far from denying society's need for judicial review as a principle-defining process that stands aside from the marketplace of expediency. And it is at the heart of the utility of such a process to proclaim the absolute principle that race is not an allowable criterion for legislative classification. The principle as such permits no principled flexibility, just as abhorrence of slavery did not. But at the same time, it cannot in our society constitute a hard and fast rule of action for universal immediate execution. This is nothing to be proud of. It is a disagreeable fact, and it cannot be wished away. It is no service to any worthy objective simply to close one's eyes to it. Yet the question persists, how does the Court, charged with the function of enunciating principle, produce or permit the necessary compromises?

The essentially important fact, so often missed, is that the Court wields a threefold power. It may strike down legislation as inconsistent with principle. It may validate, or, in Charles L. Black's better word, "legitimate" legislation as consistent with principle. *Or it may do neither.* It may do neither, and therein lies the secret of its ability to maintain itself in the tension between principle and expediency.

When it strikes down legislative policy, the Court must act rigorously on principle, else it undermines the justification for its power. It must enunciate a goal, it must demonstrate that what the legislature did will not measure up, and it must proclaim its readiness to defend the goal—absolutely, if it is an absolute one. But it is not obligated to foresee all foreseeable relevant cases and to foreclose all compromise. Indeed, it cannot. It can only decide the case before it, giving reasons which rise to the dignity of principle and hence, of course, have a forward momentum and broad radiations. But the compelling force of the judgment goes only to the actual case before the Court. If it were otherwise, another part of the justification for the existence of the power would be destroyed. For, as we have seen, the Court's peculiar capacity to enunciate basic principles inheres in large part in its opportunity to derive and test whatever generalization it proclaims in the concrete circumstances of a case. This is an opportunity that a legislature, constrained to generalize prospectively and hence in a sense abstractly, cannot have. I have remarked that the function of judicial review arises in the limiting context of cases, and yet, while the Court should not surmount the limitation, it must rise above the case. And while the Court should rise above the case, it must not surmount the limitation.

Again, when the Court legitimates a legislative action, it should also act on principle. Here, the clash between judicial review and the electorally responsible institutions is less grave. Perhaps theoretically it is nonexistent. But in actual practice, as I shall show further, the Court, when it legitimates a measure, does insert itself with significant consequences into the decisional process as carried on in the other institutions. This is a necessary consequence of the Court's power to define and apply society's basic principles.

When the Court, however, stays its hand, and makes clear that it is staying its hand and not legitimating, then the political processes are given relatively free play. Such a decision needs relatively little justification in terms of consistency with democratic theory. It needs more to be justified as compatible with the Court's role as defender of the faith, proclaimer and protector of the goals. But in withholding constitutional judgment, the Court does not necessarily forsake an educational function, nor does it abandon principle. It seeks merely to elicit the correct answers to certain prudential questions that, in such a society as Lincoln conceived, lie in the path of ultimate issues of principle. To this end, the Court has, over the years, developed an almost inexhaustible arsenal of techniques and devices. Most of them are quite properly called techniques for eliciting answers, since so often they engage the Court in a Socratic colloquy with the other institutions of government and with society as a whole concerning the necessity for this or that measure, for this or that compromise. All the while, the issue of principle remains in abeyance and ripens. "The most important thing we do," said Brandeis, "is not doing." He had in mind all the techniques, of which he was a past master, for staying the Court's hand. They are the most important thing, because they make possible performance of the Court's grand function as proclaimer and protector of the goals. These are the techniques that allow leeway to expediency without abandoning principle. Therefore they make possible a principled government.

There can be no understanding of the Court without an appreciation of the variety and significance of these techniques, most of which are lumped roughly and often disingenuously together under the rubric of jurisdiction. In a later chapter I shall deal in detail with jurisdictional doctrines, so-called, and also with other techniques and devices of the mediating way between legitimation and denial of legislative power. Actually, the decree in the *School Segregation Cases* itself exemplifies one such device. For present purposes, it is enough to assert that the Court found no insuperable difficulty in leaving open the question of the constitutionality of antimiscegenation statutes,[30] though it would surely seem to be governed by the principle of the *Segregation Cases*, and that the Court should similarly leave open such an issue as is offered by benevolent housing quotas.

There was a time, following the Civil War, when segregated public education marked a great advance toward achievement of equal citizenship for the Negro. It was no more defensible on principle then than it is now. But men of principle, concerned with providing education of any sort for newly freed slaves, readily tolerated it as a necessary compromise.[31] The Supreme Court made the grave error of lending its affirmative sanction to the practice of segregation in the nineteenth century, and doing so on principle, across the board.[32] This was the error, not failure at the early date to strike down segregation as unconstitutional. For the moment, unless and until experience should belie the hope that may animate benevolent quota proposals or demonstrate that, rather than a possibly progressive expedient, they are a retrogressive one, benevolent quotas should be allowed their season of leeway, without offense to principle. They may well be for the 1960's the equivalent of segregated schooling a century ago. This is not to say that the Supreme Court should legitimate them—only that it should leave their constitutionality undecided. Before examining, however, the jurisdictional techniques and cognate devices which would enable the Court to achieve this result, we must consider certain other approaches to the general problem of the nature and justification of judicial review.

CHAPTER 3

"The Infirm Glory of the Positive Hour"

In *Marbury* v. *Madison,* it will be remembered, Marshall derived the power of judicial review by putting the case of a conflict between an act of the legislature and the Constitution. There were only two possible ways out of such a conflict, he said. Either the Constitution controls the legislative act which is repugnant to it, or the legislative act controls the Constitution, with the upshot, in the latter instance, that the legislature has the power to alter the Constitution any time it chooses to do so by an ordinary statute. "Between these alternatives there is no middle ground." Since the supremacy of the Constitution, as the organic law, was "a proposition too plain to be contested," it became the function of the judiciary to uphold the latter and strike down the conflicting statute. The test case, again, was one to which both a statute and the Constitution applied, and the position of the Court was that it had to decide either conformably to the statute, disregarding the Constitution, or conformably to the Constitution, disregarding the statute.

If cases such as Marshall's model exist, it must be because the Constitution is a plain and specific document giving plain and specific answers to concrete questions. This, as I have noted at some length, is the fundamental assumption underlying the reasoning of *Marbury* v. *Madison,* and it is an assumption refuted on the face of the Constitution, at least in so far as the typical case is concerned. Marshall himself eloquently conceded as much in his later opinion in *McCulloch* v. *Maryland.* For Thayer, of course, the crux of analysis was a conception of the Constitution as a sweeping and flexible charter of government—a conception, that is, rooted in *McCulloch* v. *Maryland,* not in *Marbury* v. *Madison.* The same is true of the criticism current in the 1920's and '30's, to which I have alluded, and of the more recent writers I have discussed, who pick up where Thayer left off. All at least profess to agree that the Constitution is what Thayer and the later Marshall recognized it was, and that its text can serve only as the putative starting point of the process of judicial review, not as both its certain beginning and its unequivocal end. *Marbury* v. *Madison,* in other words, states the problem rather than solves it; moreover, it states the wrong problem.

Marbury v. *Madison,* however, exerts an enormous magnetic pull. It is, after all, a great historic event, a famous victory; and it constitutes, even more than victories won by arms, one of the foundation stones of the Republic. It is hallowed. It is revered. If it had a physical presence, like the Alamo or Gettysburg, it would be a tourist attraction; and the truth is that it very nearly does have and very nearly is. At any rate, most of us share, as Thayer said, in the moral approval of the lines, and it is not altogether surprising that many of us often tend to forget the faults in the reasoning. And so, in almost regular cyclical fashion, we witness atavistic regressions to the simplicities of *Marbury* v. *Madison,* to its concept of the self-applying Constitution and the self-evident function of judicial review. This is an aspect of a phenomenon to which the law as a whole, not only the law of judicial review under the Constitution, is often subject. Judges and lawyers recurrently come to feel that they find law rather than make it. Many otherwise painful problems seem to solve themselves with ease when this feeling envelops people. American law went through an era of such soothing, if not good, feelings during the first thirty years or so of this century.[1] Courts were prone in general to "find" the law and "merely" give voice to it and see to its automatic application. They "found" it in the precedents of the past century and even further back. On the Supreme Court, "inescapable answers" were "found" in the Constitution and in the gloss that earlier cases had imposed on the text. These attitudes need exploding, of course, as soon as they recur, and a school of critics who very appropriately called themselves realists, and who flourished during the 1920's and '30's, proceeded assiduously to explode them. They achieved what was in effect a return to Thayer and the main tradition. Then, however, as I shall explain, they overshot the mark. Or at least their descendants did. Being true children, perhaps, of their atomic times, they produced overkill. And eventually, as in our weaponry we may get so sophisticated as to revert to bows and arrows, so the neo-realists effected a most curious joinder with a renewed wave of literalists who are wedded to the ever-irresistible simplicities of *Marbury* v. *Madison*.

Adjectival Simplicities and the Neo-Realists, Nihilists, et al.

In 1942, when the reconstituted Court—the liberal, Roosevelt Court, as it was called—was in full flower, give or take a petal, Max Lerner had occasion to recall the "great constitutional war" of New Deal days. By and large, the Supreme Court and those who battled in its behalf were the victors of the war of 1937. And so it seemed to Mr. Lerner that it was "difficult today for any conservative group to attack the Court as a whole, because the Court rests on the essential judicial foundation for which the conservatives themselves fought so bitterly. They won that fight, and they must content themselves with the fruits of their victory, even though the taste of the fruits is sometimes bitter in their mouths."[2]

The word "conservative" in this usage tends somewhat to mislead, for it suggests that the victors of 1937 were a politically homogeneous group, or that they have remained one. But it does help to evoke the image of the political right in this country, which was arrayed in defense of the Supreme Court twenty-five years ago and which is now, a generation after Mr. Lerner wrote, rather generally and strongly critical of the Court. The interesting fact is that current attacks upon the Court from the right rest comfortably on "the essential judicial foundation" bitterly fought for and gained in 1937. For that foundation was *Marbury* v. *Madison*. And on that case, strictly read and literally carried forward, conservative opinion bases its present critique of the Court.

"Stripped to the waist, it is the obvious purpose of those who demand this procedure [President Roosevelt's proposal to enlarge the Court] to change the interpretation of the Constitution, the construction of the Constitution, hence the Constitution itself." Thus the late Senator Walter F. George of Georgia, champion of the Court, in a radio address on February 28, 1937. It was essential to government under a written constitution, he went on, that the Supreme Court have the power to interpose the will of the people, represented by the Constitution, to the will of the legislature. On March 11, 1956, Senator George signed the Southern Congressional Manifesto, which, also addicted to the nudist metaphor, detected in the *School Segregation Cases* an exercise of "naked judicial power." Avowing their continued "reliance on the Constitution as the fundamental law of the land," Senator George and his colleagues deplored the Court's decision as having "no legal basis" and as substituting "personal political and social ideas for the established law of the land." After all, that law had been "found" long ago, in *Plessy* v. *Ferguson,* when the Court held segregation constitutional. And the Constitution itself "does not mention education"!³

But the signers of the Southern Manifesto knew what they were about and were perhaps not all taken in by their own rhetoric. Theirs, as I shall try to show in a later chapter, was a sophisticated and purposive political assault. I am interested now in conservative opinion that lays some claim to objectivity, and I take as illustrative an article by Arthur Krock, published in *The New York Times* upon the occasion of the retirement of Mr. Justice Reed in February 1957.⁴ Mr. Krock, in the course of an appreciation of the career of Justice Reed, briefly surveyed the work of the Court in the preceding generation. During the 19 years of Justice Reed's tenure, Mr. Krock wrote, the Supreme Court underwent three phases: "from conservative to radical, from radical to moderate, and from moderate to radical again." Justice Reed himself was throughout a "moderate progressive"—a term, Mr. Krock concedes, which "reflects an oversimplification" but which is applicable nonetheless.

Mr. Krock here reveals a conception of the process of judicial review which is not his alone. He sees the Court as conservative in the 1920's and early '30's, when it construed the Due Process and

Commerce Clauses of the Constitution as forbidding certain measures of social and economic regulation enacted by the Congress
and by various state legislatures. Mr. Justice Reed, bringing his
"moderate progressivism" to the Court in 1938, would have none
of this. His construction of the Constitution made room for such
legislation. But the "judge-made amendments of the Constitution
implicit in the opinions of Black, Felix Frankfurter, William O.
Douglas and Frank Murphy" (ah, the radicals!) were too much
for him, and he dissented, except that he went along in the *School
Segregation Cases.* One concludes that "conservatives" tolerate no
"judge-made" amendments to the Constitution, moderates indulge
some mild ones but reject others, and radicals just go on writing
them all the time. Tax and tax, spend and spend, amend and
amend. This must be so since, as Mr. Krock notes, Van Devanter
and Sutherland and Butler and McReynolds of the old Court—the
true conservatives—thought, or would have thought, that Reed
himself, the moderate, was amending the Constitution when he
accommodated the New Deal and when he held all-white pri-
maries unconstitutional. And then comes Reed, presumably thinking the same thing of the radicals. Former Supreme Court Justice
James F. Byrnes exemplified the same conception when he joined
in the attack on the Court's *School Segregation* decision. He accused the Court of having willfully amended the Constitution in
the face of precedents that had settled the true construction of the
document.[5] This was a radical thing to do.

Such criticism derives straight from *Marbury* v. *Madison.* The
Constitution is thought to embody a clear and certain yardstick
by which to measure the actions of other branches of the government. The ideal function of a Justice of the Supreme Court is the
mechanical application of the yardstick to such actions as are duly
brought to his attention. The only qualification he is required, or
indeed allowed, to bring to the task is a lawyer's skill. Such constitutional phrases as "Due Process of Law" or "Equal Protection of
the Laws" are very much like the language in a deed, let us say,
giving one title to land "in fee simple": it takes a lawyer to tell one
just exactly what such fine print means; but a good lawyer can tell
you, and that is that. From this engaging conception, everything
follows. The Constitution, being very old, is naturally a conserva-

tive document; that is to say, conservative in the sense in which the word is used to describe the position of men in American political life. It is wary of Big Labor, inhospitable to social and economic experimentation, attached to existing racial practices, suspicious of foreign creeds, favorably inclined toward a balanced budget and a sound dollar, and probably ill disposed toward dealings with Red China; conservative in the tradition of Harry Flood Byrd and Herbert Hoover, with perhaps a touch of moderation *à la* Bernard Baruch. To be construed so as to produce such conservative results, as for a day it was, the Constitution need not be "amended." It need only be honestly read by a lawyer, in Mr. Krock's phrase, "of deep experience." The "radicals," being intent on achieving what —again, in common political parlance—are radical results, have to amend the document. To be sure, lawyers "of deep experience" made things a little sticky during the Depression, and wise "moderate progressives," having regard to the unrest of the people, were constrained to go ahead and cut a few corners. But that was a crash program, and it does not justify going on in the same fashion now.

It follows inexorably that the "radical" Justices who are engaged in "amending" the Constitution are simply a body of electorally irresponsible politicians, and that there can be no excuse for letting them exercise a veto over the actions of other politicians, who are responsible to the voters. This is somewhat—very mildly— true of the moderates as well, but it is not true of conservative Justices, for they do not make policy; they simply apply the organic law. Mr. Krock and Justice Byrnes imply just this, although it is owing to Mr. Krock to add that he does so in considerably better temper than the former Justice. Moving farther out of the temperate zone into the Equatorial Right, one is greeted by the Congressional Manifesto mentioned above, which amounts otherwise to the same thing.

What is passing strange is that there is a group of neo-realist writers who say out loud and with cheerful approval the things Mr. Krock and Justice Byrnes imply in pain and sorrow. "Among the more significant aspects of the Warren Court decisions," writes Professor Alpheus T. Mason in a book published in 1958, "especially in the civil rights orbit, is the unblushing way in which certain Justices take sides on burning issues." In the *School Segregation Cases*, he says, "the distinction between *judgment* and *will*, already tenuous, was honored only in the breach."⁶ The neo-realists—Mr. Mason may be taken as representative in this respect at least—would be no more eager to be bedfellows to Mr. Krock and Justice Byrnes than the latter would like to be theirs. Indeed, Mr. Krock and Justice Byrnes call them radicals. But they have a great deal in common just the same, being bound together by the steel hoops of those adjectives—conservative, moderate, radical—which they all apply to members of the Court. The neo-realists are aware of the difference between the Due Process Clause and deeds and leases and the like. They have not Mr. Krock's illusion that the Constitution is a clear and certain document written in early law-French, which can be translated clearly and certainly by good lawyers. But this does not greatly distinguish their conception of judicial review from Mr. Krock's and Justice Byrnes's. For they will not see that the Court should intervene under the Constitution only to vindicate what the judges deem to be ultimate values, which they may evolve only by a subtle and complex process, and to which no adjectives drawn from the political marketplace can be applicable. The neo-realists see the judges as free to achieve such immediate results as they like, when they like, without necessary relation to any particular category of principles. And they take a dim view of those judges who hesitate to act in behalf of the liberal cause of the moment as if they had about fifty votes apiece in the House of Representatives. The neo-realists call such judges what Mr. Krock and Justice Byrnes call them: conservative; and they add such choice terms as legalistic, technical, and unrealistic if, going on his pre-judicial record, they feel that the judge in question should have come out on the liberal side.

A generation or more ago, the realists taught, in the words of one of the most brilliant of their number, the late Felix S. Cohen, that "the vivid fictions and metaphors of traditional jurisprudence" are no more than "poetical and mnemonic devices for formulating decisions reached on other grounds." Or, to quote another famous passage of Felix Cohen: "Rules of logic [or of constitutional construction] can no more produce legal or moral doctrines than they can produce kittens. On the whole, it is safe to assume that those legal doctrines that claim to be the offspring of logic are either not proud or not aware of their real parents."[7] The realists were themselves taught all this by Holmes; by Felix Cohen's father and Holmes's friend, the redoubtable Morris Raphael; by Thomas Reed Powell; and by others, including Thayer himself and John Chipman Gray. But, as I have noted, this is a lesson frequently unlearned, especially in the province of judicial review, where *Marbury* v. *Madison* exerts its great attraction. The realists, who were a substantial company of original minds working in a time of great ferment, retaught the lesson vigorously and well.

Felix Cohen and some of his peers also strained to find the grounds on which a new jurisprudence might be made to rest soundly and realistically. Having established once more that judges make law, they addressed themselves to the crucial question of how and when they should do so. Cohen was not resigned to conclude that the "poetical and mnemonic devices" screened personal predilection, temporal political preferences, hunch—no more. And he was certainly not content to have it remain so.

"What a judge ought to do in a given case," he wrote,

is quite as much a moral issue as any of the traditional problems of Sunday School morality. . . . [T]his notion has no terrors for those who think of morality in earthly terms. . . . If ethical appraisals are inherent in all realms of human conduct, the ethical appraisal of a legal situation is not to be found in the spontaneous outpourings of a sensitive conscience unfamiliar with the social context, the background of precedent, and the practices and expectations, legal and extra-legal, which have grown up around a given type of transaction.[8]

It was never altogether realistic to conclude that behind all judicial dialectic there was personal preference and personal power and nothing else. In any event, that is a reality, if it be true, on which we cannot allow the edifice of judicial review to be based, for if that is all judges do, then their authority over us is totally intolerable and totally irreconcilable with the theory and practice of political democracy. However, some of the followers of Cohen and the others stopped just there.

Cohen had occasion once to quote from the *New Statesman* a variation on Bertrand Russell's "conjugation of irregular verbs"

(I am firm/You are obstinate/He is a pigheaded fool). It runs as follows:

1. I have about me something of the subtle, haunting, mysterious fragrance of the Orient.
2. You rather overdo it, dear.
3. She stinks.[9]

It has long been a tradition in criticism of the legal system, and particularly in criticism of the process of judicial review, to suggest that its conceptual constructs often have about them a subtle, haunting, mysterious fragrance of total unreality. Cohen and the school of realists were at pains to point out that the system was rather overdoing it in this respect. And they proceeded with the attempt to found the system in the reality of the proper ethical and practical considerations. Some of their followers merely mutter—or exclaim—"She stinks," and are content to let it go at that. A close rereading of the work of Felix Cohen would be good for their souls.

The final fruit of neo-realism—perhaps either arrested realism or surrealism would be more accurate—is a genial, nihilistic attitude of coexistence with the Court and its work, along with a complete lack of interest in the process by which the work is achieved, or in the proper role of that process in a democratic society. The Court itself is interesting as a mountain is said to be to a climber, because it is there. If there is any judgment to be exercised with respect to it, it is a factional, predilectional one about results. The rest is *elegantia juris,* and it couldn't matter less.

The efforts of judges and of their more concerned critics to evolve principles and to explain and justify results in terms of principle might as well be described, in the phrase of the British philosopher F. H. Bradley, as the process of finding "bad reasons for what we believe on instinct." Bradley added that "the finding of these reasons is no less an instinct." Walter Kaufmann, who quotes Bradley in his *Critique of Religion and Philosophy,* observes that "it ought to be the aim of philosophy to teach men to master this instinct and become housebroken." This is, of course, a function of the law in general, and of constitutional law in particular. It is what the realists of old labored to achieve. Let men act on rational and moral principle, and let them at any rate not be satisfied with bad reasons for what they believe on instinct. The function of judicial review is to evolve and apply, although in a limited sphere, fundamental reasons of principle on which to base men's actions, and which should cut across men's uncontrolled instincts and interests.

This is of no concern, however, to the arrested realists. They consider only the outcome of a case, not the process. Thus, in a recent book,[10] John P. Frank remarks that faulty reasoning in an opinion is a matter of "technical failure." It is all very well and good to have on the Supreme Court men of first-rate intellectual powers. But "more important than reason is the quality of creativeness." This, in turn, is evidently the capacity to come up with something new often. Astoundingly enough, for Mr. Frank at least, almost anything seems to do. He disapproves, for example, of the Court's efforts to erect rigid barriers against economic and social legislation in the 1920's and early '30's. These were results Mr. Frank dislikes. Yet he is ecstatic in his appreciation of the Court's performance in those years: "For sheer creativeness there has never been anything like it." That was a great Court. The bad Court for Mr. Frank is a sort of do-nothing Court. When he touches on the Vinson years, he sounds like Mr. Truman denouncing the 80th Congress. And he is always much preoccupied with the volume of the Court's output; productivity is the watchword in Mr. Frank's judicial universe. Brief, muscular, simply written opinions that come to a "clear, creative" conclusion are what he values, not reflective essays. The admonition to the Court in the exercise of the function of judicial review seems to be very simply: Don't just sit there; do something. Anything.

An even more striking—perhaps the ultimate—cry of nihilism has issued from Thurman Arnold, sometime Professor of Law at Yale, sometime Assistant Attorney General of the United States, and sometime Judge of the Court of Appeals for the District of Columbia. Judge Arnold was a member in high standing of the group of realists that was so fruitfully at work in the 1920's, and he retains their characteristic accents in his writing. The utterance that I have in mind is entitled "Professor Hart's Theology," and it was published in 1960, by way of answer to a paper by Professor Henry M. Hart, Jr., of Harvard, which in turn was quite critical of some of the Court's recent product. Mr. Hart's premise, stated in a passage quoted earlier, was that the Court "is predestined . . . not only by the thrilling tradition of Anglo-American law but also by the hard fact of its position in the structure of American institutions to be a voice of reason, charged with the creative function of discerning afresh and of articulating and developing impersonal and durable principles of constitutional law. . . ." Some of the Court's recent work fell short, for Mr. Hart, of this standard. Judge Arnold's thesis is as follows: "Legal theorists like Professor Hart design the clothes which conceal the person of the king and which give him his authority and public acceptance." And further: "These are the clothes which the Court must wear in order to retain its authority and public appearance." They are clothes whose worthiness Judge Arnold does not question. If men do not pursue the ideal of "reason" above "personal preference," they may succumb to the "even greater illusion . . . that personal power can be benevolently exercised." But the ideal of a process such as Professor Hart describes is, Mr. Arnold suggests, also illusion, if a pleasant one. The reality *is* personal power. The Justices will often be able to agree on a result without being able to articulate reasons for it. That is just as well. Mr. Hart speaks of a process of "maturing of collective thought." Judge Arnold's reply is as follows:

There is no such process as this, and there never has been; men of positive views are only hardened in those views by such conferences. . . . To suggest that judges who hold differing views with absolute convictions . . . are going to surrender those views, moved solely by logic and debate, is to betray a lack of knowledge of the history of the Court.[11]

As it happens, the betrayal of a lack of knowledge of the history of the Court is on the other foot. Moved not "solely by logic and debate" but by introspection, by reflection, by reason, of which logic is a tool and which debate can induce, judges have surrendered what seemed to others, and above all to themselves, "views [held] with absolute convictions." There are not a few such instances of record, some celebrated, some obscure, and one can only surmise that many more are unrecorded, some unknown even to a Justice's colleagues, and some of which the Justice concerned may himself not be fully aware. Of course, there have been judges "of positive views" who have sometimes behaved as Judge Arnold says. But why should we accept them as the norm? The fact, as Whitehead wrote, "that reason too often fails does not give fair ground for the hysterical conclusion that it never succeeds."[12] This is the point. Judge Arnold is content to suggest that there is no such thing as a process of maturing collective thought, no such thing as a process of reason, no such thing as decisions rigorously governed by principle. What is there, then? There are nine men, not responsible to us, who have "deep-seated convictions about current national problems," and who do what they like. Judge Arnold finds conditions as he describes them quite satisfactory and considers all else to be merely the theorizing of academic persons who have never met a payroll.

This is cynicism pure and simple. And here, as in other realms, cynicism is what the late Henry L. Stimson called it: "the only deadly sin."[13] As always, there is no reply to be made to it other than that if the estimate of reality on which it feeds is in any degree correct, then the reality must be changed to exactly that degree. The sin is mortal, because it propagates a self-validating picture of reality. If men are told complacently enough that this is how things are, they will become accustomed to it and accept it. And in the end this is how things will be. That is the reason such a view, or non-view, of the judicial process as Judge Arnold's must be noticed and seen for what it is.

Of Activism, Absolutes, Attitudes, and the Plain Words of the Constitution

The neo-realists, I have maintained, have most curiously married themselves to the present generation of literalists, for whom, as for their ancestors, the beginning and the end of judicial review are both to be found in the text of the Constitution. Strictly speaking, however, the neo-realists' connection with the political conservatism of Arthur Krock and former Justice Byrnes can scarcely be called a marriage. A marriage of inconvenience, perhaps, if it is one at all. I have in mind now an alliance more soundly joined and more enduringly sanctioned, both in practical considerations and in the emotions. This alliance is solemnized, among many other places, in the book by Professor Alpheus T. Mason to which I have referred. Mr. Mason is intent upon broadcasting the truth "that judges, like other human beings, are influenced by political and personal factors." As he says in his Foreword, his purpose is to dispel "the fiction that judges operate in a non-political vacuum, above personal considerations, and beyond political influences." Mr. Mason, therefore, greets with hearty approval what he perceives to be a significant aspect "of the Warren court decisions, especially in the civil rights orbit," namely, "the unblushing way in which certain Justices take sides" on current issues. "The activistic views long propounded by Justice Black *et al.,*" Mr. Mason concludes, "are now gaining ascendancy."[14] These are the banns, and the neo-realist literature is replete with them. The curious aspect of the marriage is that Justice Black and his "activist" brethren are very far from professing the exercise of any will of their own. They take sides, to be sure, but they unblushingly admit only to taking the side of the constitutional text.

Mr. Justice Black is the senior Associate Justice of the Supreme Court, having taken his seat in 1937. He is also—it can be said in his lifetime—without doubt a figure of the first importance in the history of the Court. He has been an articulate judge, and his views have long been familiar in great detail, although, as might be expected, they have not remained entirely static. In February 1960, Justice Black delivered a paper on "The Bill of Rights" at New York University Law School, which may be taken to represent at least the chief feature of his mature judicial philosophy.[15] This address marked one of the Justice's exceedingly rare extrajudicial appearances. It is valuable as a concerted statement of his position, for which the confines of cases seldom offer so full an opportunity.

There is a difference of opinion, Justice Black said, over the extent to which the Bill of Rights limits federal power. The ultimate resolution of this difference must "have far-reaching consequences upon our liberties." There are those, he said—and one has every reason to suppose that he had in mind Thayer's writings, the papers by Judge Learned Hand and Professor Herbert Wechsler discussed above, and the work of Mr. Justice Frankfurter, both in his judicial capacity and as the author of the opening address on the "Judicial Function" at the John Marshall Celebration at Harvard in 1955[16]—there are those, said Justice Black, who recognize "no 'absolute' prohibitions in the Constitution," and for whom "all constitutional problems are questions of reasonableness, proximity, and degree." This view, in Justice Black's judgment, "comes close to the English doctrine of legislative omnipotence, qualified only by the possibility of a judicial veto if the Supreme Court finds that a congressional choice between 'competing' policies has no reasonable basis."

The statement of the opposing position and the closeness to the English view that Justice Black perceives are both open to considerable question. As I have indicated, neither the theory nor the practice of contemporary judicial review has stopped with Thayer's rule of the clear mistake, which is all Justice Black concedes to those who do not agree with him. What is irrational is unconstitutional, but more has been held to be unconstitutional as well by those who take a different approach than Justice Black's. Be that as it may, he "cannot accept this approach to the Bill of Rights. It is my belief that there *are* 'absolutes' in our Bill of Rights, and that they were put there on purpose by men who knew what words meant, and meant their prohibitions to be 'absolutes.' "

To be, that is, unconditional, definite, certain. And there, stated truly enough, is one issue between judges who practice what is rather unhappily called judicial restraint and those who are readier and quicker to strike at legislative and executive actions. Justice Black, like the neo-realists, speaks readily for the quick.

Yet it is central to Justice Black's position that he enters no plea for judicial supremacy. Quite the contrary. In no sense that he will vouchsafe is it judges who shape the limitations to be imposed on Congress, the President, and the states; rather, it is the Constitution, the written Bill of Rights. "Where conflicting values exist in the field of individual liberties protected by the Constitution," says the Justice, "that document settles the conflict. . . ." Naturally enough, therefore, like Marshall in *Marbury* v. *Madison*, he goes to the text to make his case.

Starting in reverse order with the articles of the Bill of Rights, Justice Black soon reaches a point of some difficulty for one who expects to find absolute language. The Eighth Amendment prohibits the exaction of "excessive bail" and "excessive fines," and the infliction of "cruel and unusual punishments." This, says the Justice, "is one of the less precise provisions. The courts are required to determine the meaning of such general terms. . . ." But the difficulty can be overcome by excluding it from consideration. And that is not necessarily a debating tactic to be despised. Subjects for discussion must be sensibly circumscribed; no one can usefully talk about everything all at once. So the Justice, having earlier excluded the "problem of the marginal scope of each individual amendment, as applied to the particular facts," proceeds to argue that, whatever difficulties might arise in some cases, surely "admittedly excessive fines or cruel punishments" are absolutely outlawed and may not be allowed by any process of balancing reasonableness, proximity, and degree. But, after all, what is an "admittedly cruel punishment"? Is it the peacetime death penalty imposed upon Julius and Ethel Rosenberg for spying, or the thirty years' imprisonment that has been the lot of the very equivocally involved Sobell in the same case? Is it the twelve years in the death house followed by the electric chair visited upon Caryl Chessman? And is it the same today as when those "absolute" words were written? And who is to admit that it is admittedly? The people of the United States? The people of the State of California? Chessman? The Rosenbergs? The Supreme Court of the United States? Will a majority of judges do? A minority recently thought that loss of nationality is a cruel and unusual punishment. Fifty years ago, seven were of the view that a punishment consisting of a fine plus lengthy imprisonment for corruptly making false entries in public records was cruel and unusual, but two judges, White and Holmes, based a dissent upon the original meaning of the "absolute" words in question.[17]

We try another amendment. There is the Fourth, under which Brandeis, in dissent, would have forbidden wiretapping, and which for him, as for Bradley before him and for others after, speaks not only in the most stirring but in the most comprehensive language of all: "The right of the people to be secure in their persons, houses, papers, and effects, against unreasonable searches and seizures, shall not be violated. . . ."[18] Justice Black's comment is that while there will be differences of opinion concerning what is unreason-

able and thus barred by the amendment—he has himself found
to be reasonable practices that some of his generally less "activist"
brethren have struck down—"if it *is* unreasonable, it is absolutely
prohibited."

Again, the Fifth Amendment's famous phrase, Due Process of
Law, has been given effect over and above the narrow procedural
content assigned to it by early statutes at common law. Pursuant
to due process of law, after all, segregation was struck down in the
District of Columbia. There has been, says Justice Black, much
controversy over the meaning of the phrase. "Whatever its meaning, however, there can be no doubt that it must be granted." But
what has a litigant got who has due process of law, whatever that
may be? Perhaps, when he says that whatever-it-is must be granted,
Justice Black has in mind the jurisdictional and other doctrines of
"not doing" which sometimes cause the Court to stay its hand;
perhaps he wishes to suggest that the Court ought never to withhold adjudication. Justice Black, however, does not address himself in this paper to problems of jurisdiction, as they are commonly
called, and the like. Nor does he here maintain that history binds
judges absolutely. This would raise an obvious difficulty in the
present context, for if the reference were to an "admitted," very
narrow historical meaning of the Due Process Clause, much else
in which Justice Black has joined would be relegated to limbo.
But here, Justice Black insists only on the force of the text of the
Constitution, literally read. He insists that whatever else may be
true, there is a core of absolute literal meaning in the text, which
it is the duty of the judges to render and apply literally.

Having tackled the Bill of Rights in reverse order, Justice Black
rises to the climax of the First Amendment: "Congress shall make
no law . . . abridging the freedom of speech, or of the press." The
phrase "Congress shall make no law," says Justice Black, "is com-
posed of plain words, easily understood." And in a recent opinion
in an obscenity case, he added, calling italics to the aid of his assertion: "I read 'no law . . . abridging' to mean *no law abridging*."[19]
But other judges have wondered just what sort of speech it is
whose freedom is not to be abridged? And what qualifies as an
abridgment? Can it be said that the search for organizing principles adequate to the solution of a variety of free-speech problems

is flatly ended by the "plain words" of the First Amendment? Justice Black professes to think so. Two cases last year, for example, in which a divided Court upheld once again the investigating power of Congress, were quite plain for Justice Black in dissent. For him the applicable principles were

embodied for all who care to see in our Bill of Rights. They were put there for the specific purpose of preventing just the sort of governmental suppression of criticism that the majority upholds here. Their ineffectiveness to that end stems, not from any lack of precision in the statement of the principles, but from the refusal of the majority to apply those principles as precisely stated. For the principles of the First Amendment are stated in precise and mandatory terms. . . .

And further:

The area set off for individual freedom by the Bill of Rights was marked by boundaries precisely defined. It is my belief that the area so set off provides an adequate minimum protection for the freedoms indispensable to individual liberty. Thus we have only to observe faithfully the boundaries already marked for us. . . . As I understand it, this Court's duty to guard constitutional liberties is to guard those liberties the Constitution defined, not those that may be defined from case to case on the basis of this Court's judgment as to the relative importance of individual liberty and governmental power. The majority's approach makes the First Amendment, not the rigid protection of liberty its language imports, but a poor flexible imitation. . . . The Founders of this Nation were not then willing to trust the definition of First Amendment freedoms to Congress or this Court, nor am I now.[20]

It is thus quite evident that when Justice Black speaks of something that is "admittedly" within the language of the Bill of Rights or of another constitutional provision, and when he insists on the "plain words" of such provisions, he has in mind not only those core cases in which everyone might indeed admit the force of the constitutional language, as where that document speaks of civil jury trials if the amount in controversy exceeds twenty dollars, or where it limits the President's term to four years and that of a Senator to six. For Justice Black, references to "admitted" rights and to "plain words" also cover cases in which the language, as a matter of common English usage, would not generally be deemed compelling, in which the process of decision involves, for other judges, nontextual considerations, but in which Justice Black chooses to declare himself compelled by language alone.

A statement of the late Mr. Justice Roberts is generally cited as typical of the Court whose "poetical devices" the realists so effectively exploded; the Court, that is, which goaded President Roosevelt into trying to pack, or unpack, it in 1937. Speaking for the majority that struck down the New Deal agricultural program (AAA) in 1936, Roberts said that the Court in constitutional litigation "has only one duty—to lay the Article of the Constitution which is invoked beside the statute which is challenged and to decide whether the latter squares with the former."[21] This was not an exercise of power; there was no volition in it; it called for a low form of judgment only, a nearly automatic act, very much like something a machine might nowadays do; which in turn gives rise fatally, if unintentionally, to the inference that a nine-man court is an instance of featherbedding.

Mr. Roosevelt, as is well known, failed to pack the Court for whose majority Justice Roberts spoke. But time unpacked it, and by 1941, the controls were securely in the hands of those who agreed with the Court's critics—that is, with the realists, among others—and in the hands of some of the political and academic critics themselves, such as Hugo L. Black and Felix Frankfurter, William O. Douglas and Robert H. Jackson. In a few years, they cleaned up after the old Court. A great many measures which, almost everyone would concede today, denoted social and economic progress had been laid beside the Due Process and Equal Protection Clauses, or beside the Commerce Clause, and had been struck down because they were found to be round where they should have been square. Citing the outside critics and the dissents of Holmes and Brandeis and Cardozo and Stone, the reconstituted Court made clear that there were no economic and social certitudes in the Constitution against which to find these measures wanting, and that the majority of the predecessor Court had substituted its own policies, not the Constitution's, for those of the federal and state legislatures. These judicially imposed policies were themselves wrong, because they did not rest on intellectually coherent, let alone sufficiently fundamental and enduring, principles. ("Enduring," a word of hindsight, is fair, because foresight is required.) And in purporting to "find" its decisions by laying statutes beside the Constitution, the old Court had certainly obscured the actual process of judgment.

With the years, as the reconstituted Court settled in, statutes that embodied other legislative policies and raised different problems of principle came up for adjudication. Some were problems that the old majority had neglected; some were quite fresh. But they all called for exercise of the true process of judicial review, which the new majority of Justices had just reidentified and reinstituted. They required judgment under Thayer's rule, and beyond that under relevant fundamental principles, evolved or to be evolved by the Court. Yet here is Justice Black ignoring the lessons he had his share in teaching and reverting to the practice of laying articles of the Constitution beside federal and state statutes and finding, so to speak, a lack of squarage. In thus closing the square circle, he chooses to disguise, as did his predecessors of a generation ago, the process of judgment. And one is entitled to ask why.

The late Constitutional authority and constitutional wit, Thomas Reed Powell, wrote with reference to the Court of the 'twenties:

It sometimes seems that these judicial professions of automation are most insistent when it is most obvious that they are being honored in the breach rather than in the observance. They seem to appear less often when statutes are sustained than when they are condemned, less often when the Court is unanimous than when there is strong dissent. Try as I will, I cannot bring myself to admire both the candor and the capacity of the men who write such things to be forever embalmed in the official law reports. They must lack one or the other, or I must suffer from some such serious lack in me.[22]

Now, a quarter century later, the observer not only can bring himself to admire the capacity of so powerful a figure as Justice Black, he cannot bring himself not to. And it is not, in the full sense, candor that is in question. For while professing to find his answers in the constitutional text, Justice Black also often professes his passionate belief in their validity. He speaks frequently, with force and eloquence, in the accents of the dissenters, the Lilburnes and the Roger Williamses of Anglo-American history, for whom he freely announces his admiration and from whom he conceives his intellectual descent, for which we may in turn admire him. He has repeatedly made clear his belief that the results he would reach, for example, under the First Amendment would best serve "this Nation's security and tranquillity." He is given to no impersonal application of what he regards as "the explicit commands of the First Amendment"; these commands, as he reads them, have his most enthusiastic allegiance. It is not, then, that Justice Black would hide his own fundamental convictions from public view. It is just that he is in the happy position of being able to enforce as law, not merely his own convictions, but the literal constitutional text. For he ever returns us to the text and offers his results wrapped in its cellophane, with locked-in flavor, untouched by contemporary human hands. "There are grim reminders all around this world," he tells us, "that the distance between individual liberty and firing squads is not always as far as it seems. I would . . . return to the language of the Bill of Rights."[23] And so the question remains one of candor, but in a different sense. With submission, I should say that it is a question—not unknown to other disciplines —of the utility of benevolent illusions and of the justification for creating them.

In Conrad's *Under Western Eyes*, the following passage refers to what a supposed friend of a dead man should tell the grieving mother about the manner of her son's death. The dead man's sister is speaking: "It would be a mercy if mama could be soothed. You know what she imagines. Some explanation perhaps may be found, or—or even made up, perhaps. It would be no sin." The people of a democracy must be mercifully soothed when they find themselves ruled, to whatever extent, by the nine men of the Supreme Court. We know what the people imagine. They imagine that they rule themselves, and they imagine *Marbury* v. *Madison*. To the extent that this is not so, some explanation perhaps may be found or—or even made up, perhaps. It would be no sin. It has been done before.

But it is very dangerous. To begin with, the illusion is a two-edged sword, which can be turned very sharply against the Court. So, lately, has it been turned by former Justice Byrnes and by the authors of the Southern Congressional Manifesto of 1956, as well as in every State House of the Deep South. What is even more ominous, the illusion may engulf its maker and breed, as it has occasionally done, free-ranging "activist" government by the judiciary. Such government is incompatible on principle with democratic institutions, and in practice it will not be tolerated. This way lie crises such as the Court-packing fight of 1937, in which the Court, if it persists, must ultimately be the loser. The truth is that the illusion of judicial impotence and automatism may, when fostered, be first acquired by the people and last, with the accompanying feel of omnipotence, by the judges themselves. But it is also first lost by the people and last by the judges. One day the judges may abandon it too late.

Justice Black's New York University address, taken in context of a quarter century's judicial career, has been the subject of a sympathetic explication and commentary by Professor Charles L. Black, Jr.[24] Conceding that Justice Black's absolutes cannot really be deemed—how shall one say—absolute absolutes, and that they do not emerge as such from the constitutional text, and assuming that Justice Black ("an experienced judge with a long head") must be well aware of this, Professor Black reduces the address to the advocacy of an attitude. The Court, he agrees, is required again and again to strike balanced judgments, at least in defining the content of the First Amendment or the Fourth or the Fifth, and so forth. But if the judges tell themselves and the world that the constitutional language, as construed, does define absolutes, even if not "in imagined chemical purity" but "in the practical sense in which chemicals labelled 'chemically pure' are 'pure'," the tendency of their judgments and those of their posterity will be affected thereby. There will be a tendency, for example, to let more speech be heard more freely in more circumstances if the First Amendment is thought of as a literal absolute than if it is conceded that the Amendment is merely an invitation to contemporary judgment. This, in Professor Black's view, is the heart of the dispute. "Attitude," he writes, attitude governed by whether or not one elects to find absolute language in the Constitution, "is what is at stake between Justice Black and his adversaries."

Professor Black's premise, of course, is that the more speech of all sorts and the fewer restraints, the better; and one may well concede that, as a sort of working hypothesis, this is the premise that is true to the best of our tradition. Hence it is fitting that analysis and evolution should start here. But no one urges that they start elsewhere; the question is whether they should end here. It is common ground that the history of the First Amendment and its language, to the extent that it can be read to establish anything in particular, are of the first importance. To deny this would be as much as to say that tradition is to have no influence upon the Court's judgments. This would be absurd, for the Court is typically the institution of government in which tradition should and does have the greatest weight.

Obviously, however, Justice Black's address and Professor Black's variation on the Justice's theme amount to more than an argument for the relevance of tradition. Nor is Professor Black's thesis merely that the Constitution is a symbol and that it has utility as such. It is and it does, as I have noted, quite without relation to particularized meanings that may be drawn from it.[25] For many reasons that have no specific relation to the constitutional text, most of us treasure our nationhood, glory in much of our common past, and deeply want our posterity to live as we have done, in membership of this nation. These are profound and powerful feelings which few of us can express in words that have meaning to ourselves, let alone to all of us in common. And so, as in many other relations that engage our deepest selves and unite us to our fellows, we turn to symbols: the Constitution, the flag, the Supreme Court, Lincoln, Washington, the Capitol, the White House. And sometimes, for some of us, the Bill of Rights and, even more specifically, the First Amendment. But symbols, as most of us ought to know, are the outward manifestation of an inner state of feeling, and they must begin by expressing this feeling before they can significantly direct it. "A person gets from a symbol," the late Justice Jackson once remarked, "the meaning he puts into it, and what is one man's comfort and inspiration is another's jest and scorn." Referring, as it did, to the flag, this is surely an overstatement. No doubt, as Mr. Justice Frankfurter said in reply, the state uses the symbols of nationhood in the attempt to inculcate allegiance. To a degree this works and is justifiable. So the Constitution and the Court have evolved into potent symbols of continuity and unity. But there ought to be no pretense about all this; the symbol only sharpens and focuses feelings that start by being shared, however nebulously. Even so, we must guard against the danger, of which Whitehead warns, that "the symbolic elements in life" will "run wild, like the vegetation in a tropical forest. The life of humanity can easily be overwhelmed by its symbolic accessories."[26] At any rate, the "attitude" Professor Black would have us adopt is another matter altogether. The crucial point about it is that it is meant to influence an actual, supposedly deliberate decisional process in a specific direction; and it can, in my judgment, do so, if at all, only in subliminal ways.

I have referred and shall refer again to the effectiveness of authoritatively announced principles in guiding the tendency of public action. In the stress of practical affairs, exceptions to the principle may be found expedient. Nevertheless, it may be of the utmost importance to resist repudiation of the principle itself. This was Lincoln's ideological objective in fighting the Civil War, and it was important because the principle, even though compromised in practice, will, if maintained, influence the tendency of public policy. This effect on the tendency of policy is what Professor Black has in mind, I believe, when he speaks of the importance of attitude. But there is a world of difference between attributing to the Supreme Court the role of enunciating principles which will then affect the attitude of the political departments, without always rigorously governing their actions, and assigning the same function to the constitutional text in relation to the process of judicial review. In the interplay between the Supreme Court and the political institutions, all is or should be in the open. Men are not required to disguise to themselves or to others what each is doing. The system justifies and encourages each institution in acting as it does—on principle in one institution, often on interest and expediency in the others—for it thrives on the tension among them. And the integrity of the Court's principled process should remain unimpaired, since the Court does not involve itself in compromises and expedient actions. When it does not forbid them on principle, it should withhold intervention altogether, trusting to previously announced principles to exert their influence on tendency. Professor Black's "attitude" would influence the tendency of the process itself by which principles are evolved. The attitude could operate effectively, in my opinion, only so long as the judges really believed that the First Amendment, for example, is a literal absolute. The attitude will operate effectively, in other words, only on the basis of what (to borrow an adverb from Justice Black) is *admittedly* an illusion, purposefully fostered. For, admittedly, choices and judgments necessarily entered into an initial definitional process, which was judicial, which constructed rather than found the literal absolute, and which, once acknowledged, is always open to revision. A degree of dissimulation thus seems to me unavoidable, if the effort to erect literal absolutes is to accomplish anything like its professed objective. There is no such dissimulation involved in the interplay between the Court and the electoral institutions; no one is required to believe anything that is not so in order to achieve a society whose actions tend toward the path of principle, without always being uncompromisingly held to it. The effectiveness of principle is not less because we are allowed to admit that we do not live up to it when we don't.

It may not be too far off the mark to say that Justice Black's position, with Professor Black's gloss on it, amounts to this: the Justice, for our own good, would have us rise and be about the business of asserting and exercising our liberties at 7 A.M. There are those among his Brethren, to be sure, who think that 8 or 8:30 is good enough. That is a difference of principle. Beyond that, however, Justice Black thinks it insufficient just to convince the Court and the country that he is right. He does not trust us, neither now nor in future, even if convinced, to abide by the principle that 7 o'clock is the time to rise. We will, he knows, backslide, oversleep. So he labors to set our alarm clocks one hour ahead, in the expectation that when we oversleep we may nevertheless wake, without quite knowing how it happened, at what is actually the right time.

To introduce into judicial review the factor of attitude springing from illusion would be gravely to depreciate and damage the process. The process is justified only if it is as deliberate and conscious as men can make it. Its attitudes should be informed, consciously and deliberately, by tradition, so far as tradition speaks with relevance, and so far as it suits the times. But the Court should not tell itself or the world that it draws decisions from a text that is incapable of yielding them. That obscures the actual process of decision, for the country, and for the judges themselves, if they fall in with the illusion. And it is a menace, to the Court and to the country, for the reasons I gave earlier.

But why should we expect judges to fall in with an illusion that we ourselves are able easily to dispel? Because, as I have suggested, it gives them a great sense of freedom, it induces a happy activism without afterthought and sometimes even without forethought; in short, it lightens the load of personal and institutional responsibility. But behind the screen of the illusion, thus embraced, will operate—and operate less deliberately than they should—the judge's own convictions. These convictions will be decisive, even after the illusion has engulfed him; it is to these that he will have fitted his reading of "the literal meaning of the text." A judge who has not Justice Black's principles will not read his literal absolutes. The expectation, therefore, that the intentionally fostered illusion of the particular literal meaning of a particular constitutional text will significantly affect future attitudes of adjudication is itself an illusion, so long at least as our judges remain men, not electronic devices whose memories have been wired to the right precedents. This, then, would be a futile game, even if it were not otherwise inadmissible.

Justice Black, one is emboldened to surmise by Professor Black's concession, does not believe that all speech, in all forms and to all purposes, should go wholly unhindered and unregulated by government, whatever the form or purpose of the governmental action, because such is the literal command of the First Amendment. It is the other way around. He contends that this is the literal command of the First Amendment, because this is what he believes and wishes to achieve. But is it sensible to hope that, when he is gone, future judges will be converted to his views by the words of the First Amendment rather than by the merit and force of his beliefs and the record of his eloquence? Of course, the device of the literal absolutes is meant to be an instrument for the eternal vindication of certain values. Its wellspring is the galling uncertainty to which even the most ideal process of principled judgment will ever be subject. The truth is that the most fundamental of one man's fundamental presuppositions, most ideally arrived at, are not now always and will not always be another's, thus inci-

dentally proving that a nine-man court is no instance of featherbedding. And so judges fear for the survival of passionately held
presuppositions of their own and wish to preserve them for the
ages in the deathless body of the Constitution. But the Constitution is merely words—deathless words, but words. And the future
will not be ruled; it can only possibly be persuaded.

The Wonder of the Past—and Its Tyranny

Justice Black's position—that the principles he would have the
Court apply are to be found through a literal reading of the constitutional text—has also a second line of defense. I have quoted
the Justice's remark, in his New York University address, that
when "conflicting values exist in the field of individual liberties
protected by the Constitution, that document settles the conflict.
. . ." But in order to bolster what he refers to as the "plain words"
of the text, or in order to make quite plain words that will not
make themselves so, even at his bidding, Mr. Justice Black often
seeks reliance in history. The historical materials in question, to
list them in some rough order of descending probative value, are:
the records of the deliberations of the Framers of the Constitution,
of the Bill of Rights, and of the later Amendments, chiefly the
Fourteenth; evidence of prevalent opinion and conditions around
the time of the framing, which may have shaped the purposes of
the actual Framers; evidence of opinion and conditions in times
prior to the framing, knowledge of which may be imputed to the
Framers and which may again have a bearing on what they were
trying to avoid or achieve; and evidence of later opinions and
actions of the Framers and of contemporaries closely associated
with them, which may throw a backward light on what the Framers did earlier.

Such materials, like all history, have many uses and many limitations. They are of crucial significance to any conceivable process
of judicial review, and in one fashion or another, and to one end
or another, they have been consulted throughout the recorded experience of the Supreme Court. At its best, the Court has always
discharged for our society—officially, so to speak—the function

Professor Herbert J. Muller assigns to the historians' guild: "at once reviving the wonder of the past and relieving its tyranny."[27]

Justice Black, however, seeks in history, and professes to find, specific proof of the intention of the Framers in writing specific language. Thus he professes to clarify that language in its present, literal application. He is not the first judge to have made the attempt. The difficulty, however, is, first, that unless main force is applied to them, the materials have almost never been known to yield what Justice Black seeks in them; and secondly, that whenever they have been thought to do so, the result has been nothing less than to put in question the capacity of the Constitution to endure as an operative organic law.

As an example of the unsuitability of historical materials to the uses that Justice Black would make of them, let us take one of the most eloquent, as well as intellectually persuasive, passages in the extensive literature of free speech. Its author is Justice Brandeis, and it was written in what amounted to a dissent in the case of *Whitney* v. *California.* I quote a few excerpts only:

Those who won our independence believed that the final end of the State was to make men free to develop their faculties; and that in its government the deliberative forces should prevail over the arbitrary.
. . . They believed that freedom to think as you will and to speak as you think are means indispensable to the discovery and spread of political truth; that without free speech and assembly discussion would be futile; that with them, discussion affords ordinarily adequate protection against the dissemination of noxious doctrine. . . . Believing in the power of reason as applied to public discussion, they eschewed silence coerced by law—the argument of force in its worst form. . . . If there be time to expose through discussion the falsehood and fallacies . . . the remedy to be applied is more speech, not enforced silence. . . . Such, in my opinion, is the command of the Constitution.[28]

Brandeis drew out of what he considered historical evidence a broader, less immediately pointed indication of intent than Justice Black often attempts to find. The passage is nevertheless an apt illustration, embodying as it does an assumption widely indulged by many authoritative figures. For, on the basis of the most recent and most thorough scholarship, it has turned out to be extremely unlikely that "those who won our independence" believed quite this much. The received hypothesis, to which James Madison himself gave some currency after the fact, has long been, in the words of the late Zechariah Chafee, Jr., that the Framers of the First Amendment intended "to wipe out the common law of sedition, and make further prosecutions for criticism of the government, without any incitement to law breaking, forever impossible in the United States of America."[29] Professor Leonard W. Levy, in his *Legacy of Suppression*, has shown, however, that the best evidence is largely otherwise. Very broadly, it appears that in colonial times, here and in England, freedom of the press meant only freedom from prior censorship. For the rest, English and colonial libertarian thought seems to have advanced no farther than to demand that in prosecutions for seditious libel—that is, for certain uncomplimentary utterances about the government of the day— truth be an absolute defense and juries rather than judges be empowered to decide guilt or innocence. It seems possible that the First Amendment was meant to deprive the *federal* government of all authority to deal with seditious libel. Even this is far from certain, but in any event, the First Amendment becomes on this hypothesis only an instrument for the distribution of powers between the general government on the one hand and the states on the other. Very little in the way of general libertarian principles could on this hypothesis be drawn from it, and hence no well-defined restriction on the power of the states to punish what they deem to be seditious speech, whether directed at themselves or at the federal government.

Take another example. Beyond question, the Equal Protection Clause of the Fourteenth Amendment was aimed chiefly at creating new rights for the emancipated Negro race. Was it the intention of the framers of that Amendment—the Reconstruction 39th Congress—to forbid the states to enact and enforce segregation statutes? If one goes to the historical materials wih this specific question, the only answer that can emerge is in the negative. The framers did not intend or expect then and there to outlaw segregation, which, of course, was a practice widely prevalent in the North.[30]

History presents us with a similar disappointment in respect of a more complex issue under the Fourteenth Amendment. The

Bill of Rights—that is, the first eight amendments to the original Constitution—is the grand checklist of civil liberties. It deals, to mention the principal points only, with freedom of speech, of the press, and of religion, with security against searches and seizures, with freedom from self-incrimination and other procedural guarantees in criminal trials, with the right to jury trial, the right to bail, and the like. From the beginning, the Bill of Rights—which is to say, such particular principles as the federal courts might work out pursuant to it—was held applicable only to the federal government. It was not held to bind the states, which were left to deal with questions of civil liberties in their own courts, under their own constitutions or statutes. Then came Section 1 of the Fourteenth Amendment, which, in addition to Equal Protection, guarantees also Due Process of Law and provides against abridgment of "the privileges and immunities of citizens of the United States." The Fourteenth Amendment is directed to the states. It marked an extension of federal authority, a move toward uniformity throughout the nation in matters of civil liberties, to be attained by authority of the federal government. The question obviously arises, what degree of uniformity was intended, to what extent were the states to be subject to federal authority in respect of civil liberties? Another way to put the question is to ask whether the Fourteenth Amendment now makes applicable to the states all rules and principles worked out or to be developed under the Bill of Rights— rules and principles that were previously applicable to the federal government only. In a celebrated dissent in 1947, in the case of *Adamson* v. *California,* in which he was joined by Justice Douglas and by the late Justices Murphy and Rutledge, and to which he and Justice Douglas have since adhered, Justice Black argued:

My study of the historical events that culminated in the Fourteenth Amendment, and the expressions of those who sponsored and favored, as well as those who opposed its submission and passage, persuades me that one of the chief objects that the provisions of the Amendment's first section, separately, and as a whole, were intended to accomplish was to make the Bill of Rights applicable to the states.

The argument had been made a few times in the past by earlier Justices, but never successfully. Justice Black brought to its support historical materials of the sort I have listed. His dissent aroused much interest and provoked new scholarship. Within two years, Professor Charles Fairman had conclusively disproved Justice Black's contention;[31] at least, such is the weight of opinion among disinterested observers.

This sort of ping-pong between historical assertion, itself based on some scholarship, and the further, definitive scholarship that disproves it did not begin with the exchange between Mr. Justice Black and Professor Fairman, and it has not ended yet. It was vigorously and very authoritatively argued following the Civil War that the Framers intended to forbid the issuance of paper money as legal tender. As late as 1884, Justice Stephen J. Field wrote in dissent:

If there be anything in the history of the Constitution which can be established with moral certainty, it is that the Framers of that instrument intended to prohibit the issue of legal tender notes both by the general government and by the states. . . .[32]

Thayer, in his essay "Legal Tender," published in 1887, refuted the contention once and for all. Such exchanges continue, however, on other points. Other "moral certainties" are erected and promptly knocked down. In *Burns* v. *Wilson*, decided in 1953, Mr. Justice Douglas, in a dissent in which Mr. Justice Black joined, remarked that he thought it "plain from the text of the Fifth Amendment" that at least certain rights guaranteed to defendants in civilian criminal trials were intended as applicable also to defendants in trials by courts martial. To bolster this assertion, somewhat vulnerable as made, Gordon D. Henderson purported to demonstrate that the intention of the Framers was to make applicable to trials by court martial all the procedural provisions of the Bill of Rights, except the right to a jury. Within the year, two massive articles by Frederick Bernays Wiener showed otherwise.[33]

It is thus quite apparent that to seek in historical materials relevant to the framing of the Constitution, or in the language of the Constitution itself, specific answers to specific present problems is to ask the wrong questions. With adequate scholarship, the answer that must emerge in the vast majority of cases is no answer. In all the examples I have given, what we have is an assertion of an exact original intention, followed by its refutation. But the refutations disprove the assertion, they do not prove its opposite. It is not true that the Framers intended the First Amendment to guarantee all speech against all possible infringement by government regulation; but they did not foreclose such a policy and may indeed have invited something like it. It is not true that the Framers intended the Fourteenth Amendment to outlaw segregation or to make applicable to the states all restrictions on government that may be evolved under the Bill of Rights; but they did not foreclose such policies and may indeed have invited them. It is not true that the Framers intended to forbid the issuance of money as legal tender; but they did not foreclose such a policy and may indeed have invited it and hoped rather strongly that it would prove feasible. And it is not true that the Framers intended that trials by courts martial be conducted in most respects as if they were civilian trials, although, again, they far from foreclosed such a policy and quite possibly invited it.

No answer is what the wrong question begets, for the excellent reason that the Constitution was not framed to be a catalogue of answers to such questions. And, indeed, how could it have been, consistently with the intention to write a charter for the governance of generations to come—for a period, it was hoped, stretching far into the future? What sort of enormously comprehensive effort must these men have undertaken in those hot summer months in Philadelphia, and what prescience must they have been capable of, in order to be equal to such an attempt? What confidence must they have had in their ability to imagine changes in material conditions in future years, let alone changes in human knowledge and outlook? These were strong, hopeful men, it must be remembered, living at a time of burgeoning intellectual inquiry, when the best of men remembered change and looked for it. They did not believe in a stable world. They were themselves the instruments of change, innovators, tinkerers, inventors; they could not have believed that they were the last of their breed. To be sure, they did write a Constitution, and they meant by it to affect the behavior of their posterity. They provided quite specifically for certain forms of the government that must necessarily be settled and known to all, they prescribed a very general allocation of competences among the several institutions, and they handed on certain broad convictions, which they held firmly as natural truths, and which were to be the setting for the growth of the society they founded. When they dealt with more specific questions of power, they showed, in a phrase of Professors Morison and Commager, a distinct "preference of 'may' over 'must'." Structural matters aside, as the late Charles P. Curtis wrote, what the Framers said "comes down to us more like chapter headings than anything else. They put it up to us, their successors, to write the text. And why not? We are better equipped and better able than they to deal with their future, which is our present. At that, we are older and more experienced than they. They died in a younger world."[34]

All this is itself a judgment of the intent of the Framers, based on the sort of materials in which Justice Black seeks his answers. This is an answer, however, to a very different question. It is also with this different question in view that scholarship has been able to arrive at the conclusion, as I pointed out in Chapter 1, that the Framers expected the Supreme Court to exercise a power of judicial review over other departments of government. They expected it. They might have said "must," but they did not depart from the more customary "may." And they certainly had no specific intent relating to the nature and range of the power and to the modalities of its exercise. This is the more noteworthy since judicial review is an issue in the allocation of competences, the sort of issue the Framers generally did address themselves to, in terms sufficient at least to make possible the initial organization and operation of the system. Many, many other issues that are pressing today, even some that seem obvious and unavoidable to us, were not foreseen, naturally enough, and were not faced. But beyond that, many specific problems that *were* foreseen were intentionally left open for settlement by the Framers' posterity. This is characteristically true of the legal-tender problem, as Thayer showed, and, perhaps by emulation, of the Fourteenth Amendment.

The tendency of the Framers toward the open end is often accounted for simply by the political conditions of the time. A particular issue was foreseen and was discussed because it was mooted in the politics of the day. But for the sake of the success of their immediate enterprise—namely the ratification of the Constitution

—the Framers were anxious to settle only such issues as there was an adequate consensus about, and to deal with those on which opinion was divided only in such generalities as could command general assent; unless, of course, the matter was one that had to be settled in one fashion or another—usually by compromise—in order to get the government organized and operational. The Framers wanted their Constitution founded on broad popular consent. Their impulse was to avoid controversy wherever possible.

The Framers were moved also by considerations looking beyond the immediate objective of ratification. They knew, and this was perhaps their greatest wisdom, that in order to last and be stable and thus affect the behavior of posterity in any degree, a constitution must make it possible for future battles to be fought out by men who, on both sides of contested issues, can in good faith profess allegiance to the organic law and to the regime established by it. They were aware, in other words, of the function of the Constitution as the symbol of nationhood, meant to transcend and to endure beyond the fiercest political differences. It is possible to have an institution such as the Supreme Court, especially clothed with the constitutional mystique, which will intervene in special ways on special issues—rarely, subtly, mindful that the rule of principle has limits. But both Constitution and Court must remain above the day-to-day battle, and the Constitution itself, for the most part, above the battle altogether. The constitutional generalities must be capable of containing most differences and of embracing either result of most trials of political strength. Hence, as Marshall said in *McCulloch* v. *Maryland,* a constitution—or to quote him more precisely, a *constitution*—must not "partake of the prolixity of a legal code" and so seem false and alien to the people, who are expected to pour into it and draw from it the sense of union and common purpose, past and future. If a constitution purports to settle, in detail and for all time, most of the issues that are likely to be the grist of the political mill, it invites either abandonment or frequent amendment. The familiarity of amendment will breed a species of contempt and incapacitate the document for symbolic service.

Again and again, in our own states, where it has done relatively little harm, and in other countries, the validity of this assertion has been painfully demonstrated. Constitutions have tried to settle too much, promptly became and remained the focal point of political controversy, lasted for a turbulent day, and passed, taking the "regime" with them. A striking and one of the most tragic examples was the Spanish republican constitution of 1931. It contained in the greatest possible detail provisions for the disestablishment of the Spanish Church. Hugh Thomas, the historian of the Spanish Civil War, points out that if the provisions had been more general, and if, in their disposition of the educational problem, for example, they had left more to the future rather than attempting to solve everything in legislative fashion, the survival of the constitution might have been more nearly possible. As it was, "all Spanish Catholics were forced into the position of having to oppose the very Constitution of the Republic if they wished to criticize its educational or religious policy.[35]

"The whole aim of construction, as applied to a provision of the Constitution, is to discover the meaning, to ascertain and give effect to the intent, of its Framers, and the people who adopted it. . . . As nearly as possible we should place ourselves in the condition of those who framed and adopted it." This was written by the late Justice George Sutherland, a mainstay of the old Court, in 1934. It was answered in the same case by Chief Justice Hughes:

If by the statement that what the Constitution meant at the time of its adoption it means today, it is intended to say that the great clauses of the Constitution must be confined to the interpretation which the Framers, with the conditions and outlook of their time, would have placed upon them, the statement carries its own refutation. It was to guard against such a narrow conception that Chief Justice Marshall uttered the memorable warning [in *McCulloch* v. *Maryland*] . . . "We must never forget that it is *a Constitution* we are expounding."[36]

The Framers knew and Marshall knew, and perhaps by 1937 even Justice Sutherland might have begun to realize, that nothing but disaster could result for government under a written constitution if it were generally accepted that the specific intent of the framers of a constitutional provision is ascertainable and is forever and specifically binding, subject only to the cumbersome process of amendment. It is all perhaps most succinctly and tellingly put in a statement of Brandeis:

Our Constitution is not a strait-jacket. It is a living organism. As such it is capable of growth—of expansion and of adaptation to new conditions. Growth implies changes, political, economic and social. Growth which is significant manifests itself rather in intellectual and moral conceptions than in material things. Because our Constitution possesses the capacity of adaptation, it has endured as the fundamental law of an ever-developing people.

These lines were written in dissent. The strait-jacket the majority was imposing on Congress was the Seventh Amendment: "No person shall be held to answer for a capital, or otherwise infamous crime, unless on a presentment or indictment of a grand jury. . . ." The case was a proceeding in the Juvenile Court of the District of Columbia, which was begun, pursuant to Act of Congress, by information rather than by presentment or indictment of a grand jury. Having been charged with neglecting to provide for the support and maintenance of minor children, the defendant faced imprisonment in a workhouse at hard labor for six months. The workhouse in question was an industrial farm in healthy and pleasant surroundings, where inmates worked eight hours a day and were paid for it. A majority of the Supreme Court held that this punishment rendered the crime of nonsupport infamous within the terms of the Seventh Amendment, because the sentence of hard labor denoted infamy in colonial times. Brandeis, joined by Chief Justice Taft and by Holmes, dissented. Hard labor, he said, had once been a medium of disgrace. Penological opinion now (1922) regarded it more as a means of rehabilitation, of restoring self-respect. The last paragraph of Brandeis' opinion as printed in the Reports reads as follows:

But even if imprisonment at hard labor elsewhere than in a penitentiary had, in the past, been deemed an infamous punishment, it would not follow that confinement, or rather service, at a workhouse like Occoquan, under the conditions now prevailing should be deemed so. . . . "What punishments shall be considered as infamous may be affected by the changes of public opinion from one age to another." Such changes may result from change in the conditions in which, or in the purpose for which, a punishment is prescribed. The Constitution contains no reference to hard labor. The prohibition contained in the Fifth Amendment refers to infamous crimes—a term obviously inviting interpretation in harmony with conditions and opinions prevailing from time to time. And today commitment to Occoquan for a short term for nonsupport of minor children is certainly not an infamous punishment.

It was here that Brandeis added the passage quoted above, ending with reference to our Constitution's "capacity of adaptation" and consequent endurance. But although Brandeis expressed such views elsewhere, this passage was never printed, and for a very interesting reason. The draft containing the passage gained and retained the assent of Holmes, and it gained at first the assent of Taft as well. But on March 30, 1922, there came this disarmingly ingenuous letter from Taft:

As I endorsed on the opinion, I am very much pleased with your opinion in the hard labor case, except the last four or five sentences in respect to the growth of the Constitution. I object to those words, because they are certain to be used to support views that I could not subscribe to. Their importance depends, as old Jack Bunsby used to say, on their application, and I fear that you and I might differ as to their application. I object to them because they are unnecessary here. It seems to me you have sufficiently demonstrated that . . . the statute should be construed by its context not to impose an infamous punishment. . . . Now it is possible—I have felt that way myself sometimes—that these particular sentences constitute the feature of the opinion that you most like, and therefore that you don't care to eliminate them. If not, I can write a short concurring opinion, avoiding responsibility for those words. . . .

Taft saw the point, but he wanted to reserve freedom not to see it when convenient. He thought it somewhat precipitate to abandon permanently the bulwark of the literal Constitution and the intent of the Framers. These are things a judge can find comforting use for now and then. On the same date Brandeis replied to his amiable Chief: "I believe strongly in the views expressed in the last five sentences; but I agree with you that they are not necessary and I am perfectly willing to omit them."[37]

Like the text, we may thus conclude, history cannot displace judgment. And like the text, it should not, if it could. For, as Brandeis said on more than one occasion, and as the Framers themselves well knew, "the only abiding thing is change." "In change," said Heraclitus, "is rest."[38] But it is a function of the Court—in the sphere of its competence—to maintain continuity in the midst of change. Change should be a process of growth. The coloration of the new should not clash with that of the old. Change should not come about in violent spasms. Government under law is a continuum, not a series of jerky fresh departures. And so the past is relevant. Around it cluster settled ways of doing and settled expectations which, for the sake of both stability and fairness to the individual, should often, as a matter of principle, control the rate of change in society. Moreover, the recorded past is, of course, experience; it is a laboratory in which ideas and principles are tested. History is "philosophy teaching by example."[39] For these and other reasons, all obvious, history is a recurrent major theme in the Supreme Court, as it necessarily must be in an institution charged with the evolution and application of society's fundamental principles. The relevant materials are not merely those I have mentioned, which throw light on the purposes of constitutional provisions, but also further ones, relating to the past work of legislatures and, of course, most significantly, of the Court itself. The Court consults not only the origins of constitutional provisions but also, in a phrase of Holmes, "the line of their growth."[40]

But history, including precedent, how used? History, said Burckhardt, "is on every occasion the record of what one age finds worthy of note in another." Henry Adams, writing to his fellow mediaevalist Henry Osborn Taylor, said: "Your middle-ages exist for their own sake, not for yours. To me . . . the middle ages present a picture that has somehow to be brought into relation with ourselves." Or as Mr. Muller has put it:

Historians can more nearly approach the detachment of the physicist when they realize that the historical "reality" is symbolic, not physical, and that they are giving as well as finding meanings. . . . In piety and justice we try to see it as it was . . . [but] in our contemplation of the drama we see what is most pertinent for our own hopes and fears. . . . Our task is to create a "usable past," for our own living purposes.[41]

We are guided in our search of the past by our own aspirations and evolving principles, which were in part formed by that very past. When we find in history, immanent or expressed, principles that we can adopt or adapt, or ideals and aspirations that speak with contemporary relevance, we find at the same time evidence of inconsistent conduct. But we reason from the former, not from the frailties of men who, like ourselves, did not always live up to all they professed or aspired to. Lincoln reasoned, not from the Framers' resignation to the fact of slavery, but from the abolition of the slave trade and from the numerous manumissions, particularly in Virginia. In considering the Bill of Rights, we find worthy of note the stirrings of libertarian theory in colonial times, not the barbaric prosecutions. The often-invoked John Wilkes, Professor Levy makes clear, held the view that some seditious speech (although not his own) should be severely dealt with, and he was committed to this view "side by side with a rhetorical tradition that should have implied the contrary but addressed itself only to transcendant propositions uncontaminated by reality."[42] But what we find worthy of note is the rhetorical tradition and its implications, not the inconsistent commitment.

Such a use of history constructs no Procrustean beds, but it is far from laying violent hands on the findings of scholars who seek only to discover *wie es eigentlich gewesen ist*. Our interest in history, says Mr. Muller, is "more poetic than practical or scientific." But he hastens to add, with Trevelyan, that the very poetry of history consists in its truth. "It is the fact about the past that is poetic."[43] The integrity of the fact is important generally, and it is crucial particularly with respect to the First Amendment. For only a society that strives to attain truth through reason is fit to enjoy freedom of speech. Such a freedom, bestowed by judges who rest it on a historical hypothesis suspected of being (or known to be) erroneous, carries the fault of a profound inner contradiction and is a very uncertain blessing. We require to know, as accurately as may be, whence we come, in order to be aware that it is our own reasoned and revocable will, not some idealized ancestral compulsion, that moves us forward.

CHAPTER 4

The Passive Virtues

Writing in 1949, Professor Paul A. Freund noted "a remarkable core of agreement on the Court" with respect to human rights and the rights of property. He found that "the degree of concord in this area is much more important than the degree of discord. . . ." The area of discord included the debate, then at white heat, of *Adamson v. California,* in which Mr. Justice Black and three colleagues were ranged against a majority of the Court, itself abetted by Professor Charles Fairman. Justice Black argued that the Fourteenth Amendment was intended to make any and all principles of the Bill of Rights directly applicable to the states, whereas the majority held that the historical materials proved no such thing. I touched on this not insignificant difference in the previous chapter, and Mr. Freund did not omit to canvass it. Yet he found that, despite these opposed premises, the two sides often evolved the same or very similar principles for application to the states. He felt able, therefore, to "give point to the story of the Irish cleric who was asked by a parishioner what the difference was between the cherubim and the seraphim, and who answered, 'I think that there was once a difference between them, but they have made it up.'"[1] Although the sounds of dispute, old and new, remain unmuffled, it can now be said that the area of concord has in some important respects enlarged. One need only mention the *School Segregation Cases* of 1954 and their aftermath as bespeaking the Court's unity in disposing of what is surely the single most important issue to come before it, in this century at least.

More may be ventured. The conceptual distance between Mr.

Justice Black's absolutist positions, on the First Amendment, for example, and the majority's generally more "balanced" results—to use the word the Justice particularly despises—may not be the true measure of the discord between them. The extremity of Justice Black's absolutist professions is a dissenting position. It is an opposition program. Of necessity, as we have seen, there is a great deal about it that is merely tactical; Justice Black knows as well as anyone else that free speech cannot really be an absolute and that the First Amendment does not literally say any such certain thing.

A gap exists, and it is not to be minimized. The Justices do not all assess the values of speech and association alike, in all the particular circumstances that come before them. "There is something voluptuous in meaning well"—so Henry Adams reports a not altogether ill-meant remark by the French minister about President Jefferson.[2] The Justices are not all equally First Amendment voluptuaries. Moreover, as I have argued at length, the absolutist-literalist position raises a grave question of process—a question, some might say, of candor. For in propagating his absolutes, Justice Black chooses to obscure the actual process of decision. Yet there would be fewer occasions for differences in result if cases coming before the Court were viewed more closely, more narrowly, in a less apocalyptic frame of mind. On the immediate merits of many cases, more discord strikes the ear than is necessarily involved. The Court has been entering upon more arguments than it needs to resolve. This is true as well in another, more precise, and more revealing sense, which I wish now to emphasize. Occasions for differences in result would be infinitely fewer if certain techniques of the mediating way, which I touched on at the end of Chapter 2, were more imaginatively utilized.

For Brandeis, as I have mentioned, the mediating techniques of "not doing" were "the most important thing we do." But these jurisdictional techniques and like devices have fallen into something of a state of disrepair, and they are consequently in not a little disrepute. They are heavily encrusted with what Felix Cohen called "the vivid fictions and metaphors of traditional jurisprudence,"[3] and their true import is not readily made evident. They have in any event no ring; they do not resound. They cause cases to abort, and clients and their lawyers like to win and may prefer even to lose. Men come and contend for a judgment of last resort and are met with the first resort of what sounds like a legalism, a technicality. Yet these legalisms, these technicalities, remain "the most important thing." In the effort to understand and perhaps to scrape off and refurbish them, it will be well to start somewhat anew, and from the beginning.

The Vivid Metaphors of Jurisdiction— and Their Sense

The beginning was two episodes that preceded *Marbury* v. *Madison.* The first arose out of the Act of March 23, 1792, by which Congress charged the federal courts with certain fact-finding functions in respect of the allowance of pensions to disabled veterans of the Revolutionary War; their decisions being, in effect, subject to review by the Secretary of War. The Justices of the Supreme Court, severally sitting on circuit, as was then their duty, thought that they could not properly undertake performance of such tasks. The Constitution vested in the federal courts "the judicial Power" and no other, and this was the power of rendering final judgments only, not opinions liable to be administratively revised. The views of the Justices have come down to us in a report styled *Hayburn's Case,*[4] although the issue was never sharply joined, since Congress hastened to change the statute.

The second of these early episodes is rather grandly known as *The Correspondence of the Justices.*[5] On July 18, 1793, Secretary of State Jefferson addressed to Chief Justice Jay and his Associate Justices a letter reading in part as follows:

Gentlemen:

    The war which has taken place among the powers of Europe produces frequent transactions within our ports and limits, on which questions arise of considerable difficulty, and of greater importance to the peace of the United States. These questions depend for their solution on the construction of our treaties, on the laws of nature and nations, and on the laws of the land, and are often presented under circumstances *which do not give a cognizance of them to the tribunals of the country.* Yet, their decision is so little analogous to the ordinary func-

tions of the Executive, as to occasion much embarrassment and difficulty to them. The President therefore would be much relieved if he
found himself free to refer questions of this description to the opinions
of the judges of the Supreme Court of the United States, whose knowledge of the subject would secure us against errors dangerous to the
peace of the United States, and their authority insure the respect of all
parties. He has therefore asked the attendance of such of the judges as
could be collected in time for the occasion . . . to present, for their advice, the abstract questions which have already occurred, or may still
occur. . . .

The questions involved construction of treaties between the United
States and France, issues of international law, and more general
issues of the power of the federal government. The Chief Justice
and the Associate Justices, by letter to the President dated August
8, 1793, respectfully declined to answer. "Considering themselves," as Marshall said in the *Life of Washington* that he published in 1807, "merely as constituting a legal tribunal for the decision of controversies brought before them in legal form, these
gentlemen deemed it improper to enter the field of politics by declaring their opinion on questions not growing out of the case
before them."[6] They were elegant about it, but firm:

We exceedingly regret every event that may cause embarrassment to
your administration, but we derive consolation from the reflection that
your judgment will discern what is right, and that your usual prudence,
decision, and firmness will surmount every obstacle to the preservation
of the rights, peace, and dignity of the United States.

This background, if a trifle faint, assumed sharper outline once
Marbury v. Madison had been decided. If, as Marshall argued,
the judiciary's power to construe and enforce the Constitution
against the other departments is to be deduced from the obligation
of the courts to decide cases conformably to law, which may sometimes be the Constitution, then it must follow that the power may
be exercised only in a case. Marshall certainly offered no other
coherent justification for lodging it in the courts, and the text of
the Constitution, whatever other supports it may or may not offer
for Marshall's argument, extends the judicial power only "to all
Cases" and "to Controversies," and not otherwise. It follows that
courts may make no pronouncements in the large and in the ab-

stract, by way of opinions advising the other departments at their request; that they may give no opinions, even in a concrete case, which are advisory because they are not finally decisive, the power of ultimate disposition of the case having been reserved elsewhere; and that they may not decide non-cases, which do not require decision because they are not adversary situations and nothing of immediate consequence to the parties hangs on the result. These are ideas central to the reasoning in *Marbury* v. *Madison.* They constitute not so much limitations of the power of judicial review as necessary supports for Marshall's argument in establishing it. The words of art that are shorthand for these ideas are "case and controversy" and "standing." The federal courts, it is also said, may not render "advisory opinions," although the English judiciary, from whose practices in general our "judicial Power" derives, and some of our own state courts do lend their services to the other departments of government in this fashion.

It is not often that any portion of the syllogism of *Marbury* v. *Madison* accurately describes present practices of judicial review or adequately justifies their nature. This, however, is an exception. The concepts of "standing" and "case and controversy" follow as well, in their essence, from the general analysis and justification of judicial review outlined in Chapter 1 and subsumed since, and they follow for reasons not dissimilar to those cited by Marshall. One of the chief faculties of the judiciary, which is lacking in the legislature and which fits the courts for the function of evolving and applying constitutional principles, is that the judgment of courts can come later, after the hopes and prophecies expressed in legislation have been tested in the actual workings of our society; the judgment of courts may be had in concrete cases that exemplify the actual consequences of legislative or executive actions. Thus is the Court enabled to prove its principles as it evolves them. The concepts of "standing" and "case and controversy" tend to ensure this, and there are sound reasons, grounded not only in theory but in the judicial experience of centuries, here and elsewhere, for believing that the hard, confining, and yet enlarging context of a real controversy leads to sounder and more enduring judgments. "Every tendency to deal with constitutional questions abstractly," Professor Felix Frankfurter wrote a generation ago, "to formulate them in terms of barren legal questions, leads to dialectics, to sterile conclusions unrelated to actualities."[7]

It may be added that the opportunity to relate a legislative policy to the flesh-and-blood facts of an actual case, and thus to see and portray it from a very different vantage point, to observe and describe in being what the legislature may or may not have foreseen as probable—this opportunity as much as, or more than, anything else enables the Court to appeal to the nation's second thought. Moreover, the "standing" and "case" requirement creates a time lag between legislation and adjudication, as well as shifting the line of vision. Hence it cushions the clash between the Court and any given legislative majority and strengthens the Court's hand in gaining acceptance for its principles. The validity of this argument, it may be ventured, would soon be apparent if it were customary to bring statutes to court, as it were, in the very flush of enactment, while the feelings that produced them were at their highest pitch, and while the policies they embodied had as yet suffered none of the dents necessarily made, in another of Professor Frankfurter's phrases, by the "impact of actuality."[8] Of course, the time lag imposed by the "standing" and "case" doctrine may also entail the consequence that the Court will be presented with a species of *fait accompli;* it may be, as Thayer said, "that the mere legislative decision will accomplish results throughout the country of the profoundest importance before any judicial question can arise,"[9] and that this circumstance will give the Court much pause. But so it should. That is what is meant by not applying sterile dialectics to "barren legal questions." The accomplished fact, affairs and interests that have formed around it, and perhaps popular acceptance of it—these are elements, as I shall argue further, that may properly enter into a decision to abstain from rendering constitutional judgment or to allow room and time for accommodation to such a judgment; and they may also enter into the shaping of the judgment, the applicable principle itself. No doubt the T.V.A. and the Bank of the United States seemed less objectionable to the judges as established facts than they might have as abstract proposals. If this gives an edge to the decisions of the representative institutions, it is not difficult to deem it an acceptable one. But that was not the case with the N.R.A., and segregation was not upheld because it was already there.

The aspect of the "case" concept emphasized in *Hayburn's Case*—namely, that the judgments the Court is asked to render must be final—merges with the prohibition against advisory opinions, insofar as judgments subject to revision elsewhere may be thought of as merely offering advice to the revising authority. The requirement of finality is by way, also, of providing further assurance of quality in the Court's work, on the theory, often expressed by Brandeis, that "responsibility is the great breeder of men." It is further supported, both in terms of the *Marbury* v. *Madison* syllogism and otherwise, by a reluctance to invoke the judicial power except in the last resort; that is, under compulsion of a case which no one else will decide. Still, the finality or lack of it in judicial judgments is rather a matter of degree, and this is the least important, and perhaps the least rigidly maintained, element in the concept of "case and controversy" and "standing." But for the rest, as it establishes minimum standards of concreteness in adjudication, this concept goes to the heart of any acceptable process of judicial review.

One is soon recalled, however, to the difficulties to which any reliance on the reasoning in *Marbury* v. *Madison* gives rise. For it would seem also to follow from that opinion that "all Cases" of the constitutional description are justiciable and must be heard and decided. Indeed, Marshall himself was quite dogmatic about it in *Cohens* v. *Virginia:*

It is most true that this Court will not take jurisdiction if it should not; but it is equally true, that it must take jurisdiction if it should. The judiciary cannot, as the legislature may, avoid a measure because it approaches the confines of the constitution. We cannot pass it by because it is doubtful. With whatever doubts, with whatever difficulties, a case may be attended, we must decide it if it be brought before us. We have no more right to decline the exercise of jurisdiction which is given, than to usurp that which is not given. The one or the other would be treason to the constitution.[10]

But the doctrines of "standing" and "case and controversy" have in time come to mean also something entirely unrelated to the syllogism of *Marbury* v. *Madison*. They have encompassed numerous instances in which the Court did nothing else but to "decline the exercise of jurisdiction which is given. . . ." And to this end they have been abetted by, or used interchangeably (and rather unanalytically) with, overlapping doctrines, such as "ripeness" and "political question." This has caused great difficulties to the school of strict constructionists, or classicists, as Professor Louis L. Jaffe has called them, who would rest the institution of judicial review on the foundation of the opinion in *Marbury* v. *Madison,* or even on an independent, more scrupulous but quite similar process of deduction from the constitutional text.

Thus, as a first illustration, it becomes extremely tricky to place any reliance in the word "all" in the phrase "all Cases, in Law and Equity, arising under this Constitution," which is the language of Article III. If there is significance in the word as establishing the function of judicial review, because "all" cases arising under the Constitution must include those in which the power of reviewing acts of the other departments may have to be exercised, then all cases must be heard. Only if one emphasizes the preceding phrase, "judicial Power," is there room for declining to hear some cases arising under the Constitution. But in that event the question whether the text confers the power of judicial review is open on the basis of this article. For "judicial Power" is a relatively indefinite phrase, and it remains to be determined whether or not it subsumes judicial review. We are thrown back to defining our power, with no conclusive help from the recital of cases to which it shall extend.

Professor Wechsler believes that "the power of the courts [to exercise judicial review] is grounded in the language of the Constitution." He is well aware of the consequences with respect to the legitimacy of any discretionary option to withhold the exercise of jurisdiction. "For me, as for anyone who finds the judicial power anchored in the Constitution, there is no such escape [having quoted Judge Learned Hand, whose escape hatch was larger than the compartment from which it offered egress] from the judicial obligation; the duty cannot be attenuated in this way." Mr. Wechsler, indeed, goes on to quote with approval the passage from *Cohens* v. *Virginia* given above. But he makes some room for what the courts have done in fact by arguing that the "judicial Power" extends to "all Cases . . . arising under this Constitution" only when a remedy is made available by the general law of remedies, statutory or decisional.[11]

To be sure, some cases answer to this classical formulation. The general law may show that the plaintiff has no existing rights in the premises, which a statute claimed to be unconstitutional could have infringed. Therefore, the statute, even if in fact unconstitutional, could not have injured him. Therefore, in the pure sense in which, following *Marbury* v. *Madison,* we have defined these terms, the plaintiff has no standing, there is no case. That is what Brandeis showed in his famous concurring opinion in *Ashwander* v. *TVA.*[12] But in most instances, the formulation will not avail. For one thing, it leaves out of account legal rights that the Constitution itself may be held to have created.

The *Ashwander* case was this. The Alabama Power Company, a corporation organized under the laws of Alabama, had entered into a contract with the newly established Tennessee Valley Authority, under which the Authority bought from the Power Company certain transmission lines and other properties for a sum upward of a million dollars. Ashwander and others were holders of preferred stock of the Power Company. They thought the contract should not be entered into and made their views known to the board of directors, which, however, proceeded anyway. Thereupon Ashwander and the others sued the Company, seeking to have the Court enjoin it from making the contract, on the ground that the contract was illegal since the TVA was unconstitutional. The ultimate issue thus tendered was whether the federal government had power under the Constitution to construct and operate the TVA. The Court, per Chief Justice Hughes, went to the merits and upheld the constitutionality of the TVA. Brandeis, in a concurrence in which Stone, Roberts, and Cardozo also joined, held that there was no standing to sue. He assumed that there was and should be no constitutional principle protecting the right of preferred shareholders to have a say in the management of a corporation. Aside from the Constitution, neither the general federal law nor the law of Alabama created such a right. Hence, Ashwander's suit gave rise to no case. There was the scarcest, if any, showing of a prospect of loss to the Company from the contract with the TVA, let alone any showing that even if the Company might suffer a loss, it would be reflected in the earnings of preferred shareholders. Under these circumstances, given the absence of any legal right to interfere, Ashwander was not injured; he stood neither to lose nor to gain from the suit, except as he had an abstract interest in being advised of the law applicable to the Tennessee Valley Authority. Such an interest cannot make a case. As Professor Frankfurter wrote in 1938, in an article discussing *Ashwander* v. *TVA*: "The Court is not the forum for a chivalrous or disinterested defense of the Constitution. Its business is with self-regarding, immediate, secular claims."[13]

But it was a quite different matter to hold some few years later, in *Tennessee Electric Power Co.* v. *TVA*,[14] that a group of companies seeking to litigate the constitutionality of the TVA had no standing because their only claim was that the TVA injured them by competing with them, and there is no right to prevent competition "otherwise lawful." Here the companies were subject to material injury. And the question whether the Constitution protects against some forms of competition cannot be assumed away. It was held in *Pierce* v. *Society of Sisters*[15] to protect a parochial school against a certain kind of public-school competition. It was held in *Joint Anti-Fascist Refugee Committee* v. *McGrath*[16] to protect an unincorporated association from being arbitrarily listed by the Attorney General of the United States as a Communist-front organization and thus damaged in its ability to recruit members and otherwise operate effectively. And so, when the companies were held to have no standing in the *Tennessee Electric Power* case, the Court was either deciding, on the merits but without opinion, that the Constitution does not protect against competition by such a governmental unit as the TVA, or that the case was for some discretionary reason an unsuitable one in which to pass on the constitutionality of the Tennessee Valley Authority. The general law, state or federal, obviously could not affect the former holding as such, for it could not create a constitutional right. The general law, however, state or federal, statutory or common, could create a remedy against competition by instrumentalities of the federal government that are unconstitutional for independent reasons. Would that render adjudication mandatory in a case that the Court had otherwise deemed unsuitable? Perhaps not, if the remedy is a creature of state law, since special problems are thus raised.[17] But at least if the federal law creates the remedy, an affirmative answer follows from the classical position.

Note well that we have in view cases such as *Tennessee Electric Power Co.* v. *TVA*, which are "cases" in the pure, *Marbury* v. *Madison* sense,˙because as a matter of fact a palpable injury is present. If there is no injury, either material or to a right independently created by law, and if the Constitution itself does not create the right, as it was held to do in *Pierce* v. *Society of Sisters* and in *Joint Anti-Fascist Refugee Committee* v. *McGrath*, it is in my opinion extremely difficult to contend that the general law of remedies, by allowing a suit to test constitutionality, can make a case. This, in my judgment, is no more nor less than the advisory-opinion situation. It arises when a plaintiff, having no greater stake in the matter than did Mr. Ashwander, for example, baldly sues in his capacity as a citizen merely to have the law straightened out, so to speak. Or it arises, in only slightly more veiled fashion, when a plaintiff, suing to declare this or that statute unconstitutional, alleges no other interest than that of the taxpayer and is unable to show material injury, because the statute has no particular impact on him, and because there is no indication that, should he win, his burden as a taxpayer will be in the slightest affected. Such a suit was *Frothingham* v. *Mellon*,[18] which challenged the power of Congress to enact the Maternity Act of November 23, 1921. This statute appropriated modest sums of money to be apportioned among states complying with its provisions, which were aimed at reducing maternal and infant mortality. Mrs. Frothingham was able to allege only that she was a taxpayer of the United States. Quite obviously, she could not make the faintest showing that, should the Maternity Act be declared unconstitutional, the federal tax burden would be lessened and her own tax bill decreased. Her suit was dismissed. It was under very different circumstances that the constitutionality of the federal Social Security Act was challenged. Congress had levied a special social security tax for the sole purpose of funding this special program. A corporation from which this tax was owing sued to avoid payment of it, and this it would effectively have accomplished had the program been declared unconstitutional; for unlike the all-purpose income tax, this levy would have fallen—such was the will of Congress—with the statute to which it was tied. This suit was entertained.[19]

For the Court to entertain such a suit as *Frothingham* and to adjudicate the constitutional issue tendered would, in my judgment, materially alter the function of judicial review and seriously undermine any acceptable justification for it. In two important recent papers, Professor Louis L. Jaffe has argued in favor of the justiciability at least of some taxpayers', and, indeed, even just plain citizens', suits. This view emerges for Mr. Jaffe from what he conceives to be "the necessary and proper role of the judiciary." Mr. Jaffe is not unmindful of the benefits that flow from restricting the Court to the decision only of concrete cases. I cannot now do justice to his challenging treatment of an intricate subject. I may say merely that he does not seem to me to meet the order of considerations here discussed. Be that as it may, it suffices for my present purpose to point out that the thrust of Mr. Jaffe's argument is toward enlarging judicial discretion to adjudicate or to decline to do so. Mr. Jaffe would relax one fixed element—pure standing—which circumscribes that discretion. He would leave the courts quite free, however, to decline adjudication where the issue is not "clear cut" and thus "apt for judicial determination," or where it is lacking in "a desirable maturity," and he recognizes that there is a "potential correspondence between the lack of a conventional plaintiff and the lack of maturity."[20]

The classical position against which I am here contending is a good 180° removed. If a case is offered by a conventional plaintiff who has standing in the pure sense, this position maintains, the question whether or not the Court must hear it is answered by the federal law of remedies; that is, by jurisdictional statutes plus standard rules of the law of equity, themselves subject to statutory change. There is no judicial discretion to decline adjudication, no such attenuation of the duty. But many judges have thought, and most have from time to time acted, otherwise. There are numerous decisions—such as the *Tennessee Electric Power Co.* case discussed above—in which adjudication of the merits was declined despite the presence of an adequately concrete and adversary case.[21] Often the word "standing" has been made to do duty in a sense beyond the pure one. It has covered, for example, refusals to adjudicate at the instance of a plaintiff who had suffered an injury but who was thought not to be in a position to raise the ultimate issue in the clearest and most fully developed fashion. Thus, if the FCC revokes a TV station's license to broadcast, and does so without publishing charges and granting a hearing, the owner-operator of the station, an announcer employed by him, a bank that has made him a loan on the security of his license, advertisers who have used his facilities, and even members of the public who have been accustomed to take their amusement from the station's offerings—all may be materially injured. The announcer, the bank, the advertisers, and members of the TV-watching public will, however, generally be deemed to be in a poorer position than the owner-operator to tender the ultimate issue of whether broadcasting licenses may constitutionally be revoked without a hearing. Plainly, the intensity of everyone else's interest is less than the owner-operator's. No one else is likely to push so hard as he or explore the issue at expense of money and effort so deeply, for no one else has so much at stake. Nor will anyone else be able to round out the case so fully. There will be many factual facets of it that the owner-operator is best equipped to develop, since they are best known to him—such as the history of the station and all aspects of its activities and structure. Yet the announcer, the bank, the advertisers, and the station's audience all have standing in the pure sense, and there may be times when they alone are likely to raise, and may be heard to litigate, the constitutional issue.

The elements of standing of the "impure" sort just mentioned, which may be decisive of all but the owner-operator's suit in the example I have put, shade gradually into the considerations subsumed by that even more intriguing and engaging term, "ripeness." Under this compendious label, there is a gradual shift in emphasis from the position of the plaintiff to the timing of the litigation. To state the matter plainly, governmental action may well have hurt the individual plaintiff, so that his standing in the pure or constitutional sense is beyond doubt, and he may be the owner-operator rather than the announcer or bank of our hypothetical example. But the action he complains of may nevertheless be in its initial stages only; if he waits a while longer, he will be hurt more. This sounds gratuitously harsh, but the damage may not be major or irremediable. The point is that, if litigation is postponed, the Court will have before it and will be able to use, both in forming and in supporting its judgment, the full rather than merely the initial impact of the statute or executive measure whose constitutionality is in question. To put it in yet another way, pure standing ensures a minimum of concreteness; the other, impure elements of standing and the concept of ripeness seek further concreteness, in varying conditions that cannot be described by a fixed constitutional generalization. Other relevant factors go beyond not only the position of the plaintiff but also the timing of the particular litigation. They have to do with the ripeness, not of the case, but of the ultimate issue itself; they search in the largest sense, and in the full political and historical context, the relationship between the Court and the representative institutions of government. Finally, and cumulatively with the other considerations just assembled, the concept of ripeness ripens into the question, suggested in Chapter 2, of the role that principle, called constitutional law, is capable of playing in a society such as ours.

All this Mr. Jaffe would evidently allow. If the strict-constructionist or classical, *Marbury* v. *Madison* position is to be maintained, however, it is impossible to allow anything like such means of escape from the duty to adjudicate, although in fact the Court has continually, albeit erratically, availed itself of them. Moreover, the notion that the Court cannot decline to adjudicate any real "case" of which the law of remedies gives it jurisdiction pursuant to the constitutional enumeration serves to avoid a theoretical difficulty for the strict-constructionist position; but the unseverable converse—that the Court may not hear constitutional claims made in real "cases" of which Congress has deprived it of jurisdiction—creates a serious new one. Indeed, in a phrase of Judge Hand quoted by Mr. Wechsler, it should be an intolerable "stench in the nostrils of strict constructionists."[22] How is it to be squared with Marshall's syllogism? How can there be a duty to decide "all Cases" conformably to the Constitution, acts of Congress to the contrary notwithstanding, if Congress can defeat this duty by a jurisdictional act? Would not this be "to overthrow in fact what was established in theory"? Would it not seem "an absurdity too gross to be insisted on"? Congress, to be sure, is expressly author-ized by the Constitution to regulate the Court's appellate jurisdic-tion and to make exceptions in it, but that cannot be the whole answer.[23]

The standing (impure) and ripeness concepts, although ample in themselves, are not the only available devices of "not doing." Other technical labels denote concepts that are in many respects overlapping but that may import, or emphasize and make more explicit, additional considerations. Such a label, suggesting poten-tially the widest and most radical avenue of escape from adjudica-tion, is the doctrine of political questions. The classical explanation of it, given by Mr. Wechsler, is that, when the Court declines jurisdiction of a case as "political" or when, having taken the case, it declines to adjudicate the merits of this or that issue in it on the same ground, what the Court does, conformably with *Marbury* v. *Madison*, is to render a constitutional adjudication that the mat-ter in question is confided to the uncontrolled discretion of another department. This is sometimes an adequate statement of the result. It also represents, however, for Mr. Wechsler, "all the doc-trine can defensibly imply." He puts it quite plainly that

the only proper judgment that may lead to an abstention from decision is that the Constitution has committed the determination of the issue to another agency of government than the courts. Difficult as it may be to make that judgment wisely, whatever factors may be rightly weighed in situations where the answer is not clear, what is involved is in itself an act of constitutional interpretation, to be made and judged by stand-ards that should govern the interpretive process generally. That, I sub-mit, is *toto caelo* different from a broad discretion to abstain or inter-vene.[24]

It is different, just so; but one must say, with submission, that only by means of a play on words can the broad discretion that the courts have in fact exercised be turned into an act of constitutional interpretation governed by the general standards of the interpre-tive process. The political-question doctrine simply resists being domesticated in this fashion. There is, as we shall see, something different about it, in kind not in degree; something greatly more flexible, something of prudence, not construction and not principle. And it is something that cannot exist within the four corners of *Marbury* v. *Madison.*

The strict-constructionist position has difficulty also reconciling itself to the Court's two commonest devices of declining "the exercise of jurisdiction which is given." These are denials of certiorari and dismissals of appeals, whether "for the want of a substantial federal question" or otherwise.[25] The appellate jurisdiction, covering a small portion only of the total number of cases coming to the Court, is supposedly mandatory. Yet Chief Justice Warren has allowed that it "is only accurate to a degree to say that our jurisdiction in cases on appeal is obligatory as distinguished from discretionary on certiorari." Thus a decision on the validity of anti-miscegenation statutes was avoided through the dismissal of an appeal, which is to be explained in terms of the discretionary considerations that go to determine the lack of ripeness. It can be said, and indeed it is commonly assumed, that dismissals "for the want of a substantial federal question" are decisions on the merits, though without opinion. But when the Court decides the merits without opinion, it is in the habit of telling us so by issuing a summary order that reverses or affirms the judgment below. There is and has been for many years a great deal that is pure fiction in this explanation. Many are the dismissals for the want of a convenient, or timely, or suitably presented question.[26]

The certiorari jurisdiction is professedly discretionary and based on few articulated standards. The Court's own rule on the subject says that it neither controls nor fully measures the Court's discretion, and, broad as it is, the rule does not in fact do so. It may be said of the certiorari jurisdiction that it does not deny judicial review but, rather, denies it in a particular court only. But in no event is constitutional adjudication in the lower federal courts the equivalent of what can be had in the Supreme Court. It lacks, of course, the general authoritativeness. And judgment, even as it affects the immediate litigant, is constrained by the judiciary's hierarchical structure. The lower courts do not and should not as a rule base judgment on a guess of what the Supreme Court would do; they must follow what it has done in the past as best they can. No doubt, this is not a mechanical process, and the lower courts have decision-making power; but it is comparatively inter-stitial. Moreover, what of cases coming up through the state courts, in which no access could have been had, or can any longer be had, to the lower federal courts? Here, surely, we have outright denial of adjudication by an Article III court. The system, says Mr. Wechsler, "rests upon the power that the Constitution vests in Congress to make exceptions to and regulate the Court's appellate jurisdiction. . . ." But Congress has granted the jurisdiction. It is the Supreme Court that makes the exceptions, and it does so by the case, not by the category; and that is what happens, even though the exceptions are the cases that are heard rather than those that are dismissed.[27]

Misgivings about the certiorari jurisdiction, grounded in the strict-constructionist position, are nothing new. "I find it difficult," Senator Walsh of Montana, who was a lawyer of distinction, said in debate on the Judiciary Act of 1925, "to yield to the idea that the Supreme Court of the United States ought to have the right in every case to say whether their jurisdiction shall be appealed to or not."[28] And the Solicitor General of the day, the late James M. Beck, although he acquiesced in the inevitable and did not advise a veto of the Act, wrote to the President that he had always believed it to be a citizen's right to have any constitutional issue ultimately decided by the Supreme Court, "as the final conscience of the Nation in such matters."[29] Mr. Beck ever employed the eloquent phrase, but what he had in mind was the difficulty of reconciling the discretionary certiorari jurisdiction with *Marbury* v. *Madison* and *Cohens* v. *Virginia*.

The Power to Decline the Exercise of Jurisdiction Which Is Given

I have tried to show that the Supreme Court's well established if imperfectly understood practice of withholding, from time to time and in one fashion or another, exercise of the power of judicial review is hard to reconcile with the strict-constructionist or classical conception of the foundation of that power. If this were all what is called merely academic, it would be none the worse for it. Actually, however, important consequences are in play. Of course, no concept, strict, loose, or medium constructionist, classical or downright jazzy, can get around the sheer necessity of limiting each year's business to what nine men can fruitfully deal with. But strict-constructionist compunctions cause the techniques for meeting this necessity to be viewed with misgiving and to be encumbered with fictive explanations. So are other techniques of avoiding adjudication, and I would suggest that herein lies at least part of the reason for the confusion and lack of direction that has occasionally characterized their development. Some of the confusion may be in the eye of the beholder, but not all.

Beyond this, and more fundamentally, the consequences of the strict-constructionist position are in the alternative. Literal reliance on *Marbury* v. *Madison* may lead to a rampant activism that takes pride in not "ducking" anything and takes comfort and finds "protection," as Mr. Wechsler says, in the dictum of *Cohens* v. *Virginia*. Or, for those, like Mr. Wechsler, who are not unaware that judicial review is at least potentially a deviant institution in a democratic society, the consequence, as we saw, is an effort to limit the power of review and render it tolerable through a radical restriction on the category of substantive principles that the Court is allowed to evolve and declare; the consequence is, indeed, a radical constriction of the quality of the Court's function. To put it in another way, some do and some do not care to recognize a need for keeping the Court's constitutional interventions within bounds that are imposed, though not clearly defined, by the theory and practice of political democracy. Those who do recognize this need have the choice either of limiting the occasions of the Court's interventions, so that the times will be relatively few when the Court injects itself decisively into the political process, or of restricting the category of principles that the Court may evolve and enforce, with the presumed automatic result that occasions for intervention will be fewer. The first alternative sounds faintly quantitative; the second, more qualitative. To be sure, neither adjective really fits either alternative, and they are not mutually exclusive. But the difference between them is crucial.

The second, so-called qualitative alternative grievously mistakes the effect of decisions by the Court that validate legislative policies. It is this "qualitative" alternative that is represented by Mr. Wechsler's thesis of the neutral principles (see Chap. 2), which is inextricably tied to the conviction—never lacking in comfort yet fraught with risk—that there is no escape from the exercise of jurisdiction which is given. As I have indicated, a neutral principle, aside from its other, less controversial but by no means unimportant aspects, is, for Mr. Wechsler, a rule of action that the Court must be prepared to apply unrelentingly and without compromise in all future cases to which it is relevant. When such cases come up, the Court is duty-bound to decide them, and if it cannot apply even-handedly the principle evolved earlier, then that principle was not a proper one for the Court to enunciate. And if no principle, neutral in this sense, is available against which to measure and perhaps to find wanting an action taken by the other departments of government, then the Court has but one alternative, and that is to declare the action valid.

It is true enough that the Court does not approve or otherwise anoint a legislative policy when it finds it, as the formula goes, "not unconstitutional." No doubt, in one of the late Charles P. Curtis' phrases, "to call a statute constitutional is no more of a compliment than it is to say that it is not intolerable."[30] But, if not a compliment, neither is it an inconsequential appreciation. To declare that a statute is not intolerable in the sense that it is not inconsistent with the principles whose integrity the Court is charged with maintaining—that is something, and it amounts to a significant intervention in the political process, different in degree only from the sort of intervention marked by a declaration of unconstitutionality. As I argued in Chapter 1, it is no small matter, in Professor Black's term, to "legitimate" a legislative measure. The Court's prestige, the spell it casts as a symbol, enable it to entrench and solidify measures that may have been tentative in the conception or that are on the verge of abandonment in the execution. Regardless of what it intends, and granted that it often intends no such thing, the Court can generate consent and may impart permanence. Hamilton, in the 65th *Federalist*, defending the choice of the Senate rather than the Supreme Court as the trier of impeachments, doubted that the Court "would possess the degree of credit and authority" adequate "toward reconciling the people to a decision. . . ." Impeachments to the side, time has in great measure dispelled the doubt. Indeed, Jefferson, when writing to the Justices for their advisory opinion, spoke for a President who wanted their support because "their authority [would] insure the respect of all parties."

The Court's high "degree of credit" is a fact of life, and has been at least since *McCulloch* v. *Maryland* was decided, later causing President Jackson to have to contend with the constitutionality as well as the expediency of a Bank of the United States. This may be the first but it is not the only illustration of the potent quietus that the Court can place on the further agitation of once hotly contested issues. Nor is this plainly observable condition owing to a general misapprehension of the Court's doubly negative way of validating measures of the political institutions. The phenomenon is rather a necessary concomitant of a process of principled decision. Quite aside from the Court's mystic spell, how could it not make a difference in a society committed to principle as well as to electoral responsibility that a measure is authoritatively said not to conflict with principle? It needs no mistaken impression that the Court has also passed on the expediency or prudence of the measure for the fact of its validation to have significant impact. The country is currently witnessing a principled difference of opinion as well as a trial of political strength on the issue of federal aid to parochial schools. Is there any question but that the outcome of this struggle would be affected, perhaps determined, by a Supreme Court decision that federal grants or loans to parochial schools are "not unconstitutional"? Before 1954, segregated schools existed in a number of border cities and in some communities in northern states, including California, Ohio, Illinois, Pennsylvania, and New Jersey. They do not exist there now, and it is reasonable to surmise that even absent a Supreme Court intervention their days were numbered. But would a holding that segregation is "not unconstitutional" have left the situation unaffected in these communities? Would not such a holding clearly have deflected the political trend that was perceptible from the late 'thirties onward?

Declarations of constitutionality—or, if the reader can stand it, of "non-unconstitutionality"—have not only contemporaneous results but also portentous aftermaths. "Legislation," Professor Frankfurter once wrote, "is largely empirical."[31] And much of it is evanescent, and meant to be. Principle is intended to endure, and its formulation casts large shadows into the future. Today's declaration of constitutionality will not only tip today's political balance but may add impetus to the next generation's choice of one policy over another. The point is tellingly put in the dissent of Mr. Justice Jackson in *Korematsu v. United States,* one of the World War II Japanese relocation cases:

Much is said of the danger to liberty from the Army program for deporting and detaining these citizens of Japanese extraction. But a judicial construction of the due process clause that will sustain this order is a far more subtle blow to liberty than the promulgation of the order itself. A military order, however unconstitutional, is not apt to last longer than the military emergency. Even during that period a succeeding commander may revoke it all. But once a judicial opinion rationalizes such an order to show that it conforms to the Constitution, or rather rationalizes the Constitution to show that the Constitution sanctions such an order, the Court for all time has validated the principle of racial discrimination in criminal procedure and of transplanting American citizens. The principle then lies about like a loaded weapon ready for the hand of any authority that can bring forward a plausible claim of an urgent need. Every repetition embeds that principle more deeply in our law and thinking and expands it to new purposes. . . . A military commander may overstep the bounds of constitutionality, and it is an incident. But if we review and approve, that passing incident becomes the doctrine of the Constitution. There it has a generative power of its own, and all that it creates will be in its own image.[32]

The rule that the Court must legitimate whatever it is not justified in striking down fails to attain its intended purpose of removing the Court from the political arena; rather, it works an uncertain and uncontrolled change in the degree of the Court's intervention, and it shifts the direction. In the course of achieving this result, it excises a great deal of what the institution is capable of doing without undue offense to democratic theory and practice. At the root is the question—in the large—of the role of principle in democratic government. No attempt to lift the Court out of the Lincolnian tension can be successful. The rule of the neutral principles merely distorts the tension, by placing the weight of the Court most often on the side of expediency; for that weight is felt whenever the Court legitimates legislative choices on the constitutional merits. The Court is able to play its full role, as it did in the *School Segregation Cases,* maintaining itself in the tension on which our society thrives, because it has available the many techniques and devices of the mediating way between the ultimates of legitimation and invalidation. This, as I shall try to show, is the meaning of the deliberate-speed formula itself.

It follows that the techniques and allied devices for staying the Court's hand, as is avowedly true at least of certiorari, cannot themselves be principled in the sense in which we have a right to expect adjudications on the merits to be principled. They mark the point at which the Court gives the electoral institutions their head and itself stays out of politics, and there is nothing paradoxical in finding that here is where the Court is most a political animal. Thus, by way of one spectacular example, I do not think I mistake the burden of Professor Freund's argument, in a much noted article, that the Court should have avoided adjudication of the ultimate issue in the great *Steel Seizure Case* of 1952 when I conclude that the argument rests on considerations generally deemed political and fit only for legislatures. Mr. Freund contended, however, that these considerations—having to do chiefly with the need to maintain pressure on the parties for a settlement that would allow production to continue—should properly have been decisive for the Court in abstaining from judgment on the constitutional merits. Justices Burton and Frankfurter dissented from what they viewed as a precipitate grant of certiorari in the case. "The time taken" by letting the case find its way up through the lower courts in regular fashion, they said, "will be available also for constructive consideration by the parties of their own positions and responsibilities." Clearly an allusion—if not something more explicit—to factors such as those later canvassed by Mr. Freund, which could play no part—and did play no part for these same two Justices—in the ultimate principled judgment on the constitutional issue, but which could be decisive on the question of certiorari.[33]

But this is not to concede unchanneled, undirected, uncharted discretion. It is not to concede decision proceeding from impulse, hunch, sentiment, predilection, inarticulable and unreasoned. The antithesis of principle in an institution that represents decency and reason is not whim or even expediency, but prudence. And so all the significant questions are still before us. We have touched so far only on the sort of generalization that cannot resolve a single concrete case, but without the aid of which no case can be sensibly decided. What, then, are the considerations in various categories of cases? I propose to attempt an illustrative unfolding of some of the devices for deciding not to decide. I shall start with certain elements of ripeness that should be and often are reflected in the Court's denial of petitions for certiorari. Thence I shall peel down to other—perhaps they may be thought of as deeper—layers. In such an exercise, it is necessary to soak the reader in rather full details of actual cases.

Restraint: Prior and Judicial

A purposive administration of the certiorari jurisdiction would have found no room for *Times Film Corp. v. City of Chicago*.[34] Certiorari, however, was granted in 1961, and the Court divided five to four on the merits, to the accompaniment of not a little public notice. This was the case. Chicago has an ordinance requiring all motion pictures to be submitted "for examination or censorship" prior to being licensed for exhibition. An administrative appeal lies to the Mayor, and exhibition of a picture without the required license is subject to a fine of not less than $50 nor more than $100 for each day the picture is thus exhibited. The Times Film Corporation applied for a license but, when requested to present the motion picture in question, "Don Juan," for inspection, flatly refused to do so. For this reason the license was denied. Times Film thereupon filed suit in the federal district court for an injunction requiring issuance of a license and restraining the city from interfering with exhibition of the picture "Don Juan." No allegation was made describing the picture. The district judge held "that I am without jurisdiction to hear this cause on many grounds," the chief one being, in effect, that the plaintiff lacked standing in the pure sense. On appeal, the dismissal was affirmed.

The film not being part of the record, the Court of Appeals said, no one had any idea what kind of picture Don Juan was. Thus the case was reduced "to an abstract question of law." There was no telling what kind of exhibition the court would be sanctioning if it granted the relief prayed for. "It might be a portrayal of a school of crime, which, for instance, teaches the steps to be taken in successfully carrying out an assassination of a President of the United States as he leaves the White House; or shows how to arrange an uprising of subversive groups in one of our cities."[35]

"The precise question at issue here [the constitutionality of censorship by prior restraint of motion pictures] never having been specifically decided by this Court, we granted certiorari." So runs the ritual recital of the grant in the opinion of the Court by Mr. Justice Clark. It hardly needs counter-recital to establish that the Court does not grant certiorari to decide all questions that have not previously been "specifically decided by this Court." Grants and denials turn, rather, in addition to other factors, on a judgment of the importance of the issue and the suitability of the case. Now the problem of movie censorship in general happens to have a rather full recent history in the Supreme Court. For nearly a decade, starting in 1952, everything that came up was struck down.[36] Censors were ordered to keep hands off such movies as Rosselini's "The Miracle" and, most recently, "Lady Chatterley's Lover," which had been banned as "sacrilegious," "prejudicial to the best interests of the people," "immoral," or "harmful." The guiding consistency of this course of adjudication is marred, however, by the fact that only two opinions of the Court were written, the rest being summary dispositions, and that no readily applicable principle was evolved. There can be no doubt that lower courts as well as local administrators and legislators have had great difficulty making head or tail of the law the Court provided them with. And so, the issue that the *Times Film* case offered for adjudication was important, and might even be said to have ripened not insufficiently, if time alone can make for ripeness. Certiorari should have been denied, however, for other, overriding reasons of unsuitability for adjudication. These reasons do not concern standing in the pure sense. They do necessarily involve the merits.

The question of pure standing, or constitutional standing, is scarcely debatable. Times Film was in danger of being fined for exhibiting "Don Juan," which is an immediate prospect of palpable injury. The company could have avoided the prospect, to be sure, by submitting the film for licensing. But it was precisely this requirement of the law that it deemed unconstitutional. To hold that the requirement is unburdensome or that there is no right to be protected against censorship is simply to decide the merits, although in somewhat disguised fashion. There is and there ought to be no rule of constitutional standing that, in order to construct a justiciable case, a plaintiff must submit to the very burden whose validity he wishes to contest. It is necessary to comply with the other conditions of a licensing process before one can object to denial of a license on this or that specific ground, because there is no injury before the denial. But no like necessity arises before one can object to licensing altogether, for then the very requirement constitutes the injury alleged to be illegal.

But was *Times Film,* as the Court of Appeals thought, otherwise an "abstract" case? This goes to ripeness, and the answer must depend on at least an initial judgment of the merits. If a judge—and it would have to be a judge experienced in this category of cases and not a little addicted to absolutes—holds the conviction that there ought to be no governmental power whatever, no matter what the means used, to forbid the showing of any movie whatever to anyone, no matter how obscene or gruesomely offensive or incendiary it may be, or if he takes the view that a prior restraint is always unconstitutional, under any circumstances, then *Times Film* was as concrete a case as the next. For a judge who entertains the faintest doubts about the absoluteness of such absolutes, no case could be less suitable, for no case could have truncated the issue more or narrowed the line of vision more severely. Absolutes to the side, what, after all, is the issue of prior restraint?

There was a time when the issue was quite straightforward, because the difference between a prior restraint on speech and regulations by way of subsequent punishments was plain. A prior restraint—that is, a requirement that the censor, acting to enforce standards announced by statute, must approve before one may publish or exhibit—was censorship by the Crown or under the authority of Parliament. It represented, therefore, control by irresponsible or oligarchic officials. Subsequent prosecutions—meaning a system of announcing by statute standards under which publication or exhibition of certain matter is prohibited, and relying for their enforcement, not on prior censorship, but on subsequent criminal prosecutions and on their *in terrorem* effect—were subject to the safeguard of trial by jury; by the eighteenth century, a reasonably well-developed safeguard. Lord Mansfield wrote in 1754 that a conviction then obtained in such a case was the first from a London jury in 27 years. In the colonies the difference was even starker. Prior restraint meant control by officers responsive to officials in England. Subsequent punishment meant trials before local juries. The problem was to protect a majority and to foster an infant democratic process. Prior restraints were a certain means of strangling it. Jury trials came near to placing total control in the hands of the very majority whose freedom of speech was in question. This straightforward difference lay behind the abhorrence of prior restraints, expressed by Blackstone, which was so strong in the English tradition and which most of the colonists certainly shared.[37] But this particular tradition, edifying though it may be, has only the faintest present relevance. The problem today is quite different. It is not protection of the majority against irresponsible, oligarchic government; rather, it is protection of minorities against a majority in a working, deep-cutting democracy, a majority whose attitudes will be reflected by the executive as well as by the jury system. In a representative democracy, neither officials—especially appointive ones—nor juries should be allowed too wide a discretion to make policy in these matters. The legislature, as the most broadly based, deliberative institution, may have to be held fairly strictly to its own responsibility in the premises. That was the thrust of some of the decisions preceding *Times Film*. But this is a consideration that applies about equally to prior restraints and to a system of subsequent prosecutions. If there remain significant general differences between the two, they must be other ones.

To maintain that a prior-restraint statute will necessarily have a wider deterring effect on speech than a similarly drawn criminal statute simply does not bear analysis. There is a difference, however, in the timing and posture of litigation, the difference between requiring the exhibitor to apply to, and then perhaps to sue, the censor and inviting the exhibitor to act at his peril and wait for the censor to sue him. In either event, the ultimate decision will be by judges on review. In neither event can litigation be avoided. Law suits, Brandeis once said, "often prove to have been groundless; but no way has been discovered of relieving a defendant from the necessity of a trial to establish the fact."[38] But a criminal prosecution is not so easily started as a license is denied. One may well wonder why there should not be demanded of the censor a showing, or at least an allegation of reason to believe, that a film which must be submitted for examination might fall within a forbidden category. It is difficult to see why the state should be thus empowered to arrest a film, as it were, even for a day, without first making out probable cause—some substantiated grounds for suspecting—that the film may ultimately be found to be pornographic or whatever, and that its exhibition may ultimately be forbidden without offense to principles of free speech. The state cannot ordinarily arrest an individual or search his papers or effects without first making out probable cause that he has committed an illegal act, and it ought to have no greater power over the product of an individual's mind, which a motion picture may sometimes turn out to be. It is strange and unaccustomed that the exhibitor of a motion picture should have the burden of coming forward with evidence of "innocence," while the censor need prove nothing at this stage. But this is not an argument that could lead to wholesale prohibition of prior restraints.

The most crucial present-day difference between prior restraints and subsequent punishments concerns what happens to the film while litigation takes its course. If it were necessarily true that a film may be exhibited—at the defendant's peril, to be sure, but nevertheless exhibited—throughout the period of criminal litigation and appellate judgment, while it may not be exhibited during the period of civil litigation following denial of a license, then the difference would indeed be major. But this is far from a necessary consequence. Mr. Freund, for example, has strongly urged that the act of disobeying the censor and showing the film without a license should be held not to be a punishable offense if the exhibitor wins the ultimate litigation. This suggestion would equalize matters.[39]

The brief for the defendant—the City of Chicago—in the *Times Film* case ends with what is surely one of the most touching, upturned-face pleas ever made to an authoritative oracle, let alone the Supreme Court:

What, then, is the answer? It is for this Court to lead the way, for it is with this Court that the ultimate responsibility rests. The Court must adhere to the middle-of-the-road policy—a road that is flanked by two precipices. The one drops off to moral debasement, the other to witch-hunting, thought-strangulation, Puritan regimentation. Neither course is for America. This Court must take the helm and lead us—both sides to this controversy—down the middle path where motion pictures will be subject to only such prior restraint as may be necessary to prohibit the obscene, the immoral and those motion pictures which tend to produce a breach of the peace and riots.[40]

The case is hardly imaginable in which the materials for such a judgment could be scantier. The only thing to be said in favor of *Times Film's* suitability for adjudication is that portions of the Chicago ordinance have been construed in another case by the Illinois Supreme Court.[41] For the rest, and despite descriptive testimony in the record, no case could throw less light than did *Times Film* upon the actual workings of the licensing operation in Chicago. In no case could there be less opportunity to consider in detail and concretely the ramifications of prior restraints, or to assess ways of removing their most objectionable features. Had it been alleged that the showing of "Don Juan" could not be forbidden under any of the provisions of the ordinance, as construed by the Illinois Supreme Court itself, the city might have demurred, and the question of probable cause would thus have been brought into focus. Another of the crucial aspects of the issue of prior restraint would have been raised if the film had been exhibited for one day without a license, so that a criminal prosecution might result—which, at the maximum cost of $100, is not a prohibitive thing to ask of defendants able to bear the over-all expense of litigation. And, of course, going beyond the question of the differences between prior restraint and subsequent punishment, there was no way of evaluating the validity under the First Amendment of any regulation, by whatever means, as applied to this film, for the Court was not allowed to know anything about it. All for the excellent reason that the case was framed that way, to force upon the Court an either-or proposition.

Thus the short of it is—to borrow a figure of Mr. Freund—that the real issues must be dealt with at retail, whereas the parties here offered one issue at wholesale. This, as I have said, represents an initial estimate of the merits; namely, that the Court should not impose an absolute prohibition outlawing all prior restraints across the board. But we know that five judges were prepared to hold something quite different, though far from inconsistent—namely, that in some circumstances, however restricted and narrowed, prior restraints are constitutional. On its substantive merits, as an ultimate judgment of the present outer limits of the principle of free speech, there can be little, if anything, to object to in such a holding, and *Times Film* was a perfectly suitable case in which to announce it. It is a quite separate question, however, whether or not the Court ought to legitimate, even by means of so narrow a holding, prior-restraint censorship, and the decision of this question should not be permitted simply to go by default. Its resolution should turn on the Court's assessment of the wisdom, the prudence of prior restraints, and on the likely effect, in current social and political circumstances, of the judgment of legitimation. These are, to be sure, legislative considerations. They can form no proper part of a principled judgment. The Court cannot, consistently with its *raison d'être*, legitimate a legislative measure, let alone strike it down, on grounds such as these. It should not, finding that the Congress or the President needs the support of its authority for a worthy or necessary measure, as a majority of the Justices may deem it, proceed to legitimate it, even though, like the relocation of the West Coast Japanese in 1942, the measure collides with principle. But the question in *Times Film* was whether prudential considerations, as a majority of the Justices see them, might govern a decision to withhold legitimation—a decision, that is, to abstain from intervention in the political process. Nothing in the justification of the power of judicial review forecloses such a decision by the Court, so grounded, for here is no conflict with the theory, no interference in the practice, of political democracy.

All that was in fact decided in *Times Film* was the issue exactly as tendered. The majority dealt—the Chief Justice's dissenting alarms notwithstanding—with motion pictures only, for motion pictures may be deemed different even from television in impact and most signally in the numbers and nature and situation of any single audience; movies, like the theater, address themselves to groups of people in public places, not to the individual in the home. This is not to say that they are unprotected by principles of free speech. It is simply to assert what is readily observed— that movies are neither books nor newspapers nor even television, and that Justice Clark's statement on behalf of the majority that he was speaking of motion pictures only may be fully credited. As it concerns the movies, the majority's holding was merely that there is no absolute right to exhibit all films without prior submission to censorship—all films, perchance including one which contains "the basest type of pornography, or incitement to riot, or forceful overthrow of orderly government. . . ."

This is not very far-reaching doctrine. But there can be little doubt that the decision—especially since it was rendered in an unconcerned opinion, which treated the power to censor as if it hardly differed from a municipality's sewer-maintenance functions—will have radiating consequences, and that these will be to encourage Comstockian tendencies. The Court's previous adjudications, confusing as they were, and no doubt in part because of their lack of clarity, at the very least rendered censorship uncertain of ultimate effectiveness. Some state courts and some communities even misinterpreted the Court's decisions as invalidating all motion-picture censorship. Certainly it can be said that the Court had been having, and might expect its previous adjudications to continue to have, a dampening effect on censorship.[42] The *Times Film* decision bids fair to inaugurate an opposite trend. Is this a consideration not properly addressed to the Court? It is unreal to think that by putting such matters out of view the Court keeps itself out of politics. Actually, it merely abandons control of the direction in which, inevitably, its decisions on the merits do influence public opinion and the political institutions.

An absolute prohibition on prior restraints is not, as I have maintained, a proper principle for the Court to impose. It is neither a proper neutral principle, in Mr. Wechsler's sense, nor a proper principled goal, because it does not proceed from moral or other considerations that are sufficiently clear cut and deep cutting to override countervailing ones. If it were an adequate principled goal, the Court might have announced and enforced it in this case, expecting to allow room for accommodation and compromises, if any, that might prove necessary in practice by means of one or another of the devices for withholding future judgments on the merits. It is, as I have argued, decidedly the Court's function to proclaim principled goals, including some that it foresees may be incapable of immediate, full attainment. In no way does this demean the process of reason or the durability of principle. It would be a quite different matter, however, for the Court to proclaim an absolute which is not merely unattainable in practice, but untenable as such on principle. In the one case, the Court undertakes to influence the tendency of public action toward an end of whose validity it has no present doubt. In the second, the element of manipulative dissimulation inheres unavoidably. Herein, as I suggested in Chapter 3, appears to lie one of the differences between Justice Black's absolutist position and the approach generally adopted by a majority of the Court.

But to have said this is not remotely to suggest that good reasons are lacking for an attitude of extreme hostility to prior restraints. The differences between prior restraints and other regulations of speech are relatively slight and capable of being minimized even further or eliminated altogether. Yet certain imponderables come into play.[43] There is, after all, a peculiarly galling indignity in having to submit the work of the mind, in whatever form, to official approval before being permitted to issue it—even at one's peril—for the assessment of the public and the judgment of posterity. Moreover, a certain attitude of mind seems always to be engendered in professional censors (or perhaps it propels people into the profession), which results in excesses and stupidities such as are impressively recited in the Chief Justice's dissent in the *Times Film* case. A system of subsequent prosecutions does not call for professionalism in censors; it is administered through the general law-enforcement hierarchy. There is not enough in this to form the basis of an absolute principle outlawing censorship, but there is enough for a prudential judgment that censorship should not be lightly encouraged; enough, therefore, to have caused the Court to withhold the sanction of constitutionality by the comparatively inoffensive expedient of denying certiorari.

There would have been offense, to be sure—continued uncertainty and confusion—to the legislators and administrators, the front-line officials, as Professor Henry M. Hart, Jr., calls them. Certainty, like stability, is one of the values served by the law, but it is not always the highest. Moreover, the issue being what it is, and the materials of judgment having been truncated as they were, the likely adjudication on the merits was the one actually handed down, and it is scarcely the ultimate in shafts of light. That leaves offense to the party moving for relief, whose situation ought generally to be one of the decisive considerations, although it cannot be *the* decisive one. But the Times Film Corporation elected— presumably by way of a gamble—to frame this sort of case. Had the case been fleshed out more, Times Film would have run the risk of an adjudication on the merits that avoided the broad issue tendered. But, in light of the disposition of seven previous cases, this is to say that Times Film would have run the risk of winning its case. It guarded itself effectively.

To the extent that the decisive considerations at the certiorari stage have been accurately isolated here, the Court's practice whereby four votes are sufficient to bring about the grant of a petition is brought into doubt. Of course, nothing has been said to shake the assumption that denial of certiorari is not an adjudication of the issues tendered, let alone an affirmance of the judgment below. A denial is an avoidance of adjudication of the merits. But it is clear also that there are times when avoidance should rest on merits of its own, and it is not clear why a majority of the Court should lack the power to make this judgment. While the rule of four is in effect, however, it would seem to dictate that once certiorari had been granted in *Times Film,* the action could not be reversed. The argument revealed nothing new about the case in respect of the relevant considerations, and a single case is involved, not a category.[44] And so the appropriate disposition called for after argument was a jurisdictional dismissal for lack of ripeness.

Ripeness: A Colloquy on Birth Control

The problem in the *Times Film* case—mishandled, though we cannot say ignored, by the Court—was twofold. The suit, as plaintiff framed it, was not ripe for a principled judgment setting limits on the power of government to censor by prior restraint. On the other hand, the issue whether *any* prior restraints are permissible under any circumstances, even just of motion pictures, was itself not ripe for adjudication, although it was adequately presented on the facts and pleadings of this case. Only one outcome on the merits was open to the Court on principle—legitimation; and this was unwise in its tendency. We enjoy, after all, more freedoms (which is to say, more convenient social disorderliness) than the rule of principle should, or the judges could, guarantee us. But where freedom makes special claims, though they fall short of principle, the judges have no duty officiously to encourage majoritarian forces of order, which will speak for themselves readily enough when they feel the need.

Just a few months after it decided *Times Film*, the Court declined to adjudicate the merits of a case testing the constitutionality of anti-birth-control statutes. The Court did so on the basis of sound, prudential considerations that differed from those rejected in *Times Film*, although they were of the same order. Unlike *Times Film*, the birth-control case was ripe for adjudication either way of the ultimate issue tendered. As a case, it was wholly, not half, ripe. But the issue itself was not ripe at all, for reasons having to do with the proper interplay between the function of the Court and the responsibilities of legislatures.

Connecticut forbids the use by any person of "any drug, medicinal article or instrument for the purpose of preventing conception." Violations are punished by fines of not less than fifty dollars or imprisonment of not less than sixty days nor more than one year, or both. No Connecticut statute specifically forbids the sale or distribution of these devices, but the state does generally punish, as if they were the principal offenders, accessories who assist or counsel others to commit any offense. *Tileston* v. *Ullman*,[45] decided in 1943, was an unsuccessful attempt to have the Court pass on the constitutionality of the Connecticut law. Dr. Tileston alleged that he was prevented from giving professional birth-control advice to three patients whose lives would be endangered by child bearing, but he did not allege any infringement of his own rights, nor even any particular inconvenience to himself, and the patients in question were not parties to the suit. The case was dismissed on the ground that Dr. Tileston lacked standing—whether of the constitutional or of what I have called the impure sort is not clear.

If the trouble was that Dr. Tileston was trying to protect himself by invoking the rights of others—namely, his patients—then impure standing was the point. Provided that the moving party to a suit is in fact injured, there is constitutional standing to litigate any defect in the statute that inflicted the injury, without further need to relate the particular defect to the plaintiff and his particular injury. All else is discretionary—the search, in varying circumstances, for further concreteness. But Dr. Tileston had omitted to allege that he himself was in any respect threatened with harm— either material or in the nature of an infringement of a pre-existing legal right, constitutional or otherwise. "The complaint," as the Court noted, "set out in detail the danger to the lives of appellant's patients in the event that they should bear children, but contained no allegation asserting any claim under the Fourteenth Amendment of infringement of appellant's liberty or his property rights." Dr. Tileston was deterred by the prospect of prosecution from advising birth control, but he did not indicate in what respect he would suffer if he refrained from giving the advice. This being so, he may be seen as a public-spirited bystander, whose only interest —on the allegations he elected to make—was in clarification of the law. The question, then, is one of constitutional standing, and the answer is that there can be none in such circumstances, save perhaps under the majority opinion in *Ashwander* v. *TVA*. But Brandeis was, after all, right.

In three suits brought up for decision together as one case, styled

Poe v. *Ullman*,[46] in 1961, the omissions of pleadings and parties that frustrated *Tileston* v. *Ullman* were well and truly supplied. Dr. Buxton, one of the parties, sued in his own right, alleging that the Connecticut law prevented the full, conscientious exercise of his profession and thus injured him in violation of the Fourteenth Amendment. Two other plaintiffs, suing under fictitious names, were patients of Dr. Buxton's who alleged that their health would be endangered unless contraception could be prescribed for them. Excruciatingly enough, these attempts to obtain adjudication also failed, although in very different fashion and for a more intricate and interesting reason.

Like *Tileston,* these were suits under the Connecticut Declaratory Judgment Act, alleging that the defendant State's Attorney "intends to prosecute any offense" against the Connecticut anti-birth-control statutes. The State's Attorney admitted this allegation, and the Connecticut Supreme Court held the statutes applicable and valid. The considerations on which dismissal of the subsequent appeal to the United States Supreme Court was eventually based became apparent upon the argument. As Professor Fowler V. Harper, counsel for plaintiffs, stated in answer to questions from the Bench, there has never been any enforcement of the Connecticut law against persons who use contraceptives. In the opinion of Assistant Attorney General Raymond J. Cannon, of Connecticut, arguing for defendant, a sale of contraceptives, even if the use intended was merely to prevent disease, would violate the statutes, despite a letter dated September 15, 1954, quoted in plaintiff's brief, from the State Commissioner of Food and Drugs to the Secretary of the Bridgeport Pharmaceutical Association, which gives it as the Commissioner's judgment that since diaphragms have therapeutic and other uses, there is no reason why drug stores may not fill a physician's prescription for them. In any event, both Mr. Cannon and Mr. Harper stated to the Court that contraceptives are notoriously sold in drug stores, and that there has never been a prosecution for such sales. There have been, Mr. Cannon told the Court, two police-court prosecutions for vending-machine sales, which were successful and were not appealed. And in 1940, two doctors and a nurse were successfully prosecuted for aiding and abetting violation of the statute in the operation of a birth-control clinic, which was closed, with the result that no more such clinics have been operated in Connecticut. This is the entire history of the enforcement of the statutes.[47]

"So the matter is entirely academic," Mr. Justice Frankfurter said to counsel for the defendant on the argument. "I suppose so," replied Mr. Cannon.[48] But it hardly was. The highest court of the state, in the *Tileston* case as well as in this case, had construed the statutes to forbid and make punishable dissemination of birth-control information privately, by a doctor to his patients. Dr. Buxton alleged that he was a law-abiding as well as a prudent citizen and that the statute deterred him from prescribing contraceptives. This is something only Dr. Buxton can know. Whether prosecution is very likely, likely, possible, or even improbable, the incidence of some deterrent effect cannot be gainsaid. The matter was not academic at the time of the argument; it became so by decision of the Supreme Court.

The point of Mr. Justice Frankfurter's opinion announcing the judgment of the Court, as Justice Harlan was able to show in dissent, was not that the plaintiffs had no constitutional standing, not that the controversy was feigned or unreal, and not, as in *Times Film*, that it was "so artificially truncated as to make the cases not susceptible to intelligent decision."[49] The point was that the office of the Court, even in a perfectly real, concrete, and fully developed controversy, is not necessarily to resolve issues on which the political processes are in deadlock; it may be wise to wait till the political institutions, breaking the deadlock, are able to make an initial decision, on which the Court may then pass judgment. If the Court was not "to close our eyes to reality," it had to find that the situation in Connecticut in respect of the use of contraceptive devices by a doctor's prescription was most curious. The influences that favor the objective of the law cannot—or perhaps will not[50]— summon sufficient political strength to cause it to be enforced; the assumption being that in respect of a consistent practice in an area of continuing public concern, enforcement or nonenforcement of the law is, in its way, a reflection of political pressures. The influences that oppose the law cannot summon sufficient political strength to cause it to be repealed; attempts have been made from 1923 onward, and they have failed. All this is not known to be the fact with regard to sales from vending machines or the establishment of birth-control clinics. A prosecution involving a clinic is now winding its way up to the Court, and it will be a different matter.[51] But the case before the Court in 1961 concerned neither vending machines nor clinics. Had the attempt been to obtain a decision on the statute as applied to vending machines or to clinics, this case should have been dismissed as lacking concreteness—dismissed, that is, for a failure of ripeness in a quite elementary sense.[52]

When the Connecticut anti-birth-control statute was enacted, in 1879, as part of a wholesale attack on what was then deemed obscene, under the title "An Act to Amend an Act Concerning Offenses against Decency, Morality and Humanity," it was the product of very different political forces and a very different climate of opinion.[53] There is nothing astonishing about its survival under other patronage and to other ends today. But, having regard to the total lack of enforcement in circumstances such as those of the case before the Court, it is evident that the statute does not speak the present will of dominant forces in the state. It represents at present a deadlock of wills, from which the Court was asked to extricate the state. This may be the reality more often than we know or care to acknowledge. But this time it was demonstrable. Such a deadlock, in such circumstances, nevertheless constitutes a species of effective law, in the degree complained of by Dr. Buxton and his patients. But it is law by default. And it does not follow—except from the dictum in *Cohens* v. *Virginia*—that the Court owed an adjudication to Dr. Buxton and his patients.

For anyone prepared not to heed Thayer's admonition that the "tendency of a common and easy resort to this great function [of judicial review], now lamentably too common, is to dwarf the political capacity of the people, and to deaden its sense of moral responsibility"[54]—for anyone so disposed, the Court's judgment in *Poe* v. *Ullman* is nonsense. But if the case is seen as having presented the Court with a choice between, on the one hand, a constitutional adjudication that would cooperate with the state's political institutions in their efforts to evade their own responsibility for decision and, on the other, an act of judicial abstention that might help to set in motion the process of political decision, then the result appears in a very different light. The truth is that neither the Connecticut legislature nor the prosecuting authorities have ever faced the issue in its present significance and in context of the present political configuration. The legislature has voted against repeal. But that is not the same as voting to enact a statute,[55] and the difference is peculiarly crucial, as I shall argue further, in circumstances of nonenforcement. Prosecutors have dealt only with a clinic and two vending machines. For the rest, all they have ever done has been, literally, to demur as occasion offered. They have acquiesced, this is to say, in shifting the decision to the Court. A device to turn the thrust of forces favoring and opposing the present objectives of the statute toward the legislature, where the power of at least initial decision properly belongs in our system, was available to the Court, and it is implicit in the prevailing opinion. It is the concept of desuetude.

This, it must be said, is not an everyday, familiar doctrine of Anglo-American law. Nor is desuetude, however, as Mr. Justice Douglas remarked in his dissent in *Poe* v. *Ullman,* "contrary to every principle of American or English common law. . . ." It is squarely inconsistent with Mr. Justice Douglas' opinion for the Court (which the Justice does not cite) in 1953, in *District of Columbia* v. *John R. Thompson Co.*[56] But, happy as it was in the result, that was an exceedingly hard case, which may perhaps be excused for the kind of law it made. The Court did not there consider, and it has not elsewhere canvassed, the reason of the thing. The question is not—as it was with bootlegging, an illustration of Justice Douglas—whether, in the words of an English judge, "because a certain number of people do not like an Act and because a good many people disobey it, the Act is therefore 'obsolescent' and no one need pay any attention to it. . . ."[57] The question is whether a statute that has never been enforced and that has not been obeyed for three quarters of a century may suddenly be resurrected and applied. The civilians, more bound to codes though they are, have sometimes recognized the doctrine. "Wherefore very rightly this also is held," John Chipman Gray quotes from Julianus, "that statutes may be abrogated not only by a vote of the legislator, but also by desuetude with the tacit consent of all." And Gray points out, with his usual freshness, that formal rejection of the doctrine by the courts does not necessarily mean failure to apply its substance. "It is not as speedy or as simple a process to interpret a statute out of existence as to repeal it, but with time and patient skill it can often be done."[58]

The strongest claim that the idea of desuetude has to naturalization in American law is consanguinity, not only with practices of statutory construction, but with the well established doctrine—conventionally regarded as a constitutional principle inherent in due process of law—that statutes may be declared void for vagueness. As Anthony G. Amsterdam's brilliant recent analysis[59] has shown, vagueness is vague; the doctrine has several meanings and serves more than one end. There are times when it does import a substantive adjudication, as when a statute is so worded that it is likely to deter a great deal more than it actually forbids, and this unearned increment of deterrence causes it to intrude into an area that it may not constitutionally regulate. All criminal statutes deter more than they forbid. None can wholly avoid carrying this penumbra of inexplicit deterrence, except by resort to mathematical formulae instead of language. Generally and within limits, this is intended and is either all to the good or a matter of indifference. But a statute may deter conduct that should on principle be altogether free from governmental regulation. When a court finds this to be the case and holds the statute void for vagueness, it renders a substantive adjudication based on constitutional principle. And it can do so unembarrassed by any problem of constitutional standing.

There will be, in such cases, a difficulty of impure standing shading into a question of ripeness if the defendant's behavior, to which the statute was applied, falls within the area that *may* be constitutionally regulated. Such a defendant has constitutional standing because he is obviously subject to an injury from which he would be saved if the statute were voided. But, just as obviously, his is not the most suitable case for adjudication of the issue tendered, which turns on the effect the statute may have on persons differently situated and engaged in, or deterred from, quite different activities. Yet it may be true that by hypothesis no more suitable case can ever be constructed, because those who are unjustifiably deterred will never be prosecuted, and what deters them is precisely the prospect of litigation. Whether the statute is so broadly drawn as to have such deterrent effect and whether those whom it deters should be protected against it (although they are unlikely to be prosecuted) is the issue on the merits; and if the answer is at least initially yes, then no riper case raising the issue can be expected.[60] It was, therefore, nothing short of disingenuous for the late Chief Justice Vinson to suggest, in *Dennis* v. *United States*,[61] the original Smith Act prosecution, that a claim of vagueness in the statute could not properly be heard from leaders of the Communist party, who had been found by a jury to have "intended to initiate a violent revolution whenever the propitious occasion appeared." The Act punishes, among others, those who "teach" "the propriety of overthrowing or destroying" the government by force and violence, and those who become members of any "society" that so much as "encourages" the "overthrow or destruction" of the government. The defendants' argument was in essence that all sorts of peaceable discussion of even a theoretical right of revolution would be deterred, although perhaps not punished, by these provisions, and that their effect was therefore inconsistent with principles of free speech. Chief Justice Vinson's reply was an allusion to problems of constitutional standing: "A claim of guilelessness ill becomes those with evil intent"—*i.e.*, the *Dennis* case defendants. This was simply a failure to meet the contention, not in any fashion an adequate answer to it.

There are other instances when a court's finding that a statute is inadmissibly vague (but not necessarily void *in toto* for that reason) signifies no substantive adjudication of the sort discussed above but is, rather, a device for avoiding such a constitutional judgment. In such cases, courts often talk a great deal about fair notice or warning to the individual. Although, as Holmes observed, "it is not likely that a criminal will carefully consider the text of the law before he murders or steals," yet "it is reasonable that a fair warning should be given to the world in language that the common world will understand of what the law intends to do if a certain line is passed."[62] And there are situations in which people do read the penal code, or have it professionally explained for them. Moreover, the general outlines of the law—or its lack of sufficiently definite shape, and hence its brooding, overreaching threat—tend to be noticed by those who may be specially affected, at the time of enactment, through later news of prosecutions, or through word-of-mouth reports from persons who have the law called to their attention. But Holmes, impartially endowing with the permanence of his prose the arguments on both sides of the issue, also remarked elsewhere that "the law is full of instances where a man's fate depends on his estimating rightly, that is, as a jury subsequently estimates it, some matter of degree. If his judgment is wrong, not only may he incur a fine or a short imprisonment . . . he may incur the penalty of death."[63] In any event, the fair-warning factor can hardly be decisive, or even significant, where a statute is not self-enforcing (that is, does not rely entirely on the criminal process and its deterrent effect but is enforced in the first instance administratively, through the issuance of direct orders tailored to individual circumstances). With an administered statute, there is no duty to obey and no peril to the individual before the administrator acts, and his action is ample warning. A decisive consideration here, as Mr. Amsterdam demonstrates, is, rather, that a loosely worded statute allows latitude for "discontrol, irrationality, and irregularity," for erratic, prejudiced, discriminatory, or overreaching (the adjectives are all Mr. Amsterdam's) exercises of authority.[64] The danger is greatest from administrative officials—particularly from petty officials—but it should be guarded against as well with prosecutors, who have power to harass, and with judges and juries. Hence this is a relevant consideration in self-enforcing criminal statutes as well as in administered ones.

The evil at the root of the risks Mr. Amsterdam emphasizes is irresponsibility. A vague statute delegates to administrators, prosecutors, juries, and judges the authority of *ad hoc* decision, which is in its nature difficult if not impossible to hold to account, because of its narrow impact. In addition, such a statute delegates authority away from those who are personally accountable, at least for the totality of their performance, to those who are not, at least not directly. In both aspects, it short-circuits the lines of responsibility that make the political process meaningful. And so it is far from a sterile conceptualism to say that a vague statute delegates power to make decisions that do not derive from a prior legislative decision and that do not, therefore, represent the sovereign will, expressed as it should be. Of course, differences of degree are vital. Much will depend on what sort of decision is delegated, how much of it, and to whom. Be that as it may, when the Court finds a statute unduly vague, it withholds adjudication of the substantive issue in order to set in motion the process of legislative decision. It does not hold that the legislature may not *do* whatever it is that is complained of but, rather, asks that the *legislature* do it, if it is to be done at all. Herein, chiefly, lies the kinship with the idea of desuetude.

A vague statute may leave too much undone or may delegate the wrong thing to the wrong official. The disused statute rises above—or falls below—such differences of degree. It leaves all undone. One would be foolish, of course, to expect continual expression of the legislative will through continual reconsideration of the statute book. But normal law enforcement indicates the continuity of will, because it conduces to legislative reconsideration when in fact dominant opinion turns—although greater strength does have to be mobilized to repeal a statute than to resist its enactment. Only through normal enforcement can the effects of a law be generally felt, with the consequence that there is a chance of mustering opposition sufficient to move the legislature. When the law is consistently not enforced, that chance is reduced to the vanishing point. For consistent failure to enforce is itself a political concession to the opposition, and it will satisfy at least some portions of it. And so that "ease of obtaining new legislation," of which Gray speaks as leaving "little occasion to apply the doctrine of desuetude," is nullified.[65] The unenforced statute is not, in the normal way, a continuing reflection of the balance of political pressures. When it is resurrected and enforced, it represents the *ad hoc* decision of the prosecutor, and then of the judge and jury, unrelated to anything that may realistically be taken as present legislative policy. Undoubtedly, a consistent future course of prosecution will restore the situation to normal and reopen those channels to legislative reconsideration which, being unobstructed, can support the presumption that the statute book speaks the continuing political will of the state. But of such a consistent course there is no assurance after seventy-five years of nonenforcement, and the first prosecution, at any rate, has all the vices of an *ad hoc* official decision.

To be sure, the criminal code is not enforced in all its parts against all transgressors all the time. Society is not willing to invest quite so much of its resources in the criminal process, and it doesn't need to. Hence every criminal statute necessarily vests in prosecutors some discretion to pick and choose cases and defendants. It is a discretion governed by professional standards—imprecise though they be. All observers of the legal order will readily recognize its normal exercise and will readily distinguish it from erratic or discriminatory action under an unduly vague statute or from a consistent, total failure of prosecution over time, which allows a statute to fall into disuse. That prosecutors do, over time, nullify certain statutes, altogether or in some of their possible applications, everyone knows, although the fact is not often so well documented as in the case of Attorney General (later Mr. Justice) Robert H. Jackson's refusal, consistent with the action of his predecessors, to enforce a loose District of Columbia criminal-libel statute, except against a very narrow category of offenses.[66]

The books are full of dead-letter statutes.[67] They make good comic filler at the foot of newspaper columns. The books are full also of more sinister enactments, which are used to prosecute only with exceptional, discriminatory selectivity, and are used most often administratively, short of prosecutions, to blackmail and harass and cajole people.[68] Such statutes are not infrequently found impermissibly vague, when prosecution and appeal bring them to light—and ought to be so found even more often than they are. If this is not "contrary to every principle of American or English law" or an unjustifiable interference by the federal Supreme Court with the institutional arrangements of the states, then, in the appropriate case, neither is the device of desuetude. The same end is served. The Court declines to frame and decide an issue of principle, declines to render a judgment overcoming decisions of the political institutions, because it finds that these institutions have not made a deliberate and responsible prior decision. In the vagueness situation, the legislature has left a decision at once too narrow and too important to relatively irresponsible officials. Desuetude occurs because a series of prosecutors have registered, relatively responsibly, the play of political forces which, being in fine balance, could will no more than that the statute remain unrepealed but quiescent. Responsible government, however, is a function of imbalance; that, not equipoise, is what is meant by the expression "the balance of political forces." When a prosecution at last occurs, it denotes at least the beginning of the imbalance natural to operational government, but it reflects it irresponsibly, through the wrong institution and process, precisely as does a prosecution under a vague statute.

It may be added that the element of the absence of fair notice in obsolete statutes is not to be minimized, despite such deterrent effect as the statute may retain for the well-informed and ideally law-abiding and prudent citizen. Fair warning as a factor in a holding of desuetude would be much more soundly based on the realities of the common experience with the criminal law than it can possibly be in the usual vagueness case. Regardless of two declaratory judgments in over seventy-five years (those in *Tileston* and in the present case), the total absence of prosecutions is surely the operative fact for the great majority of the people of Connecticut. It is bound to have greater significance than the imprecision of statutory language.

The prevailing opinion by Mr. Justice Frankfurter in *Poe* v. *Ullman* did not in so many words hold that the Connecticut anti-birth-control statute had been nullified by desuetude in its application to the use of contraceptives by a doctor's prescription. But it did rest on this flat statement: "The undeviating policy of nullification by Connecticut of its anti-contraceptive laws throughout all the long years that they have been on the statute books bespeaks more than prosecutorial paralysis." And the opinion declined on this ground to reach what would otherwise be a ripe, justiciable issue. There might have been nothing amiss in language a shade more explicit. But the guarded expression is characteristic of our law in the initial stages of a doctrinal development. The consequence of the opinion, nevertheless, must be that a prosecution of persons situated as are Dr. Buxton and his patients would fail on the ground of desuetude. It has to be noted, however, that Mr. Justice Brennan's brief concurrence, making a majority, amounted only to a discretionary vote against adjudication, for reasons that are none too scrutable.

It may be that the exquisite balance registered by the disused yet unrepealed Connecticut statute is just what suits the people of Connecticut. It may be that the deterrent effect on unusually well-informed and tender consciences, plus a moral posture of the statute book agreeable to a certain portion of the population, plus the unhindered practice of birth control by another and in some measure also by the same portion—it may be that the sum of these things is exactly what is wanted. It is, as I have remarked, a species of law by default. And such it can remain; no constitutional judgment of the Court prevents. A finding of desuetude in the circumstances of *Poe* v. *Ullman* neither strikes the statute off the books nor activates it; the effect is precisely that the Court does not tinker with the equilibrium. There is no difficulty there. The harder question is why the Court should not relieve Dr. Buxton of his embarrassment. But the constitutional issue that Dr. Buxton raised is not free from doubt. The result of adjudication might have been to uphold the constitutionality of the statute. There may be occasions when the deterrent effect of a disused statute is, or can be surmised to be, stronger than it was possible to deem it on the facts presented in the argument of *Poe* v. *Ullman*. Then perhaps the Court should reach the merits of the statute's constitutionality. Even then, judicial review would sap the quality of the political process, because it would tend, much more than normally, to be exercising initial rather than reviewing judgment. *Poe* v. *Ullman*, at any rate, was an extreme instance. No amount of theorizing about the nice equipoise desired by the people of Connecticut can overcome the distinct impression left by a consistent course of legislative and official conduct that the political institutions, as well as the forces playing on them, being sorely beset by indecision, wanted the Court to solve their birth-control problem for them. No doubt, the evident disposition, indeed eagerness, of the political institutions to pass the question to the Court might minimize the eventual shock to the pride of political power, which is always occasioned by the Court's principled judgment. And it might not, for heaven knows what confident expectations of this or the other result are harbored by amateur Court-watchers. In any event, the point here is not the clash of wills between the representative institutions and the Court; granted that this clash would be relatively minimal.[69] The point is the effect on the sense of responsibility and the self-reliance of the political institutions and of their constituents. If Catholic opinion in Connecticut and officials who are responsive to it cannot decide whether it is wise or self-defeating to forbid the use of contraceptives by authority of the state,[70] it is quite wrong for the Court to relieve them of this burden of self-government. However much judicial review may always—but uncertainly, inconclusively, and unavoidably— "dwarf the political capacity of the people," it should surely not do so knowingly, demonstrably, avoidably. One day the people of Connecticut may enjoy freedom from birth-control regulation without being guaranteed it by the judges, and it is much better that way, if possible, even at some intermediate cost to Dr. Buxton.

Political Responsibility and Congressional Investigations

The Court in the birth-control case engaged in a sort of colloquy with the political institutions, begun by way of questions and answers at the argument, stylized and brought to a Socratic conclusion in the prevailing opinion. The upshot was the framing of conditions to invite a responsible legislative decision. The method of the colloquy—calling the political institutions to draw near the bench, for all the world like counsel in a lawsuit tried to a jury, there to be drawn out on their deliberate purposes, to be urged to clarify them and thus perhaps to reduce the issue, all "out of the hearing of the jury," which is to say outside the framework of the final, binding process of judgment—this method, as I have tried to show, is implicit in the vagueness cases on which the holding in *Poe* v. *Ullman* builds. And it was this method that the Court began to employ a decade ago in its approach to the intractable problem of congressional investigations. More recently, however, the Court has gone to the constitutional merits in congressional-investigation cases, and has legitimated government action which it could not very easily forbid but which need not have been turned into "the doctrine of the Constitution," there to gain "a generative power of its own."[71]

The first of the cases growing out of our recent generation of investigations that the Court brought up for full consideration was

United States v. *Rumely,* decided in 1953.[72] It was a well-selected case, and if one may say so, it stands as a textbook illustration of the Court's awareness and control of the implications and possibilities of its role.[73] Rumely had collided with a committee empowered by a special resolution of the House to investigate "all lobbying activities intended to influence, encourage, promote, or retard legislation." Rumely's organization sold far-right political tracts, and he declined to reveal to the committee the names of those who made bulk purchases. The Court gracefully conceded the indispensable and far-ranging nature of the "informing function of Congress," as Wilson called it.[74] But it emphasized as well the obvious ways in which this function can impinge on what might be thought to be First Amendment freedoms, and it construed the resolution as not authorizing the questions that were put to Rumely, despite considerable legislative history to the contrary, including, of course, the action of the House in citing Rumely for contempt. "So to interpret," said the Court, "is in the candid service of avoiding a serious constitutional doubt." And: "Whenever constitutional limits upon the investigative power of Congress have to be drawn by this Court, it ought only to be done after Congress has demonstrated its full awareness of what is at stake by unequivocally authorizing an inquiry of dubious limits."

The next important event was *Watkins* v. *United States,* decided in 1957.[75] Watkins's inquisitor was the House Un-American Activities Committee, whose charter authorizes it to investigate

(i) the extent, character, and objects of un-American propaganda activities in the United States,

(ii) the diffusion within the United States of subversive and un-American propaganda that is instigated from foreign countries or of a domestic origin and that attacks the principle of the form of government as guaranteed by our Constitution, and

(iii) all other questions in relation thereto that would aid Congress in any necessary remedial legislation.

Watkins was a labor-union official. Asked whether he had been or was then a member of the Communist Party, he answered no to both questions, although he allowed that he had "freely cooperated with the Communist Party. . . ." When he was asked further whether certain named persons had to his knowledge been members of the party, Watkins declined to answer, asserting his belief that these questions were "outside the proper scope of your committee's activities." The chairman told Watkins that the committee was authorized "to investigate subversion and subversive propaganda . . . for the purpose of remedial legislation." The questions, the chairman said, were pertinent to such an inquiry, and he directed Watkins to answer. But Watkins maintained his refusal, and a citation for contempt followed. Reversing a conviction, the Supreme Court made obeisance to "the informing function" and drew attention also to limitations on it which it might be necessary to impose under the Constitution. But the Court reached no such issues. "It would be difficult to imagine a less explicit authorizing resolution," the Court said, than the one under which this committee operates. "Who can define the meaning of 'un-American'?" ("To inquire into the nature and history of the real-estate pool," exclaimed Mr. Justice Miller in 1881, in *Kilbourn* v. *Thompson*,[76] sounding similarly astounded, but with much less justification. "How indefinite!") Given the nature of this charter and the equally cloudy remarks of the chairman in directing Watkins to answer, and given the fact that under the contempt statute only failure to answer "pertinent" questions is punishable, that statute suffered from the infirmity of vagueness as applied in this case.

So stated—and a special concurrence by Mr. Justice Frankfurter took pains to state it just this narrowly—vagueness here means very strictly lack of fair notice or warning. But it is open to question how realistic an application of this element of the doctrine the case marks. The chairman's explication of the committee's mission did nothing to dispel the vagueness of the authorizing resolution. He did, however, direct Watkins to answer the questions as being, in the committee's view, pertinent. There was no lack of warning in the elemental sense of cases where the chairman failed to direct the witness to answer, or where his order was inexplicit or ambiguous.[77] The contempt statute penalizes refusal to answer "any question pertinent to the question under inquiry." The chairman afforded notice of what the committee thought it was inquiring into and of what it deemed pertinent. If vagueness persisted, it was not because Watkins remained without authoritative warning of the meaning of the statutory word "pertinent" as applied to his situation; it was, rather, because the notice should not in the Court's judgment be deemed authoritative; it was, in other words, because the committee should not have this much discretion to decide what is "pertinent." That is an issue of vagueness, but not of fair notice.

Two years later, in *Barenblatt* v. *United States*,[78] the Court, dividing five to four, held the *Watkins* case to the narrow and none too tenable ground mentioned above, reached the constitutional merits, and placed the crown of principled legitimacy upon the modestly inclined head of the House Un-American Activities Committee. In 1961, *Wilkinson* v. *United States* and *Braden* v. *United States*[79] reaffirmed *Barenblatt*. But the majority opinion in the *Watkins* case was more broadly and soundly based than has thus been made to appear. It rested on more elements of the vagueness doctrine than fair notice, and as such it carried forward what might be called the process of avoidance and admonition that was begun in *Rumely*. The power to investigate, the Court said in *Watkins*, although exercised by committees, is the power of the Houses of Congress. The broader the authorizing resolution, the greater "the discretion of the investigators." Under this resolution, "the preliminary control of the committee exercised by the House of Representatives is slight or nonexistent." For the Committee "is allowed, in essence, to define its own authority, to choose the direction and focus of its activity." There is thus opened "a wide gulf between the responsibility for the use of investigative power and the actual exercise of that power." Wide-ranging investigations may place in issue constitutional protection of individual rights and thus call for a "critical judgment," which the Court is in a poor position to make because "the House of Representatives itself has never made it."

This, in the statement and in the application, is, as we have seen, an element of the doctrine of vagueness that has more substance and is more frequently decisive than the fair-notice factor. In the realm of federal legislation other than the criminal code, it goes by the name of the doctrine of delegation. As such, it does not have an illustrious past, which perhaps accounts in part for the failure of the *Watkins* opinion to gain acceptance. But this is no reflection on its validity or utility. The Court has since early times paid lip service to the delegation doctrine in terms of the polarities of the separation of powers. Formulas were developed that come as near to lacking any and all content whatever as anything in the annals of case law.[80] And unlike other "poetical devices,"[81] this doctrine was denied even the tarnished dignity of serving as a screen for what were actually decisive considerations. For decades no case was disposed of in its name. For decades the Court would recite something about the separation of powers and go on to decide the case regardless. Then, in the dark year 1935, at the height of the Court's war on the New Deal, came *Panama Refining Co. v. Ryan* and *Schechter Poultry Corp. v. United States,*[82] in which the recitals were as of old, except that the Court did not go on to uphold what Congress had done, regardless; this time the doctrine bit. The ill repute of those cases has stuck to the delegation doctrine, and not until the *Watkins* opinion was it ever made effective again; not until the *Watkins* opinion was there ever a statement by the Court of its substance.

To say that the doctrine of delegation is concerned with the separation of powers is merely to invoke a symbol. No doubt, as one of its side effects, it tends to support the checks and balances of the system, but the important checks and counter-checks are, after all, built into the governmental scheme in more binding ways. To say that the doctrine facilitates control by the Court of official action that might otherwise be erratic or capricious is, again, to notice a byproduct and to beg the question somewhat by assuming that judicial control (the irresponsible leading the unrepresentative) is necessary or desirable and can be effective. Other controls are possible and have been tried—through the President alone exercising power to appoint, remove, and guide; through either House or through Congress as a whole, acting by simple or concurrent resolution without approval of the President; and through committees of Congress.[83] These mechanisms share with judicial control and administrative policy-making the fault of electoral irresponsibility or, at best, fragmented responsibility. The doctrine of delegation is concerned with the sources of policy, with the crucial joinder between power and broadly based democratic responsibility, bestowed and discharged after the fashion of representative government. It follows that the doctrine should be as applicable to the relationship between Congress and one of its committees as between Congress and the administrative. The members and staff of a congressional committee have, of course, no more of a national electoral mandate than does the Federal Communications Commission or a special assistant to the Third Assistant Postmaster General. The committee and its staff are a part of the bureaucracy, although the bureaucracy of Congress rather than the executive.

"Delegation of power to administration is," however, "the dynamo of the modern social service state."[84] It has made possible the vast, pervasive growth of the administrative process, which few now would, and no one could, abolish. When should the Court recall the legislature to its own policy-making function? Obviously, the answer must lie in the importance of the decision left to the administrator or other official. And this is a judgment that will naturally be affected by the proximity of the area of delegated discretion to a constitutional issue. The more fundamental the issue, the nearer it is to principle, the more important it is that it be decided in the first instance by the legislature. In the peculiar desuetude situation, when the legislature cannot be said to have made and sustained any decision at all, not even the decision to delegate, it may be that no additional criteria need come into play. Where delegation, properly speaking, has occurred, however, as in the usual vague statute—as, indeed, some delegation, if only to the courts, takes place in all enactments—the incidence of criminal sanctions is the first significant factor. But it is not alone decisive. A judicial judgment remains to be exercised concerning the importance of what has been relegated to official discretion. This is not a principled constitutional judgment, denying or affirming the power of government to do this or that. It precedes such a judgment and avoids it, and is itself in the nature of an estimate. Its end is to pose a question, not to impose an answer. This is perhaps all the Court can ever do with respect to most congressional investigations—but one was entitled to expect that it would follow the *Rumely* case, which dealt with a one-shot investigation only, by doing no less.

Nothing can better exemplify the tension between expediency and principle in American government than does the problem of

congressional investigations. It is easily said that there are constitutional limits to the power to investigate—that is, limits
grounded in principle and to be enforced by the Court. Thus the
government conceded in the *Watkins* case, and the Court recited,
that there is "no general authority to expose the private affairs of
individuals without justification in terms of the functions of the
Congress." Congress, it was held in *Kilbourn* v. *Thompson* (1881),
may not conduct an investigation unrelated to legislative purposes.
It may not, the Court said in *Barenblatt,* set itself up in place of
the judiciary to adjudicate guilt. And the power to investigate, as
the Court also affirmed in *Barenblatt,* is subject to "the relevant
limitations of the Bill of Rights," including the First Amendment,
and including, one would suppose, what is perhaps most compendious, "the right to be let alone."[85] But there is only one limitation that has been imposed with continuity, if hardly with complete effectiveness, and that is the privilege against self-incrimination.[86] The restriction to legislative matters may have meant something in 1881, although not in *Kilbourn* v. *Thompson* itself; it does
not mean much today, having regard to what are now the acknowledged concerns of Congress. Moreover, the informing function
serves not only Congress but the public, for law with us is effective
by consent, and Congress should have the power to generate consent by making known the facts that lead it to legislate. There are
no doubt some barriers capable of principled formulation that
might be imposed under the First Amendment.[87] But they cannot
normally be the same ones as may be applicable to the governmental power to regulate, for Congress must be allowed to investigate in order to learn enough to know that it should not
legislate. Anything else is "to require of senators that they shall
be seers,"[88] or is an aspect of the illusion of immutable, self-applying absolutes enclosing an area of permissible governmental
power like some international line drawn on a map. Fittingly
enough, Mr. Justice Black's dissents in the *Wilkinson* and *Braden*
cases contain some of the most striking expressions of the literalist-
absolutist conception (see Chap. 3). But for those for whom the
governing rules of our day were less firmly and less completely
prepackaged 180 years ago, facts and conditions, which are yet
to be uncovered when the power of investigation is put into ques-

tion, are essential not only to the enactment of legislation but most often also to principled constitutional judgment by the Court. James M. Landis said it, concisely and one might have hoped finally, a generation ago:

Relationships, and not their probabilities, determine the extent of Congressional power. Constitutionality depends upon such disclosures. Their presence, whether determinative of legislative or judicial power, cannot be relegated to guesswork. Neither Congress nor the Court can predicate, prior to the event, the result of investigation.[89]

In sum, the power to investigate operates of necessity under a suspension of many otherwise applicable rules. This includes not only substantive principles but such procedural ones as the right to an impartial judge, the right to the showing of probable cause, and the right to confrontation and cross-examination. Congress must have the means to inform itself and the general public of conditions that require, or *may* require, remedial legislation, and to do so massively, dramatically, and expeditiously. This imports a visitorial power to invade privacy almost at will. It can also import, and often does, a power to condemn and punish by exposure and humiliation and so to damage or destroy people, materially or otherwise, not much less effectively than by criminal prosecution, although quite without the safeguards that surround the latter. Yet it seems impossible to tailor a full suit of principled rules specially for congressional investigations, as has been or can be done with quasi-judicial administrative agencies, grand juries, and courts-martial.[90] An investigation that invades what would otherwise be protected privacy or that summarily destroys an individual may be a self-serving frolic, or it may answer an urgently felt need. Most often, this is the real dividing line between investigations that should be permitted and those that should not. But, as the Court said in *Watkins,* "Only the legislative assembly initiating an investigation can assay the relative necessity of specific disclosures." The Court can see that it does.

It remains to account for the recent decision in *Hannah* v. *Larche.*[91] By a statute as precise as could be wished, the Federal Civil Rights Commission was empowered to investigate denials of voting rights. The Commission is not an accusatory body; it wields no criminal sanctions. But it can wield the great power of exposure. It operates, both by its charter and by its own rules, under procedural safeguards that would do great honor to the average congressional, and perhaps even to the average administrative, investigation. For example, the Commission proceeded in this case by probable cause, made out in writing under oath. But its rules do not provide for confrontation of witnesses with their accusers or for the right to cross-examine, and its charter is silent on these points. There is thus in play a fixed and abidingly important principle of our society, to which this commission, like congressional investigative committees, constitutes an exception. To have held this sort of procedure impermissible on principle might have gravely crippled the informing function. But the alternative was not legitimation on principle, across the board, of a course of action which may be expedient, even necessary, well intentioned, and fairly widespread, but which is, in these circumstances, at least, unprincipled. Nor did the delegation doctrine offer the sole alternative at this stage of the case. *Hannah* v. *Larche* was a suit to enjoin hearings that had not yet begun. An injunction had issued below. The Court should have quashed it and dismissed the suit as not ripe. Further proceedings would have made clearer just what the Commission was proposing to do and just what the consequences were for the complaining witnesses. The Commission is bound by its statute to receive in executive session evidence that tends to defame, degrade, or incriminate. It might have done so here and thus cured all that could be complained of. Or everything might have ended in a plea of the Fifth Amendment. Enforcement of the Commission's subpoenas, in any event, requires action by a federal court.

Political Responsibility and Security Dismissals

The *Watkins* case, although now apparently repudiated, does not stand alone in the books, even aside from *Rumely*. Among its companions, *Kent* v. *Dulles*,[92] a much more difficult case for the result reached, retains unimpaired authority and, one may hope, influence. The ultimate issue in *Kent* was the constitutionality of the government's asserted power to deny passports to citizens found or believed to be members of the Communist party or of what are loosely called Communist-front organizations. Denial of a passport, under present law, prevents the person concerned from leaving the Western Hemisphere. In its full ramifications, the issue is enormously perplexing, and it has carried a high emotional charge. It arises from what many people regard as obvious requirements of the cold war. On the other hand, it touches the noble claustrophobia that is endemic to free men. But the Court reached no such issue. Rather, it held that passport denials on grounds of Communist and like affiliations cannot be permitted because they are not properly authorized by statute.

The case was more difficult than *Watkins* for this reason. In *Watkins*, immense discretion was delegated, which the Un-American Activities Committee never narrowed in the administration. It has claimed and exercised all the discretion initially delegated, and the end is not yet; the full reach of the power is unpredictable, for no one can tell where the Committee may take it next. Subsequent actions of the House—appropriations, contempt citations —may, for the sake of argument, be deemed to have ratified what the Committee did in the past; prospectively, they can only be said to have continued the grant of the widest discretion. In *Kent* v. *Dulles,* the original grant of statutory authority to deny passports was easily as broad. But discretion had been administratively narrowed to reasonably well-defined categories of cases, of which this was one. Normal methods of statutory construction would therefore lead one to conclude that a congressional ratification in 1952 amounted prospectively to an affirmation of administrative authority as limited to the categories of cases in which it had hitherto been exercised. It can thus be said that there was a legislative policy applicable in the circumstances of *Kent* v. *Dulles.* But, as in *Rumely,* it was not wholly explicit. Were freedom to travel less jealously regarded, it might have sufficed. In "the candid service of avoiding a serious constitutional doubt," it need not have, and did not. But this is a step beyond holding Congress to its responsibility for a policy decision that it has failed to make— altogether or with sufficient particularity. This was remanding to Congress for a second look—not for the necessary initial decision, but for orderly, deliberate, explicit, and formal reconsideration of a decision previously made, but made back-handedly, off-handedly, less explicitly than is desirable with respect to an issue of such grave importance.[93] The same merely implicit statutory authorization was good enough to support denial of a passport on the traditional and well-agreed ground that the applicant was a fugitive from justice or was travelling to further garden-variety criminal activity (*e.g.*, the fabled figure of the international jewel-thief); but it would not do in the hotly contested area beyond. The Court's action in remanding the issue to Congress bore some fruit. Hearings and quite extensive consideration followed, and a relatively moderate and well-drawn bill passed the House. In the Senate there were hearings and a number of bills, but in the end no legislation, at least not yet.[94]

Another of the wise and honorable companions to *Watkins* and *Rumely* is *Greene* v. *McElroy*,[95] decided in 1959, the year after *Kent* v. *Dulles*. The government here caused a security clearance to be withdrawn from Greene, an executive officer of a defense contractor. As a direct consequence, Greene lost his job. There was no quarrel over the power to discharge; the ultimate issue was that the government had acted on the basis of confidential information from witnesses whom it did not make available for confrontation and cross-examination. But this procedure had not been specifically authorized either by the Congress or the President. Citing *Watkins*, the Court held that official discretion could not be allowed to impose "substantial restraints on employment opportunities of numerous persons . . . in a manner which is in conflict with our long-accepted notions of fair procedures."

Curiously enough, although it was *Watkins* all over again (indeed, an easier *Watkins*, not a more difficult case of remanding for a second look), *Greene* v. *McElroy* had its authority impaired by a 1961 decision that is rather squarely in point. This was *Cafeteria and Restaurant Workers Union* v. *McElroy*.[96] Rachel Brawner, in whose behalf the Union sued, was a short-order cook employed by a private contractor who operated a cafeteria at the Naval Gun Factory in Washington, where classified weapons are developed. Mrs. Brawner needed clearance and a badge in order to come to work, and had obtained them. One fine day both were withdrawn on the ground—as stated in officialese—that she did not "meet the basic security requirements as regards entrance." No charges were made known, and there was no hearing. It would serve, the admiral in command said, "no useful purpose." The Supreme Court, Mr. Justice Stewart writing, held that the Admiral of the Gun Factory was authorized to short-order cooks in this fashion, and that it was all quite constitutional.

The admiral's authority was derived from naval regulations approved by the President, which provide:

> In general, dealers or tradesmen or their agents shall not be admitted within a command, except as authorized by the commanding officer. . . .

The question was whether employees of contractors may be summarily deprived of their jobs "within a command." Wherein, so far as failure to address itself to this question is concerned, does the above prose differ from the following, under which *Greene* v. *McElroy* was disposed of?

> Classified defense information shall not be disseminated outside the executive branch except under conditions and through channels authorized by the head of the disseminating department. . . .

There is, said Justice Stewart, "the illuminating gloss of history." It shows that the Gun Factory is government property, and that the government may exclude anyone from it. But it shows nothing concerning procedures in security dismissals such as Mrs. Brawner's. The commanding officer's power can hardly be absolute, as Justice Stewart said it was, although at another point he seemed himself to doubt it.[97] Assuredly the commanding officer of an aircraft carrier docked in New York Harbor has absolute authority to order all visitors off at 5 P.M.; but may he order Jews off at 3, or may he order that anyone be put off by being dumped in the sea?

But let us assume that the "gloss of history" does illumine the commanding officer's absolute authority. There was authority—that is, total discretion—in *Watkins* and *Greene*, and there was more detailed authority in *Kent* v. *Dulles*. Why, in contrast with those cases and with *Rumely*, was there this time no judicial performance "in the candid service of avoiding a serious constitutional doubt"? Plainly because the Court suffered no constitutional doubt. But why? It is not arguable that Mrs. Brawner was not injured. The Court maintained that she was not injured much, but that was not her view, since the only other job offered her by her employer was one that she was unable to accept, in an inconvenient out-of-town location. The Court might for good reason decline adjudication of an issue, taking into consideration that the injury to the moving party is in the Court's view *de minimis*. But it is surely startling to encounter the constitutional principle that the government must grant hearings to private persons before inflicting palpable injury, except that it need not do so when the injury, though undoubted and bitterly complained of, seems slight. Such an estimate, prudently considered along with other factors, may determine ripeness; it can scarcely form the content of an "impersonal and durable"[98] principle of the Constitution. A short-order cook, after all, should have as much right to her humble job as Mr. Greene has to his career.

The decisive factor for the majority, it may be ventured, is to be found in the unsubstantiated, and on this record unprovable, statement that the reason advanced for Mrs. Brawner's dismissal was "entirely rational," supplemented at the end by the casual suggestion that perhaps the admiral "simply thought that Rachel Brawner was garrulous, or careless with her identification badge." Perhaps the Gun Factory, like the West Coast in 1942, is a place from which jittery commanders must be allowed to ship people out on hunch, without asking or being asked any questions. One doubts it. But if this is necessary and expedient, no amount of ratiocination can divine the fact, and the Court cannot know and has not demonstrated it. The Court should have required a responsible policy decision, as it did in *Greene*. Certainly it should not have sanctioned such goings-on now, if ever.

There are, of course, in government as in private employment, relationships that require—because of their intimacy, or in order to complement high political responsibility with commensurate authority—that the superior have arbitrary power to rid himself of his subordinate. A hearing then would be nonsense, because it could come to nothing. It can be asserted with confidence that the relationship between Admiral Tyree of the Gun Factory and Mrs. Brawner of the Cafeteria was nothing of the sort. Despite

Andrew Jackson and his spoils system, which really raised quite
different issues, hearings are now the norm, and for the most
fundamental of reasons.[99] Mrs. Brawner was the subject of an exception for which no principled justification has been put forward.
It is not the function of the Court to construct such exceptions.

The Well-Tempered Case, the Fielder's Choice, and the Uses of Procedure and Construction

The various devices, methods, concepts, doctrines, and techniques that I have discussed—and I have tended to use the terms
rather interchangeably—all serve the same end, of course. They
are all techniques of "not doing," devices for disposing of a case
while avoiding judgment on the constitutional issue it raises. This
common aspect is what I have sought to emphasize. But it will
have been observed that these avenues of disposition also differ
from one another—scenically, if not in final destination. They
differ in the degree to which they have or lack significance of their
own; the degree to which they are merely means, in themselves
quite neutral, to ends otherwise determined. It is plain, for example, that most denials of certiorari and many dismissals of appeals are entirely neutral means. They are only names given to the
result. Similarly, when a case that is fully developed, or, as one
might say, well tempered, is dismissed because the issue that it ten-
ders is thought to lack ripeness, as the issue whether *any* prior restraint may *ever* be allowed lacked ripeness in *Times Film Corp.* v.
City of Chicago—in such circumstances, the word "ripeness" is
merely a conclusionary label. A determination, however, that in
other respects *Times Film* was underdeveloped and lacked ripeness *as a case* has a great deal more significance in itself. It constitutes an extension of the requirement of concreteness which, at its
minimum of pure standing, is justly erected into a constitutional
principle. Yet, though quite significant, the concept of ripeness of
the case does not operate independently and is not alone decisive.
As I have shown, it is in substantial part a function of a judge's
estimate of the merits of the constitutional issue. A case may be
ripe for one judge but not for another, depending not on their

understanding of the fixed concept of ripeness but on the contours of the ultimate constitutional principle each would evolve and apply. And so it appears that the methods of "not doing" may be classified on a scale of intrinsic significance. On this scale, the doctrines of vagueness and delegation stand high, and the related concept of desuetude is at something of an apex.

It follows that there are limits to the occasions on which these doctrines and devices may be used, limits that inhere in their intellectual content and intrinsic significance. Indeed, with the possible exception of what I have called ripeness of the issue, which is merely a catch-all label for a certain order of considerations relating to the merits, none of these techniques totally lacks content of its own, and none is thus always available at will. Even the device of certiorari has some intrinsic meaning and will not be readily usable on all occasions. This is doubly true of the other concepts I have dealt in. Yet one or another of them will generally be available, and there will often be room for choice among two or three, and room certainly for an election whether or not to resort to any. We have had steadily in view the process of election—the elements that enter into a decision to avoid a constitutional issue. That has been the theme of the chapter, and it needs yet further elaboration. I propose now to focus as well on the process of selection of one rather than another method of avoidance, and I shall put forward also two additional techniques that I have not expressly commented on as yet.

As I have suggested, a consideration that will influence the process of selection and perhaps, too, that of election is the immediate position of the moving party. From the vantage point of the moving party's nearest present interest, some of the avenues of disposition we have considered differ from each other not only scenically but also in destination. Thus the plaintiffs in *Times Film* and in *Hannah* v. *Larche* should have lost, as in *Poe* v. *Ullman,* the birth-control case, plaintiffs did lose; on the other hand, Messrs. Rumely, Watkins, Kent, and Greene won, and so would Messrs. Barenblatt, Wilkinson, and Braden and Mrs. Brawner of the Cafeteria have done, had the techniques of the earlier cases been employed. The atypical cases in this list are *Times Film* and *Hannah* v. *Larche.* They are the only ones that were, in part at least, not ripe as cases. This could scarcely be said of the others. The truth is that most law suits, if allowed to develop naturally by parties whose dominant purpose is to defend their immediate interests at the least expense and inconvenience, thus saving litigation for a last resort—most law suits that are allowed, in other words, to mature under conditions normal in the legal order—will readily afford the Court a choice of several grounds, often including one ground of intrinsic but nonconstitutional significance, on which to rest a decision protecting in some measure the interest that is sought to be vindicated by appeal to a novel or broad constitutional principle.

This was true of the six movie-censorship cases that preceded *Times Film,* none of which was lost. Coming to more renowned instances, there was room for choice, as is well known, in *Marbury* v. *Madison* itself; the section of the Judiciary Act of 1789 purporting to give the Supreme Court original jurisdiction to hear such a suit as William Marbury's might easily have been construed not to do so, and thus the question of its constitutionality would have been avoided, although as it concerned the parties the result would have been the same. And there was room for choice in the *School Segregation Cases,* as there had been in their predecessors.[100] In several cases, starting in the late 1930's, the Supreme Court ordered that Negroes be admitted to white universities, on the ground that other facilities provided for them were not equal. In doing so, the Court did not by a word reaffirm what was assumed to be the applicable constitutional rule—namely, the doctrine of separate-but-equal facilities. Indeed, it would have been the judgment of most lawyers that the Court rather undermined the doctrine. Nor, on the other hand, did the Court in these earlier cases announce any new principle. In the *School Segregation Cases* of 1954, the Court might have reached the same result with respect to the parties before it, again without undertaking either to overrule or reassert the separate-but-equal doctrine. In the cases from Delaware, South Carolina, and Virginia, there were findings of present inequality of facilities. In the District of Columbia case, the Negro children's complaint had been dismissed on the pleadings, and there were no findings of any sort. The Kansas case presented many special features, including the fact that only elementary schools were segregated. Its findings of present equality, themselves not unqualified, could have been treated as less conclusive or less adequate than they were actually made to appear. The Court did not do so because, in the fullness of prior cases and of that litigation, it had ripened the principle that was in fact announced. Surely this judgment must be made by the Court, not by the parties to a litigation. There is enough fortuity in this as in other processes of government, and almost no matter what the basis on which the Court makes such judgments (provided that it acts, when it does, only in response to the pressure of concrete litigation), it is surely likely to take a larger view of interests and of affairs than private parties will bring to bear.

As Professor Louis H. Pollak has well said and substantially demonstrated:

Judicial authority to select the most apt of several possible avenues of decision is a sensitive and a powerful weapon. Utilized with sophistication, it complements the Supreme Court's broad discretion as to which cases the Court will entertain, and in what sequence. It is a weapon which strengthens the wielder, but which tests him as well.[101]

Unripe cases, framed as *Times Film* and *Hannah* v. *Larche* were framed, are attempts to deprive the Court of its authority to select; they are attempts to force the Court's hand. In law suits of this ilk, the moving party takes a calculated risk, and there is no need to spill many tears over its fate when the case is lost through outright dismissal. In a well-tempered case, however, the moving party has a much stronger claim to individual justice, and this claim must be balanced against the Court's judgment that the issue as such is not ripe, owing to conditions over which the parties have no control. The pressure for individual justice is, of course, all the stronger when one may fairly surmise that the tendency of the Court, if pushed to the wall of principled judgment, would likely be to vindicate the moving party's constitutional claim. How should a man feel who has lost on what he must regard as a technicality, having asserted a principle that two years later, in a similar case, carries the field? In such circumstances there will be an impulse to employ the methods of vagueness or delegation, or the devices of procedure and construction that I am about to illustrate.

For these can produce an immediate result favorable to the party seeking the shelter of the Constitution without causing the Court to adjudicate issues it should not.

Yet the equities on the side of the moving party will vary in intensity. They were a good deal less than overpowering in the birth-control case, and they might have been thought relatively weak in Mrs. Brawner's situation. This is not an argument relevant to the issue of principle itself. It can only make more palatable the use of a device of avoidance that works against the moving party. In any event, the policy of avoidance, if otherwise applicable, must prevail, despite hardship to the litigant and despite what is in other circumstances a strong policy in favor of authoritative and speedy pronouncement of governing rules. There are crucial differences—which, of course, the opinions in *Marbury* v. *Madison* and *Cohens* v. *Virginia* seek to obscure—between the role of the Supreme Court in constitutional cases and the function of courts of general jurisdiction. The latter sit as primary agencies for the peaceful settlement of disputes and, in a more restricted sphere, as primary agencies for the vindication and evolution of the legal order. They must, indeed, resolve all controversies within their jurisdiction, because the alternative is chaos. The Supreme Court in constitutional cases sits to render an additional, principled judgment on what has already been authoritatively ordered. Its interventions are by hypothesis exceptional and limited, and they occur, not to forestall chaos, but to revise a pre-existing order that is otherwise viable and was itself arrived at by more normal processes. Fixation on an individual right to judgment by the Supreme Court is, therefore, largely question-begging.

It will not do to exalt an individual claim to particular justice over all other problems that adjudication may have to solve and over all other consequences that it entails. It is not justice for the Court to take unto itself, *ad hoc*, a function that it cannot, over the run of causes, perform with more benefit than harm to society. Nor is it justice in a democracy to enlarge authoritarian judicial power at undue cost in the effective and responsible functioning of the political institutions. "Congress," said Mr. Justice Black in a recent case, "has a right to a determination of the constitutionality of the statute it passed. . . ." And in another case it seemed to

Justice Black "unfair to Congress for this Court to refuse to decide whether its Act can be fully enforced."[102] The quaintness of the expression locates the fallacy in the conception. Congress is an institution of government. It has no rights; it has functions, and it may have duties. So does the Supreme Court, and it is hardly possible for the Court to violate a right of Congress by respecting the latter's function and thus limiting its own.

And so neither Dr. Buxton's crisis of conscience nor that of his patients—nor, again, the presumed desire of the political institutions of Connecticut for a decision (or their "right" to one?)— could force constitutional adjudication in circumstances in which the Court was better advised to withhold it. So also the Court, discounting the interest of the moving party, dismissed outright a case raising the constitutionality of state antimiscegenation statutes.[103] Perhaps Virginia, whose statute was in question, had a "right" to a decision, although the clamor from those quarters has been something short of deafening. Actually a judgment legitimating such statutes would have been unthinkable, given the principle of the *School Segregation Cases* and of decisions made in their aftermath. But would it have been wise, at a time when the Court had just pronounced its new integration principle, when it was subject to scurrilous attack by men who predicted that integration of the schools would lead directly to "mongrelization of the race" and that this was the result the Court had really willed, would it have been wise, just then, in the first case of its sort, on an issue that the Negro community as a whole can hardly be said to be pressing hard at the moment, to declare that the states may not prohibit racial intermarriage? Similarly, though for variant reasons, a case of the kind projected in Chapter 2, testing the constitutionality of benevolent quotas, might, all else failing, be dismissed outright. Following *Kent* v. *Dulles*, certiorari was denied in three cases in which passports had been refused on grounds that created further difficulties for the technique employed to relieve Mr. Kent.[104] Finally, and again at the expense of the moving party, the Court should have declined to take jurisdiction in *Shelton* v. *Tucker*, the case discussed at some length in Chapter 2. This would have been a course infinitely preferable either to legitimation of a highly disagreeable and probably ill-intentioned statute, or to the unintelligible constitutional judgment in fact rendered. Happily, there are times when, even though such methods as vagueness and delegation may be difficult to press into service, the Court can avoid constitutional adjudication without causing hardship to litigants, by resort to special rules of procedure or to techniques of statutory construction, or both. An instance was *Garner* v. *Louisiana,*[105] decided in December 1961, the first case to confront the Court squarely with the sit-in problem outside the relatively more manageable context of interstate transportation. The issue in sit-in cases, broadly speaking, is this: Under the Fourteenth Amendment, as construed in the *School Segregation Cases,* no state may segregate governmentally owned or operated facilities, and the prohibition extends to administrative and judicial as well as to legislative state action. It applies to all facilities, from schools to golf courses. Nor may a state impose a policy of segregation on privately owned and operated facilities. But the Fourteenth Amendment is not held to forbid private discriminations. It has not been held to reach policies of segregation voluntarily adopted by individuals or groups on their home, business, or club premises. Yet many such private policies are ultimately effective only under the protection of the state. Hence a private policy of segregation on privately owned premises may differ from a state-enforced policy in degree only; the effectiveness of both may finally depend on the police power of the state. To be sure, the impetus for adoption of the former *is* private rather than official, and the two differ, therefore, in pervasiveness of effect and in symbolic significance. Nevertheless, the statement that the Fourteenth Amendment forbids only segregation by state action and not private discriminations formulates a delusively simple issue. The question really is, what places and activities should be deemed so private that, in respect of them, the state should be allowed to protect—albeit implicitly only—voluntarily adopted policies of segregation, just as it enforces other privately made policies and protects the enjoyment of other liberties in the course of maintaining the general legal order? The difficulty of this question needs no emphasis, and it will naturally not receive a sudden, total judicial answer.

The *Garner* case concerned peaceful—indeed, virtually soundless and motionless—sit-ins at lunch counters in Baton Rouge, Louisiana. As a majority of seven on the Court felt, the case offered a quite unsuitable occasion for so much as making a beginning toward a principled solution of the vast problem I have outlined. It was the first such case on the Court's docket (followed and to be followed by others). Now, to say that any first case is always a poor one in which to pronounce new principles is no doubt an overgeneralization. And yet it is not far wrong. A sound judicial instinct will generally favor deflecting the problem in one or more initial cases, for there is much to be gained from letting it simmer, so that a mounting number of incidents exemplifying it may have a cumulative effect on the judicial mind as well as on public and professional opinion. Moreover, an initial series of inconclusive dispositions will often provoke the Justices to reflect out loud, as it were, about approaches to an enduring solution, without as yet assuming responsibility for imposing one. They may do so—as, indeed, they did in the *Garner* case—by way of oblique remarks or heavily pregnant negatives in the opinion of the Court, or individually, in concurrences or dissents that reach the merits. Although such inconclusive ventilation of the issue is not by any means equally deliberate, it is the equivalent of the technique of the trial balloon, which is widely employed by the institutions that depend on public opinion more directly than does the Court.

Aside from being first, the *Garner* case suffered also from having arisen in what may be termed an obsolete statutory context. The defendants in *Garner* were prosecuted and convicted under a general "disturbing the peace" statute. More recently, Louisiana and other southern states have been "defending themselves" against the sit-ins under either conventional or new statutes which make it a specific offense to refuse to leave the premises of another when requested to do so. Such statutes of course pinpoint the problem more exactly. It is under such statutes that most other cases will come up. As the special concurrence of Justice Harlan in the *Garner* case indicates, it might make a considerable difference, once the merits of the issue were reached, what sort of statute convictions were obtained under. By reaching the merits now, the Court would therefore be dealing in effect with an aspect of the problem that is no longer current. This was unnecessary in

Garner, even though it is possible that the aspect of the problem presented by "disturbing the peace" statutes is relatively easier than what may have to be faced in time under trespass statutes. But then, nothing may have to be faced, or what must be faced may arise in a different social and political context. As many a southern and border city has demonstrated, the sit-in problem is soluble—and beyond a doubt best solved—by processes other than judicial.

Garner thus being far from the ideal vehicle for adjudication of the sit-in issue, a denial of certiorari would have been indicated, except that it would have been extremely harsh on the defendants, who were under sentence of four months in jail, three months to be suspended upon payment of a fine of $100.[106] The vagueness doctrine might have provided an alternative and more equitable course of disposition. The Louisiana statute in question defines "disturbing the peace" as doing various specific things, for example, fist fighting or appearing drunk, "in such a manner as would foreseeably disturb or alarm the public." It adds as also punishable "commission of any other act in such a manner as to unreasonably disturb or alarm the public." The defendants in *Garner* were convicted under this last-quoted clause. But broad as it may seem, this standard is of respectable lineage and has a traditional core of meaning that the legislature is likely to have had well in mind and that prosecutors, courts, and juries may be trusted to elaborate, reasoning by analogy in fairly disciplined fashion. In the degree in which the statute delegates the power of decision to prosecutors, courts, and juries, it may, as concerns the generality of foreseeable situations, be deemed to delegate only relatively ordinary, unimportant, and harmless power. In this instance, application of the statute touched an important constitutional issue. But the statute will not commonly do so. Hence it is quite unlike the usual vague enactment, certainly unlike the authorizing resolution in *Watkins,* both because it does represent a substantial, distinct legislative decision, and because what it leaves undone is, seen as a whole, of minor importance. Differences in this area are of course arguable, and I do not mean to suggest that it was wholly out of the question to find this statute vague. But such a conventional "disturbing the peace" statute is rather different from vagrancy statutes, widespread as they may be, which are greatly more open-ended and more dubious substantively as well, or from a statute delegating authority to punish through such a newly coined and hence more vacuous phrase as "known to be a member of any gang consisting of two or more persons.[107] I mean merely to suggest that application of the doctrine of vagueness presented difficulties.

And so a majority of the Court reversed the convictions on the procedural ground that the state had introduced no evidence at defendants' trials to show that the public was being unreasonably disturbed or alarmed. Therefore, whether or not defendants' conduct may constitutionally be punished, the elements of the offense as defined in the Louisiana statute had not been proved, and the convictions of course had to fall. As a procedural rule, this may fairly be deemed idiosyncratic. It will seldom be provable that certain conduct has a tendency to disturb or alarm the public, or, for example, that a certain speed or other transgression in the handling of a car constitutes driving that will endanger life or property. These are not matters of provable fact; they are prophecies, which is to say, matters of inference to be drawn from facts. Such an inference may sometimes depend on a particularized segment of experience, which is not generally shared. But it will often depend, as here and as in hundreds of trials, upon common knowledge, for which the trier of the facts, judge or jury, is spokesman. It is not credible that a conviction of disturbing the peace would be reversed for lack of evidence that the public might be alarmed, if all that was shown was that a person walked into a drug store naked and just sat there, like these demonstrators, with his "mere presence." Nor is it believable that a similar conviction based merely on proof that a man walked into Carnegie Hall, sat in the front row, and refused either to leave or to produce a ticket would be struck down because there was no evidence that the public might be unreasonably disturbed. The defendants were Negroes sitting at a white lunch counter; and as Justice Douglas, who differed from the majority and spoke to the merits, pointed out, this was Louisiana.

Of course there will be cases when inferences such as are here in question will have to be bolstered by more evidence than this record contained. If, for example, a person walked into a restaurant in Atlantic City in a bathing suit, one would want to know what the custom was at that place and time. And if there was no showing on this point at all, such a holding as the Supreme Court's in the *Garner* case would follow naturally. In the *Garner* case itself, it may be added, an inference other than that taken by the trial court is at least possible. There have been southern cities in which sit-ins led not to disturbances but to fairly quiet integration —though following, to be sure, concerted civic effort. Nevertheless, everything else being equal, the Court would normally have left to the local trier of facts the choice of which inference to draw. Surely the decisive factor in *Garner* was that everything else was jarred into being unequal by the looming presence, in the background, of a momentous constitutional issue. All this is not to say that the holding in the *Garner* case is intellectually untenable. It it to say only that by its own intrinsic significance such a holding was not necessarily to be expected or even likely. It is explained and justified as probably the most suitable and certainly the narrowest method of avoidance consistent with the equities that favored the defendants, the method with the fewest surrounding implications. For the upshot is merely that this prosecution failed for reasons that are easily curable without resort to the legislature.

The result in the *Garner* case may thus be regarded as a colloquy with the trial court. It tells the trial court that if convictions are to be had in cases such as this, under this statute, the trier of fact must expressly face the question of probable public alarm and disturbance, and must place the basis for his conclusion in the trial record. This may not ordinarily be required and is here required in order further to define a grave constitutional issue and allow it further to mature. When the vagueness concept, as we have analyzed it, is applied, the colloquy runs not to a trial court but to the legislature; and it covers broader ground. It poses more of a question and puts it to an institution in which getting answers is harder and takes more time and effort. The Court then tells the legislature that if there is to be regulation in the area touched by the vague statute, the legislature must itself make the regulation, deciding just what kind it wants and just where. In the mine run of its applications, it was difficult to say that the "disturbing the peace" statute left to officials decisions too important to be left unmade by the legislature. Hence the more restricted question, posed in colloquy with the trial court rather than with the legislature.

But what we have seen so far in this chapter does not exhaust the resources of the vagueness doctrine. It is possible—and would have been possible in the *Garner* case—while employing the concept of vagueness, and without tailoring special rules of procedure, to narrow the scope and consequences of the colloquy, although its addressee must remain the legislature. I have not had occasion to emphasize the point before, but it is obvious that vagueness and delegation can come into play only after it has been determined what, if anything, the legislature intended by the statute it enacted. This determination is a matter of statutory construction, depending on the common usage of words and on such objective evidence as one can find of the purpose the legislature had in view. Conclusions on this prior question of ascertainable meaning are highly fallible, but they must in any event be drawn. Statutes do not apply themselves. And so judges may find that the legislature meant nothing beyond projecting broad outlines, to be filled in by officials. That was *Watkins,* and that, chiefly, is the kind of statute I have so far held in focus. But it may be found also that the legislature conceived the statute as applicable to several fairly distinct classes of situations. The statute will then generally be deemed not vague, for, though its language might have appeared indefinite, it does, on the evidence, embody a limited legislative decision responsibly made. The Court will declare this decision as the statute's true meaning, thus binding all who must act under it. There are instances, however, when the language of the statute and evidence of the circumstances of its enactment may show a legislative purpose to cover not only relatively distinct classes of core situations but also undefined further ones, left to official discretion. A statute may, in other words, have both a core that is not vague and surrounding outlines that are. If, in the case before the Court, the attempt is to apply the statute to one of the outlying situations, as to which there was no distinct legislative decision, the statute may be held vague as applied. This is a formula meaning that the statute is too vague to be so applied or, if you will, is vague in part, the part that is vague being the one now before the Court.

In situations such as I have just described, the concepts of
vagueness and of delegation may take on the form of a canon of
statutory construction. It may be said that the statute is vague as
applied; or the result may be verbalized as a construction of the
statute, holding it not applicable. In either event, the reason for
the result will have been that a decision was delegated to officials
and to judges which is too important to be made by anyone but
the legislature. This method, using the language of statutory construction, is widely employed, and not only when constitutional
issues would otherwise have to be adjudicated.[108] Such was
the method by which the Sherman Antitrust Act was at last held
not applicable to union activities aimed at exerting labor's economic bargaining power. Such, again, was the technique employed to circumscribe and save a portion of the remarkably ill-
drawn civil-rights statutes of 1866 and 1870. It is a technique that
might have been employed—and should have been—to construe
the federal Mann Act, which forbids the white-slave traffic but also
includes a phrase punishing transportation of females in interstate
commerce "for any other immoral purpose." The latter provision
has had erratic application to activities that may not be overly edifying but that were not deliberately proscribed by Congress.[109]
The formal statement of the decision in *Rumely* v. *United States*
was also in terms of construction of the committee's authorizing
resolution, for the word "lobbying," on which everything de-
pended, has a core meaning that is not difficult to define and that
Congress plainly had had in mind. Finally, as I have noted, *Kent*
v. *Dulles* construed the statute there in question so as to save the
Secretary of State's authority to deny passports in certain distinct
and relatively noncontroversial classes of situations. In *Kent* v.
Dulles, and perhaps also in *Rumely,* it was difficult if not impossible to make an objective showing of legislative purpose that differentiated between the so-called core situations, as to which application of the enactment was permitted, and the outlying ones,
as to which the statute or resolution was held vague. But then,
those were cases that, on particularly sensitive and intractable
issues, demanded, not merely that there be a deliberate exertion
of legislative authority, but that it be explicit and thus more acutely
responsible than usual. Legislators are likely to be more acutely
aware of just what they are being asked to do if the language of

a bill clearly defines what is aimed at than if the language is relatively broad, although its concrete application is clarified in debate or is defined *post facto* by the Court on the basis of what was common knowledge at the time of enactment and may therefore fairly be imputed to the legislators.

Mr. Justice Harlan was prepared to hold the statute in the *Garner* case vague as applied. Innocent and unimportant as it might be in the common run of other situations, the statute here raised a constitutional issue; and its application here—whatever may be said of its core meaning—could be viewed as a decision left to prosecutors and juries, or at least not explicitly made by the legislature. The analysis fits easily with *Rumely,* with *Kent* v. *Dulles,* and with many other vagueness-as-applied cases. Those are, however really *delegation*-as-applied cases, the difference being that they arose under federal statutes. I have indicated that the vagueness-as-applied concept manifests itself as a technique of statutory construction. And, apparently at least, there's the rub. For while the federal courts sit to construe federal statutes, the general rule is that state courts are the authoritative interpreters of state statutes, and that the Supreme Court takes the meaning of a state statute as the state court gives it.[110] And the rule is surely sensible. Statutory construction at least starts with a factual inquiry, which depends on a sophisticated and practiced ability to understand a legislature's records and its ways—an ability the Supreme Court may be presumed to have with respect to Congress, and each state court may be thought best to possess *vis-à-vis* its own legislature. Hence, when the Supreme Court conducts colloquies with the state legislatures, the state courts act as intermediaries—quite literally, as interpreters.

In *Garner,* the state court, by way of a summary and rather impenetrable opinion, held that the Louisiana legislature had intended the "disturbing the peace" statute to be applicable to sit-ins. (Perhaps a remand to the state court for clarification of its opinion would have been yet another way out.) But the state court is an intermediary in the vagueness colloquy; it does not take the place of the Supreme Court. The state court can say that a statute is the expression of the legislative will, but it cannot say that it is, in the circumstances, a sufficiently explicit one; else the Supreme Court would have to take the state court's word in all vagueness cases, and would most assuredly have had to do so in *Poe* v. *Ullman*. Thus it was open to the Supreme Court to hold the statute in *Garner* vague as applied, because insufficiently explicit, on the analogy of *Rumely* and *Kent* v. *Dulles*. But the Louisiana legislature, in a new statute to which I referred earlier, had already specifically addressed itself to the question of sit-ins, to which such a holding by the Supreme Court in *Garner* would have invited its attention. Therefore, a holding that the statute was vague as applied, quite like a constitutional adjudication itself, would have dealt with an aspect of the problem that is no longer current and would thus have unnecessarily thrown doubt on an otherwise serviceable and unobjectionable state statute. For this reason, again, the narrowest sort of disposition, with the least possible radiating consequences, was indicated; and that was the disposition in fact made.

The procedural technique in this case was narrower than vagueness in the guise of statutory construction, which, in turn, would have been narrower than vagueness as we have previously analyzed the concept. But this relationship among the three devices is not a stable one. A procedural holding may entail more far-reaching consequences when it is less idiosyncratic than it was in this case, and when, owing to its intrinsic significance, it covers a wider range of situations. And vagueness-as-applied may be a more final judicial action than a holding that the statute as a whole is vague, because the question it poses for the legislature may be less provocative and therefore more likely to be allowed to go unanswered. There are no set rules of selection, nor can there be, given all the variables.

The Political Question and the Resources of Rhetoric

The culmination of any progression of devices for withholding the ultimate constitutional judgment of the Supreme Court—and in a sense their sum—is the doctrine of political questions. In *Times Film Corp.* v. *City of Chicago*, the ultimate constitutional issue would not answer to any absolute principle; something equally principled but more malleable was called for. It was, in any event, well within the Court's competence to evolve, although not in the case before it. In *Poe* v. *Ullman* and in the *Garner* case, the constitutional issue was again fit for judicial decision, although not just then. By contrast, the complex of investigation, passport, and security-dismissal cases discussed above turned ultimately on issues that bring into question the very capacity of judicial judgment. Here "the candid service of avoiding a serious constitutional doubt"[111] needed to be performed for the added reason that the doubt should, perhaps, be avoided permanently.

In *Greene* v. *McElroy*, the case of the withdrawal of security clearance, which Mr. Greene won in the end on delegation grounds, the government had prevailed in the court below. The operative reason was that the case was thought not to present a justiciable controversy—a controversy, said the opinion of the Court of Appeals by Judge Washington, "which the courts can finally and effectively decide, under tests and standards which they can soundly administer within their special field of competence." The ultimate question was Greene's fitness to be entrusted with state secrets, and "any meaningful judgment in such matters must rest on considerations of policy, and decisions as to comparative risk, appropriate only to the executive branch of the Government. . . . In a mature democracy, choices such as this must be made by the executive. . . ."[112] Such is the foundation, in both intellect and instinct, of the political-question doctrine: the Court's sense of lack of capacity, compounded in unequal parts of (a) the strangeness of the issue and its intractability to principled resolution; (b) the sheer momentousness of it, which tends to unbalance judicial judgment; (c) the anxiety, not so much that the judicial judgment will be ignored, as that perhaps it should but will not be; (d) finally ("in a mature democracy"), the inner vulnerability, the self-doubt of an institution which is electorally irresponsible and has no earth to draw strength from.

The case does not exist in which the power of judicial review has been exercised without some such misgivings being applicable in some degree. But the differences of degree can on occasion be satisfyingly conclusive. There are cases of which no more need be said than what Maurice Finkelstein said of *Dred Scott* v. *Sand-*

ford: "A question which involved a Civil War can hardly be proper material for the wrangling of lawyers." No doubt, *Luther v. Borden,* which arose out of Dorr's Rebellion in Rhode Island, and which Taney's Court declined to decide, was such a case.[113] Another and extraordinarily apt illustration is extrajudicial.

In 1877, following the disputed election which brought the country as close as it has ever come to a Latin American sort of crisis, a special Electoral Commission awarded the presidency to Hayes. The decisive vote on this commission was cast by Justice Joseph P. Bradley of the Supreme Court, serving extrajudicially together with four of his colleagues. The rest of the commission consisted of Senators and Representatives, who split along party lines, as did Bradley's four colleagues. Bradley himself, it is said, finally made his decision on the ground "that a Democratic triumph would mean national disaster."[114] But, as Professor Charles Fairman has since shown, "the great question" for Bradley was, in fact, whether Congress was entitled to go behind election returns or had to accept them as certified by state authorities. This is an issue of principle. "So far as I am capable of judging my own motives," Bradley wrote later, "I did not allow political, that is, party, considerations to have any weight whatever in forming my conclusion." And then this altogether admirable sentence: "I know that it is difficult for men of the world to believe this, but I know it, and that is enough for me."[115] Believe it now we must, but the point is that in the circumstances the issue of principle was trivial, it was overwhelmed by all that hung in the balance, and it should not have been decisive, except as people were prepared to accept any decision for the sake of having one, including a flip of a coin. Bradley must have been the only man in the country for whom "the great question" was simply what he saw it to be. Given the fact that on both sides fraud could not be disentangled from fraud, the real great question was not fit "for the wrangling of lawyers."

There are problems, as Mr. Jaffe has written, that "are of the sort for which we do not choose, or have not been able as yet to establish, strongly guiding rules. We may believe that the job is better done without rules. . . ." We may also believe, Mr. Jaffe adds, "that even though there are applicable rules, these rules should be only among the numerous relevant considerations."[116]

But this, as I shall argue, is a very different category of cases. Civil wars to the side, it is quite plain that some questions are held to be political pursuant to a decision on principle that there ought to be discretion free of principled rules. The existence of such discretion may be considered, not generally, but with particular relation to the interest of a particular complainant, which it is held to override. The basis of the decision will be the same, but the point is then put in terms of standing. This is a pity, for it befuddles a concept that has, as we have seen, a useful original significance.[117] Recognition of foreign governments and unilateral abrogation of treaties fall in this discretionary category. So also, in effect at any rate, does the nature of the general welfare for whose promotion the federal government may tax and spend. Uniform *geographic* restrictions on travel by American citizens would appear to present this kind of political question; also, which *nationalities* of aliens may be excluded or deported. But the italics are crucial. And with respect to the general welfare, travel, and alien matters, only the nature and coverage of the substantive regulation are deemed discretionary; procedural matters are not the same thing. Moreover, this political-question area is to be distinguished from such a power as that of Congress to regulate interstate commerce, which is plenary and almost without practical limit, but which is yet not given up as wholly discretionary.[118]

These are discretionary functions of the political institutions which are unprincipled on principle, because we think "that the job is better done without rules." There is no reason that their legitimacy as such should not be affirmed by the Court, as it sometimes has been. Such questions call for no avoidance; they call for principled adjudication. The same result would follow should a cabinet officer sue for back pay on the ground that the President had dismissed him arbitrarily, because of his race, and without a hearing. As the present consensus about the impeachment of President Johnson would indicate, it is not difficult to articulate the reasons that the President should have such arbitrary power. His whim should rule, because it is desirable to enlarge as much as possible his personal political responsibility, and this demands a special kind of loyalty and responsiveness of his immediate subordinates.[119] But it is not arguable on principle that the security of the nation can be served only if all employees of the government and of its contractors are made subject to dismissal on whim or hunch. Nobody contends that—given a substantive standard that takes account of the government's high interest—the adversary process of proof and refutation is not suited to achieving the soundest factual determinations here, as in the administration of criminal justice. Security officials contend only that it is often necessary to proceed otherwise, for reasons which the same necessity causes to remain largely obscure. To this unknowable necessity the courts may have to yield, because of such misgivings as Judge Washington voiced, but no principled judgment circumscribing a desirable area of discretionary power is possible.

At the very least, it is surely true that the question just described, which is of the divisible sort last mentioned by Mr. Jaffe, is different in that the decision whether it should be ruled by principle will be circumstantial and varying. Whether congressional investigations should inquire into matters generally held private and whether they and other inquisitions should damage careers and reputations without benefit of adversary safeguards are like questions. The answer cannot be, across the board, yes, we have no principles; let expediency rule, and political responsibility and the craft of state. It can only be, yes, in contravention of principle, if necessary, in the same way in which, by disagreeable necessity, many Negro children do not yet attend integrated schools, although they are entitled to do so on principle; in the same way in which the measures mentioned by Mr. Wechsler that take race into account to reduce *de facto* segregation and benevolent racial housing quotas may be allowed their day. The judgment of necessity is prudential. The Court sometimes makes bold to undertake it for itself and to cause principle to prevail, usually when the subject matter is well within its experience, as in the administration of the criminal law, or when its own political sense (which can be treacherous) tells it that the necessity has abated, or when it can draw on some fairly stable body of knowledge to disprove the necessity. Otherwise the Court is capable of only a tentative estimate.

Even when it is ultimately constrained to yield to necessity, however—to yield, this is to say, to the judgment of the political institutions—the Court can exert immense influence. It may be unable to wield its ultimate power as an organ of government charged with translating principle into positive law; but it need not abandon its concomitant role of "teacher to the citizenry."[120] The power to which Marshall successfully laid claim is not the full measure of the Court's authority in our day. And the Court's arguments need not be compulsory in order to be compelling. Many of the devices of not doing engage the Court, as I have shown, in colloquies with the political institutions. By their very nature, with hardly a word spoken in further explanation, vagueness and delegation, for example, ask for a legislative affirmation of just what it is that necessity demands. But the Court can at the same time do more. It can see to it that the political judgment of necessity is undertaken with awareness of the principle on which it impinges. In American life, the Court is second only to the presidency in having effectively at its disposal the resources of rhetoric. Hence—*vide* the opinions in *Rumely, Watkins* and *Greene*— the Court can explain the principle that is in play and praise it, and thus also guard its integrity. It can do so even when no device is available for authoritatively drawing the political institutions into a colloquy near the bench. For the Court can speak over their heads to the nation. It has done so, and done so productively, as indeed have individual Justices writing in dissent.[121] Oral delivery of opinions and dissents by the Justices, on Mondays at cherry-blossom time in Washington, to a small knot of lawyers and circulating crowds of high-school students—this may be in large part a symbolic ceremony only. But it does symbolize something. No one should underestimate the dominion of ideas in a nation committed to the rule of principle as well as to majoritarian democracy. Acknowledging the limits of the rule of principle and its fragility when it passes them must not plunge one into such an underestimate.

One point is, in any event, of transcendent importance. The role of the Court and its *raison d'être* are to evolve "to preserve, protect and defend" principle. If the political institutions at last insist upon a course of action that cannot be accommodated to principle, it is no part of the function of the Court to bless it, however double-negatively. Where the judicial process has been

invoked defensively—as, for example, in *Greene* v. *McElroy*—
outright dismissal of the suit is the solution, after all other devices
have been exhausted. In the congressional-investigation cases,
where the criminal process is invoked, the solution, all else failing, is to deny the process to Congress and require it to use its
own, at the Bar of each House. There is nothing shocking about
this. Defendants, to be sure, would lose the benefit of jury trials,
but there is not a great deal of content in what goes to the jury
now. Thus, authority of the committee and pertinency of the question do not.[122] Intervention by the Court would still be possible on
habeas corpus.

The congressional-investigation, security-dismissal, and passport cases are decided in the shadow of the doctrine of political
questions; some, like *Barenblatt* and Mrs. Brawner's case, are decided in its teeth, as I have suggested, but, throughout, with no
explicit mention by the Court of the doctrine and the considerations underlying it. In recent times, the notable cases that have
turned explicitly on the doctrine of political questions and have
brought it signally to the fore have been those dealing with the
problem of legislative apportionment. The story begins with a
leading case decided in 1946. This was *Colegrove* v. *Green*.[123]
The basis of the complaint in *Colegrove* is concisely stated in a
dissent by Mr. Justice Black. (Conditions exactly as described no
longer obtain. The state has been redistricted several times since.)
Suit was brought by a group of voters living in congressional election districts in Illinois,

the respective populations of which ranged from 612,000 to 914,000.
Twenty other Congressional election districts have populations that
range from 112,116 to 385,207. In seven of these districts the population is below 200,000. The Illinois Legislature established these districts in 1901 on the basis of the census of 1900. The federal census of
1910, of 1920, of 1930, and of 1940, each showed a growth of population in Illinois, and a substantial shift in the distribution of population
among the districts established in 1901. But up to date, attempts to
have the State Legislature reapportion Congressional election districts
so as more nearly to equalize their population have been unsuccessful.

In 1931, the Illinois legislature did pass a reapportionment act, but
it was struck down by the state courts, which reinstituted the

1901 arrangement. The situation in Illinois was hardly an isolated one. The consequence of such malapportionment is that the vote of residents of the underrepresented districts is debased; it is worth substantially less than the vote of residents of the smaller districts. The low-population districts are, of course, generally rural, whereas the densely populated districts are chiefly urban.

The disadvantaged voters in *Colegrove*, contending that their right to equal protection of the laws under the Fourteenth Amendment was thus violated, asked that the Illinois authorities be enjoined from holding any further elections based on the malapportioned districts; they asked for a decree, in other words, ordering further congressional elections in Illinois to be at large, until such time as the legislature reapportioned the state more equitably. The Court denied this or any other relief in a prevailing opinion written by Mr. Justice Frankfurter. Having regard, he said, to "the effective working of our government," the issue is revealed "to be of a peculiarly political nature and therefore not meet for judicial determination." Further: "Nothing is clearer than that this controversy concerns matters that bring courts into immediate and active relations with party contests. From the determination of such issues this Court has traditionally held aloof. It is hostile to a democratic system to involve the judiciary in the politics of the people." And: "The short of it is that the Constitution has conferred upon Congress exclusively authority to secure fair representation by the States in the popular House and left to that House determination whether States have fulfilled their responsibility. If Congress failed in exercising its powers, whereby standards of fairness are offended, the remedy ultimately lies with the people." And finally, in a much-quoted sentence: "Courts ought not to enter this political thicket."

It is necessary first to understand what the decision in *Colegrove v. Green* is not. It does not say that the Court may never interfere with the election process, or that there are no judicially enforceable constitutional principles that apply to elections. For the Court has interfered consistently for some fifty years to enforce the Fifteenth Amendment's guarantee that "the right of citizens of the United States to vote shall not be denied or abridged by the United States or by any State on account of race, color, or previous condition of servitude."[124] Nor—although I have quoted a passage that tends in this direction—can *Colegrove* rest on the proposition (espoused, as we saw, by Mr. Wechsler) that the Constitution, properly interpreted, confides to Congress exclusive authority to regulate congressional elections. For plainly the Fifteenth Amendment cuts across any such exclusive authority, and as a matter of interpretation of the text, there is no readily apparent reason why the Fourteenth Amendment's guaranty of the equal protection of the laws should not similarly cut across and similarly authorize judicial intervention. To be sure, the Constitution specifically empowers Congress to make or alter regulations about the times, places, and manner of holding elections for Senators and Representatives, and it confers upon Congress the duty to apportion Representatives among the states "according to their respective Numbers," and to "be the Judge of the Elections, Returns and Qualifications of its own Members." But there is no textual reason that these duties and functions of Congress should be deemed proof against judicial intervention, any more than the language of the Commerce Clause, which provides that "Congress shall have Power . . . To regulate Commerce with foreign Nations, and among the several States, and with the Indian Tribes," is read to foreclose judicial review. Again, *Colegrove* is in no sense a standing case. The disadvantaged voters in *Colegrove* were injured, and their claim had all the desirable immediacy. Finally, the decisive factor in *Colegrove* could not well have been the difficulty or uncertainty that might attend enforcement of a judicial decree. It comes easily enough to mind that the foreseeable difficulty in the *School Segregation Cases* was graver, and that the difficulties in many earlier and later Fifteenth Amendment cases were not appreciably less serious.

Colegrove is a political-question case, and the only remaining inquiry is whether it holds that apportionment—at least so far as the lower House of the federal Congress is concerned—is a matter of the sort for which we have no rules, and as to which we "believe that the job is better done without rules," or that it is of the sort to which rules are applicable, although they "should be only among the numerous relevant considerations." There is nothing in the opinion or in our political and legal traditions to support the first proposition; there is everything to affirm the second.[125] The principle of equal representation of qualified voters is surely an aspiration of American democracy, and yet consistently throughout our history, the political institutions have found it necessary or expedient to modify the principle and to represent, not only people, but interests, groups and regions.[126] In a diverse, federated country extending over a continent, organized as a representative, not a town-meeting, democracy, we strive, after all, not only for responsive, but for truly representative government, which reflects the electorate and is at the same time stable and effective.

All would be relatively simple if one could assert with moral certainty that inequality of individual representation in whatever form is intolerable on principle, as inequality in the legal status or treatment of the races is wrong in all its forms. But, however it may seem to the inhabitants of Memphis, Atlanta, New York, or New Haven, that is simply not a tenable position. The principle of the *School Segregation Cases* is one that judges may hold and proclaim with present certainty, although pragmatic compromises may remain necessary for a time. But one cannot with like moral confidence proclaim the principle of equal individual representation, holding everything else to be a temporary if necessary evil. Experience and reflection on the country as it is in fact force the conclusion that the principle of equality of individual representation can be only a partial guide to solution of the problem. And neither the Court nor anyone else has succeeded in evolving something more malleable and yet still principled, which, though present conditions might not allow for its sudden and complete execution, might yet be proclaimed as *the* governing rule. It remains in large part, perhaps unfortunately, a task of pragmatic trial and error to construct representative deliberative institutions that are responsive to the views, the interests, and the aspirations of heterogeneous total constituencies, and that are yet not so fragmented or finely balanced as to be incapable of decisive action; that are capable of decisive action, yet identified with the people, and so containing within themselves the people's diversities as to be able to generate consent. Equality of representation is one goal, and the only principled one, among many. It must be accommodated to the others, and no principled way of doing so has as yet been discovered. Who, after all, remembering the Weimar Republic or the Fourth French Republic, favors proportional representation? As Mr. Wechsler has written in a classic essay on the federal arrangement, the need is for "government responsive to the will of the full national constituency, without loss of responsiveness to lesser voices, reflecting smaller bodies of opinion, in areas that constitute their own legitimate concern."[127] The same thing is true, of course, on the smaller scale of the states.

The need is met—imperfectly, no doubt—not by one but by a troika of institutions, each answering to a differently weighted constituency, with the executive's normally being the most straight-out majoritarian. (The only partial exceptions are unicameral Nebraska and unit-vote Georgia.) And the institutions sometimes trade constituencies. The federal Senate used to be the redoubt of localism, but, owing to the Seventeenth Amendment and the rise of the city, it is now much less so. The role has been largely assumed by the more fragmented (and yet more disciplined) House, in which many isolated or obsolescent interests now find representation and some power. It should be added that power in American government has for generations gravitated steadily to executives, who are, of course, a significant part of the legislative process, exercising functions both of initiative and approval. Yet another consideration is the stability and vitality of a two-party system. Further, cities have substantial functions of self-government, and their elective heads are themselves influential forces in the state and federal legislative process. And finally, in the present American system, the influence of the individual vote is not all that counts in government or even in elections; command of wealth and of the means of communication and persuasion go for much, and most groups exercising such command are urban.

All this is to say that the Court cannot undertake to regulate practices of apportionment. To do so would be "hostile to a democratic system"; it would be "to involve the judiciary in the politics of the people," since apportionment is necessarily a very high percentage of politics with a very small admixture of definable principle. In race relations, the proportions are reversed. Some have wondered why the doctrine of political questions was not deemed relevant enough even to mention in the decision of the *School Seg-*

regation Cases. This is the reason. And there is yet another, closely related. In the *School Segregation Cases*, the southern states, claiming necessity among other considerations, defended practices that were not merely deviations from an incomplete, partially applicable principle but the fundamental negation of an emergent one, which the Court was to be prevented from proclaiming. Necessity was relied on to perpetuate an operating principle that was wrong and that the Court itself had mistakenly proclaimed at a time when the whole matter should have been deemed a political question, at least with respect to schools. As to apportionment, if I may iterate the argument once more, in words recently spoken by Mr. Justice Frankfurter:

Manifestly, the Equal Protection Clause supplies no clearer guide for judicial examination of apportionment methods. . . . Apportionment, by its character, is a subject of extraordinary complexity, involving— even after the fundamental theoretical issues concerning what is to be represented in a representative legislature have been fought out or compromised [a task itself not fit for judicial performance]—considerations of geography, demography, electoral convenience, economic and social cohesions or divergencies among particular local groups, communications, the practical effects of political institutions like the lobby and the city machine, ancient traditions and ties of settled usage, respect for proven incumbents of long experience and senior status, mathematical mechanics, censuses compiling relevant data, and a host of others.[128]

But that still makes only for the sort of political question as to which principle "should be only among the numerous relevant considerations." It does not make for the sort of question as to which we "believe that the job is better done without rules." While the Court in *Colegrove* was therefore unable to formulate a dominant principle, even as a goal, it did not see it as its function, on the other hand, to bless the expedient arrangements made by the political institutions, or to abandon the single relevant principled goal, which is equality of representation, and the benefits that might be had from its influence as such. There was no judicial review in *Colegrove*, no checking of political action, and no legitimation.

Since the spring of 1962, it may seem that *Colegrove* is no more.

A certain tendency to animism affects lawyers when they talk of cases, and they communicate it to interested laymen. Animated cases rise, struggle, and conquer, or are vanquished by, other cases. And so *Baker* v. *Carr*,[129] the great Tennessee apportionment case decided on March 27, 1962, is thought to have vanquished *Colegrove* v. *Green*. But caution is advisable. The millenium has not arrived for urban voters. A crack in the judicial gate that should not have been closed in *Colegrove* v. *Green* has now been pried open, but the gate has not swung on its hinges. Urban voters will be snatching defeat from the jaws of victory if they now concentrate all their energies on law suits and focus their hopes of ultimate success on the judiciary.

Apportionment of the General Assembly of Tennessee, which consists of two chambers, is such that counties with populations, respectively, of 2340 and 3084 have exactly the same representation as counties inhabited, respectively, by 25,316 and 33,990. Plaintiffs in *Baker* v. *Carr*, being urban voters disadvantaged as indicated, sued in the federal district court for a declaration that this inequality of representation abridged their right to the equal protection of the laws, and sought an order enjoining state officials from holding any further elections under the law creating the inequality. That law was passed in 1901, the same year that Illinois last apportioned its congressional districts before *Colegrove* v. *Green*. At the time of *Colegrove* v. *Green*, there had been no reapportionment in Illinois in over thirty-five years. At the time of *Baker* v. *Carr*, there had been no reapportionment in Tennessee in over sixty years. The district court dismissed *Baker* v. *Carr* outright, on the authority of *Colegrove* v. *Green*. Reversing, the Supreme Court reinstated the suit and directed the district court to proceed to trial and judgment.

Nothing in the prevailing opinion in *Baker* v. *Carr* affirms the essence of what was denied in *Colegrove* v. *Green. Baker* v. *Carr* does not hold that the Court is a fit body to take over from the political institutions—or from an inscrutable Providence that has surely also had a hand in the matter, as many an ironic turn in the nature and role of those institutions demonstrates—the pragmatic management of the complex and often curious adjustments that have made us a democracy and maintained us as such. That would have been too much like playing de Gaulle to the American Republic, and we are not so distracted as all that. The point decided was not what function the Court is to perform in legislative apportionment, and certainly not whether it is to take over full management, but whether it can play any role at all. Alluding to Thayer's rule of the clear mistake, the Court indicated that its function might be to impose a requirement of rationality. But Thayer's rule can lead nowhere in this instance, for most apportionments can be deemed irrational only if the legislature is *a priori* foreclosed from pursuing certain purposes, such as over-representation of some or of all rural areas. The question is, should such purposes be foreclosed, should they be foreclosed in all circumstances, and why? What is the dominant principle? To this question the Court gave no answer; indeed, it failed to ask it. The decision in *Baker v. Carr* may thus be read as holding no more than that, Tennessee having last been malapportioned sixty years ago, the situation there is the result, not of a deliberate if imperfect present judgment of the political institutions, but merely of inertia and oligarchic entrenchment. In the face of so faint an assertion, if any, by the political institutions of their own function, the principled goal of equal representation had enough vitality to enable the Court to prod the Tennessee political institutions into action. *Mutatis mutandis, Baker v. Carr* is *Rumely* and *Kent v. Dulles,* if not *Watkins* or *Greene v. McElroy.* The Court here opened a colloquy, posing to the political institutions of Tennessee the question of apportionment, not answering it for them.

The judgment in *Baker v. Carr* is likely to generate effective pressure for legislative action, which may ameliorate the inequity somewhat. The pressure will be effective, more easily so, one may expect, than decrees in some school cases have been. If election officials are ordered to hold no further elections before the legislature enacts a new apportionment law, defiance is conceivable, of course. But there is no police state among the fifty, and public opinion will not tolerate either the breakdown of state government or its constitution in what will widely be regarded as illegitimate fashion. Nor will governors, who are more responsive to the full electorate. Once a new apportionment statute has been passed, curing the situation in some degree, there will be little more that the judicial process can or should do. Yet we will, apparently, witness not a little constitutional experimentation by lower federal and by state courts; and even the Supreme Court may enter the "political thicket" in states where no branch of government, not even the executive, rests on the majoritarian principle.

There is one danger, however, whose spectre rises from the Court's opinion in *Baker* v. *Carr*. In some future case—perhaps in order to correct misreadings by lower courts of its present rather enigmatic pronouncement—the Supreme Court may see it as its function, not merely to let an apportionment be, but to legitimate it. This, as I have argued at length, would be grave error. If one may use proper nouns to name judicial errors, as is sometimes done with diseases, we should call this Plessy v. Ferguson's Error, after the case that legitimated segregation in 1896.

I have emphasized in this chapter the area of choice that is open to the Court in deciding whether, when, and how much to adjudicate; and I have discussed the order of considerations that I believe should determine the choice. The process so described is not that of principled constitutional adjudication. Nor, however, does it license predilectional, sentimental, or irrational judgment. The quality of disinterestedness, which is one of the chief factors in the formation of principled judgments, remains an essential requirement here also. No doubt, it is not an easy attainment for the human judges, who, as Chief Justice Taft once remarked, are "the only ones we have," and whom, he added, "we must treat with that in mind."[130] The Justices have their being near the political marketplace, in which the effects of their judgments are felt. But the system embodies elaborate mechanisms for their insulation. And a number of controls are built into their craft, which they practice under the scrutiny of a profession whose expectations and approval must matter to them. The judges are argued with publicly and they debate privately. Then they generally articulate their decisions in public, with supporting reasons, then to be argued with again and again. We may expect that they will in fact be insulated from the party contest and that they will cast out merely personal, group, or class interests and prejudices, taking instead, so far as humanly possible, a more detached and more encompassing view of public issues. This expectation sometimes proves overly sanguine; but no more so with respect to the kind of decision canvassed in this chapter than with respect to the ultimate function of principled constitutional adjudication, and with lesser consequences in the case of the former.

I have not addressed myself, in this chapter or elsewhere, to the role of the lower federal courts, of which the Supreme Court is the hierarchic head. Some of the methods and devices I have discussed are obviously not open to use in the lower courts. Some are, and as to them, the system of precedent, by which the Supreme Court instructs the lower courts and employs them as its agents, will serve. Throughout, of course, the lower courts can act in constitutional matters as stop-gap or relatively ministerial decisionmakers only.

CHAPTER 5

Neither Force nor Will

In Chapters 1 and 4, I have examined critically the classical, or, one might say, official, position with respect to the establishment and justification of judicial review. For reasons of analytical convenience, I endeavored in Chapter 1 to state very generally an alternative justification, before attempting to define what it was I was justifying. Subsequently, I proceeded by way of both criticism and affirmation to consider in somewhat greater detail the nature and reach of the power of judicial review, as it has been exercised and viewed in the American tradition. The thesis that emerged was this. The power extends over a broad range of public issues in our system. As de Tocqueville remarked in a much-quoted passage, "Hardly any question arises in the United States that is not resolved sooner or later into a judicial question." Ranging as widely as it has and as, on the premises I accept, there is no reason it should not, judicial review brings principle to bear on the operations of government. By "principle" is meant general propositions, as Holmes called them, deeming their formation the chief end of man, though he felt obliged at the same time to spray them with his customary skeptical acid;[1] organizing ideas of universal validity in the given universe of a culture and a place, ideas that are often grounded in ethical and moral presuppositions. Principle, ethics, morality—these are evocative, not definitional, terms; they are attempts to locate meaning, not to enclose it.

Exercising a function of this description, however imprecise, in a society dedicated both to the morality of government by consent and to moral self-government, the Supreme Court touches and should touch many aspects of American public life. But it would be intolerable for the Court finally to govern all that it touches, for that would turn us into a Platonic kingdom contrary to the morality of self-government; and in this world at least, it would not work. If one takes the rule of law to mean the full and unrelenting dominion of the Court's principles wherever and whenever applicable, then the problem becomes one of limiting, and limiting with extreme severity, the kind and thus the number of principles the Court is permitted to evolve and apply. Professor Wechsler is compelled to strive for such a solution, although in seeking to achieve it he seems to me to ignore the play of the Court's legitimating power. This is a power that the institution necessarily possesses and exerts, and Mr. Wechsler is unable to strip the Court of it, nor is he concerned with attempting to do so. Other solutions based on the premise of an obligation always to decide lead either to a manipulative process, whose inherent, if high-minded, lack of candor raises issues of its own, or to the abandonment of principle and the involvement of the Court in judgments of expediency, as a second-guesser of the political institutions; or, more commonly, to both. Thus they result in a process that, for me as for all commentators in the tradition in which I write, can have no justification so long as it is divorced from direct political responsibility. But this premise and this posture of the problem are false ones. The means exist and are in vigorous use for providing a wide-ranging and effective rule of principle, while at the same time eschewing full dominion and affording the necessary leeway to expedient accommodation. These means I dealt with at length in the previous chapter, calling them loosely and with benevolent intent "the passive virtues."

The Relativity of Virtue

The contention central to my thesis has been that the Court exercises a triune function: it checks, it legitimates, or it does neither. I have dwelt on each component not a little, but the differences among them require further analysis. For often enough, to do neither is to do something else. When the Court denies certiorari, summarily dismisses an appeal, or otherwise dismisses a case outright for lack of ripeness, to be sure, it pretty well refrains from doing anything at all. Even then it may be permitting its previous judgments to continue to have a certain effect, or it may be allowing lower federal or state courts to engage in constitutional experimentation. Only then, however, if at all, does the Court really suffer prior decisions of other institutions to stand untouched. When it employs a device such as vagueness, delegation, statutory construction, or procedure, the Court frustrates or checks, at least in the case before it, a prior legislative or official decision. These, then, can be called devices of not doing, or passive virtues, only comparatively.

In conventional classification, most of them are not so called at all. Delegation and vagueness are viewed as full-fledged constitutional doctrines, resting, respectively, on the principle of the separation of powers and on the due-process principle of fair warning. The procedural holding of the majority in the *Garner* sit-in case was also stated in constitutional terms. The trial court's inference, without proof, that the sit-ins disturbed or alarmed the public, said the Supreme Court majority, was "a denial of due process." A decision that speaks the language of statutory construction, on the other hand, is not deemed constitutional, even when the considerations that underlie it might just as well have been called vagueness or delegation. These flights of nomenclature can be explained, though not justified. Vagueness and delegation decisions, and the procedural decision in *Garner* are called constitutional because if they are not, then, in the conventional view, the Court has no authority to make them. If the Court is not prepared to declare a state statute or court proceeding unconstitutional, on grounds of vagueness, delegation, procedure, or what-have-you, then it must hold it not unconstitutional. Procedural decisions in the federal context need not be constitutional, because the Court may function as administrative head of the federal court system, in the absence of a supervening Act of Congress. Again in the federal context, a result framed in terms of statutory construction need not be called constitutional, since—fictive as it may be to do so in many instances, such as *Kent* v. *Dulles*—the Court imputes the statutory meaning at which it arrives to Congress, rather than avowing it as its own product. But a state statute, as I have noted, although it is brought to judgment by the same process, may not be construed (for reasons that are valid enough when genuine construction is in question), and so it is held vague as applied, which is labeled a constitutional decision.

Underlying the conventional nomenclature must be the assumption—or something very much like it—that a constitutional adjudication is any decision that checks the will of other institutions of government by means of a judge-made rule. Consistency is then achieved by erecting the fiction that the results of certain exercises in statutory construction are not judge-made. But even if we correct for consistency without resort to fiction and call certain statutory-construction decisions constitutional also, the fact remains that such a classification of the Court's work lacks discrimination. It does not describe with as much accuracy as is attainable what the Court actually does; it fails, indeed, to take account of glaring differences. Moreover, the differences thus blurred are highly relevant when one comes to inquire, not only what the Court actually does, but what it should do; when one comes, that is, not only to describe, but to assess the function critically and to justify it. For, unlike constitutional doctrines properly so called, the devices of vagueness, delegation, procedure, and construction leave the other institutions, particularly the legislature, free—and generally invite them—to make or remake their own decisions for prospective application to everyone in like cases, and often in some fashion even to the litigant immediately concerned. What is ordered in the meantime radiates little of general consequence; and what is frustrated or checked is often a decision derived, if at all, only in an attenuated or remote way from the legislature or an elected executive, and actually made by officials. Now, from the point of view of the theory and practice of democracy, such officials stand in closer relation to the electoral process than does the Court, but there is not between them and the Court the gulf that exists between the latter and the truly representative institutions, such as the legislature or elected executives.

A constitutional adjudication, we might better posit, is one that checks the will of the political institutions, now and for an indeterminate future, or that legitimates their action and stiffens, rein-

forces, and in some measure directs their purpose, now and in time
to come; all on the basis of principle, which necessarily reaches
far in the minds of men as well as in their immediate conduct,
promising application in widening spheres. The principle can be
revised or reversed—at least in theory—only by the Court itself.
The other institutions, however remote or close their connection
to the electoral process, are bound. Decisions that purport to bind
must be principled; else they are not proper—which is to say, not
justifiable—exercises of the power of judicial review. Such was
the premise, it will be recalled, of the criticism I put forward in
Chapter 2 with respect to *Shelton* v. *Tucker,* the case of the Arkansas statute that required teachers in the public schools to reveal
their organizational affiliations. But it may appear that there was
an element of circularity in that criticism and that there is one in
the formulation I have just essayed. A constitutional adjudication,
I am saying, is required to be principled because it is binding. But
its effectiveness as a binding adjudication, and perhaps even its
capacity to bind at all, are themselves functions of its foundation
in principle. The principle on which it rests lends to the successful
prosecution or defense of a law suit by this or that litigant the
significance, now and in the future, that I have described. The
principle promises application in widening spheres; the principle
affects, even aside from future applications by the Court itself, the
tendency of public policy. Otherwise, adjudication does no more
than to dispose of a discrete controversy. There would seem to be
little point in objecting to it as *ad hoc,* for it carries no consequences of particular moment, scarcely even the promise of its
own multiplication; and it can hardly be said to encounter in very
serious form what I called in Chapter 1 the counter-majoritarian
difficulty. It is, rather, principled adjudications that should give
the critic pause. Moreover, can it really matter much that the
Court labels its decision constitutional? The effect of a vagueness
decision, or of the holding in the *Garner* sit-in case, is not altered
because the Court, following the conventional nomenclature, calls
it constitutional. The Constitution, Charles Evans Hughes once
remarked, while he was at the Bar, is what the judges say it is.
This is a rather simplistic statement and was much misunderstood.
In any event, can it be true that a constitutional decision is what

the judges say is one, and that we are then to assess it critically as if it were?

But I have greatly overstated the argument as to the supposed circularity. To begin with, it does matter that the judges call a decision constitutional, or at least that they do not call it anything else. For thus they invoke the ultimate instrument of their power. They have, as Hamilton said, neither force nor will, neither the sword nor the purse; they have only society's striving for the rule of principle, its readiness to receive principle from the Court, and its strong, habit-formed inclination to accept, to accord and harmonize, to obey. Like the Pope, the Court takes on an ultimate dimension *dum ex cathedra loquitur*. To have said in *Shelton* v. *Tucker* that it was unconstitutional to require Mr. Shelton to reveal his NAACP membership was to strike a certain chord. The result, to be sure, was a false note. Nevertheless, a certain order of expectations was triggered. It is, in a phrase of Thayer, no light thing to do that. In the main, there are three courses of conduct that can erode and would finally defeat the rather miraculous American phenomenon of the rule of judicial principle. One is the attempt to push its dominion past natural limits. Another is manipulation —though to the highest of ulterior ends, no doubt—of principles that are not tenable for their own sakes. A third is to call the name of principle in vain, until even its genuine invocation ceases to produce the reflex of acceptance. Moreover, such a decision as *Shelton* v. *Tucker*, with its false note, was, of course, ineffective in practice well beyond the degree of ineffectiveness that inheres in the natural limits of the rule of principle. Even so, because of what it purported to be, it had and may retain for some time an inhibitive influence on the political institutions in Arkansas and elsewhere. Future actions or proposals requiring similar disclosures of teachers and other public employees will be subject to attack and resistance based on the opinion in *Shelton* v. *Tucker;* ambivalently founded resistance and ambiguous attack, but, by the same token, difficult to meet. It is not equally objectionable for the judges to call a vagueness decision, or the procedural decision in *Garner*, constitutional. This is still undesirable, but more nearly an innocent misnomer. For such a decision, no matter what it calls itself, does describe its own narrow and exclusive consequences.

Perhaps the upshot is that a constitutional adjudication should be defined as being a decision that either (1) checks or legitimates actions of the political institutions on the basis of principle, or (2) purports to do so and is in fact neither principled nor supportable on any other ground. Whatever it calls itself, and whether or not it actually proceeds from principle, a decision of the Court must be self-conscious; it must be intelligible, rational, candid. In no circumstances can it begin to be justifiable unless it meets the irreducible implications that the very words "court" and "judge" have for centuries conveyed in our tradition; unless, in short, it is disinterested. Self-conscious intellectual candor in finding and following a rational path to decision is one of the chief assurances of disinterestedness. We seek it, indeed, also in other processes of government, although they are more readily subject to direct control than the judiciary; for example, the administrative process. And we consider it a crisis when we find rationality lacking.[2] We exempt only, if at all, the most representative of political institutions. But never the judiciary, never above all, the Supreme Court, even when it does least and less than least, as in dismissing cases outright. Expediency dictates that the judges be then excused from articulating reasons, but not from reason itself.

The passive devices that I have canvassed do not produce constitutional decisions. They do not check or legitimate on principle. They are not themselves principled, they do not operate independently, and the variables that render them decisive cannot be contained in any principle; if they could be, these variables would for the most part be alone decisive. But the passive devices have intrinsic, rational significance. The Court's authority to employ them derives from its ultimate function of rendering principled adjudications; for this is a function that can be wisely and fruitfully exercised only if the Court is empowered also to decide whether and when to exercise it. The presence in the case of the ultimate issue of constitutional principle is the source of the Court's authority to make a lesser decision, by way of vagueness, delegation, and the like. When the doctrine of delegation is used in nonconstitutional cases coming up from the federal administrative agencies, it will be because Congress has chosen to give the Court supervisory power over the administrative process, and the doctrine is employed as conducive to the wise exercise of that power, with a view to the proper allocation of competences among officials, courts, and legislators.[3] And when the doctrine of vagueness decides a case even though no separate constitutional issue is present, it will be because in the circumstances the fair-warning factor is peculiarly relevant.

The passive devices are thus justified as lesser rational alternatives to an otherwise unavoidable principled judgment, which would, in turn, be unwise in the given circumstances. The devices are lesser ones because they work relatively no binding interference with the democratic process. This last statement, although I have endeavored to support it, invites further analysis. It is important to inquire into the practical effect and to question more closely the virtue of devices of not doing, such as vagueness and the like. For it comes quickly to mind that the legislature's freedom of action and its readiness to make its response in colloquies with the judiciary are qualified by an inertia that constitutes a major force in our busy modern representative bodies. And so the Court's decision, although relatively passive, has an active edge; although not constitutional, it may affect the legal order for some time. Too much must not be made, however, of the Court's edge. The legislature and the executive are not so inert as all that. They will often fail to reply to a nonconstitutional decision because, in the absence of pressure to the contrary from affected groups, they accept it; or because, being very narrow, it does not matter; or because, while the decision runs counter to administrative policy, they themselves had and have no policy in the premises, and are unable, or do not for the moment care, to develop any. But there are dozens of instances, in the federal context, of congressional reversal of the Court, and many more instances of the most fruitful interplay between the Court and the legislature or the executive, following colloquies initiated by the Justices.[4] And there are surely dozens in the states that remain uncollected and unstudied. There are even whole series of interrelated occasions when the Court and Congress engaged, as has been well said, in " 'responsive readings' of the developing law in an area where the legislative and constitutional domains, and the responsibilities of Congress and the courts, are blurred."[5]

As a practical matter, not merely theoretically, in all the illustrations I have given, decision proceeding from one of the devices of not doing was palpably a lesser decision than a constitutional adjudication striking down the challenged action would have been, and less consequential as well than a legitimating judgment. It is worth reiterating, for example, that in the vagueness, desuetude, and delegation cases, and in the *Baker* v. *Carr* legislative-apportionment case, legitimation would have had, and in some of the examples I gave did have, the effect of fixing important policy decisions that the political process had touched on only tentatively, lightly, or comparatively irresponsibly, if at all. This is not to mention the effect on the policy choices of another day. Yet the passive virtues are relative virtues. They are exercises of judicial power; whether lesser ones depends on the alternatives. It cannot always be true in practice that the effect of a passive device, though not radiating from principle, is necessarily narrower, less pervasive, than the consequences of some constitutional adjudications.[6] Normally it will be so, but to say "always" would be to try for too much neatness. It is no use; the judicial process cannot be automated. The passive devices, producing decisions that fall short of constitutional adjudication, and constitutional doctrines properly so called are all points on a continuum of judicial power. And if, having regard to actual consequences, one views exercises of the power as ranging from the extreme of a denial of certiorari at one end to that of the judgment in the *School Segregation Cases* at the other, it is evident that not all constitutional decisions have the same weight, the same reach, the same binding quality; not all encounter with equal degree of shock the counter-majoritarian difficulty; some are nearer the passive end than others.

I propose now to undertake a sketchy survey of a few further sections of the continuum. I have no illusions about the possibility of an exactly calibrated progression from one end to the other—from the passive low of a denial of certiorari to the active heights of the *School Segregation Cases*. But I shall start somewhere near where I left off in the last chapter, with doctrines that do, or purport to do, less than other ones and that might have been classified among the passive virtues. I shall try to show why they were not.

The Mysteries of Motive

A method of judicial control has been persistently advanced which would go a long way toward solving the congressional-investigation and legislative-apportionment problems that I have discussed. It might solve as well the benevolent-quota conundrum and other problems left in the wake of the *School Segregation Cases.* Yet it would—at least apparently—stop short of adjudicating the ultimate and broadest constitutional issues involved. This method, with which I dealt briefly in Chapter 2, would make motive decisive. The Court, as Justices Black and Brennan have suggested, might judge of the "chief aim" of an investigating committee and hold invalid an investigation the "dominant purpose" of which is not "to gather information in aid of law-making or law-evaluation but rather to harass . . .[the witness] and expose him for the sake of exposure."[7] Similarly, the Court might find that the "chief aim" behind a gerrymander was not to accommodate, in the usual fallible pragmatic fashion, the several objectives to be served in the setting up of representative institutions, but to discriminate against a certain class of voters. Again, the Court might determine that the "dominant purpose" embodied in a pupil-placement statute was, not a general educational one or even the desire to provide an orderly transition, without loss of quality, from a segregated to an integrated school system, but the maintenance of as much segregation as federal authorities can be made to swallow.

The established view is that inquiries into motive are not open in the Supreme Court. "There is a wise and ancient doctrine," said Mr. Justice Cardozo, "that a Court will not inquire into the motives of a legislative body or assume them to be wrongful." "The process of psychoanalysis," he remarked, must not be carried into such "unaccustomed fields."[8] This is the position that was taken from the first, if without reference to the newer arts. Marshall, as I pointed out in Chapter 1, stated it quite early in *Fletcher* v. *Peck.* Thomas M. Cooley, in what was for years a standard law-student's treatise, puts it as follows, with supporting reasons:

The validity of legislation can never be made to depend on the motives which have secured its adoption, whether these be public or personal, honest or corrupt. . . . [T]o make legislation depend upon motives would render all statute law uncertain, and the rule which should allow it could not logically stop short of permitting a similar inquiry into the motives of those who passed judgment. Therefore the courts do not permit a question of improper legislative motives to be raised, but they will in every instance assume that the motives were public and befitting the station. They will also assume that the legislature had before it any evidence necessary to enable it to take the action it did take.[9]

Such is the received tradition. But it is too simple to suffice. It happens, for example, that the remarks of Cardozo quoted above were written in dissent from a majority that would no doubt have subscribed to Cooley's formulation and Marshall's before him, but that in a given case saw it otherwise.

Some of the difficulty is due to confusion between, on the one hand, a finding of motive properly speaking (what Cardozo called psychoanalysis) and, on the other, a determination of "purpose" which, as I suggested in Chapter 2, is either the name given to the Court's objective assessment of the effect of a statute or a conclusionary term denoting the Court's independent judgment of the constitutionally allowable end that the legislature could have had in view. Thus the quest for the "chief aim" or "dominant purpose" of a congressional investigation need not be regarded as an attempt to diagnose true motive, as if legislative action were a neurotic symptom that the Court is obliged to trace to its cause. Rather, the conclusion that the "dominant purpose" was to expose for the sake of exposure may simply be a function of a restrictive conception of the investigative power. If the power is seen as having distinct limits, it becomes possible quite objectively to assess the only significant effect of a given investigation as having passed the limits; and it is then acceptable—indeed, usual—judicial diction to speak of the "purpose" of the investigation as being constitutionally forbidden. But if the line of vision takes in as allowable all the possible uses of the power of Congress to inform itself and the public, if the power is seen also as enabling Congress to generate consent for legislation already decided upon, or to lay the factual foundation for a decision not to legislate—then the significant effects multiply without passing the limits of the power, and the search for the impermissible "dominant purpose" does become an exercise in psychoanalysis. The trouble with the suggestion of Justices Black and Brennan may be, not what it leads to, but what it proceeds from; not that the Justices use the phrases "chief aim" and "dominant purpose" as euphemisms for motive, and that they would thus lead us into inadmissible psychoanalysis, but that they proceed from an inadmissible restriction of congressional power. The second alternative is a principled constitutional judgment, but, as I have argued, not a tenable one; the first bears the heavy burden of almost uniform authoritative rejection. And so confusion becomes the route of escape.

The confusion between motive and the very different construct that does duty in constitutional adjudication under the name of "purpose" is evident also in the altogether too easy transition that some commentators make between the standard Fifteenth Amendment voting cases and those raising the legislative-apportionment problem. Of this easy transition, *Gomillion* v. *Lightfoot*,[10] the famous Tuskegee gerrymander case of 1960, provided dramatic illustration. It was widely thought to put in question the doctrine of *Colegrove* v. *Green* and, when ultimately decided so as to strike down the gerrymander, though with no hint of overruling *Colegrove*, it was deemed to represent movement by the Court in the direction of employing the method of motive. But *Gomillion* was really a simple case, if an extraordinary one, in which the traditional concept of "purpose" was used with no confusion about motives.

The city of Tuskegee, Alabama, was a sensible square on the map. In 1957, the state legislature changed the city's boundaries so that it came out, as Mr. Justice Frankfurter wrote in the opinion of the Court in *Gomillion*, "a strangely irregular 28-sided figure." The effect of this "essay in geometry and geography" was to remove from the city "all save only four or five of its four hundred Negro voters while not removing a single white voter or resident." Segregated government! Now, state legislatures have all the power in the world to paint on the map the boundaries of their political subdivisions. No inquiry into the motives that may have governed the choice of this shape was undertaken by the Court in *Gomillion*. The Court, to be sure, did hold that neither this power nor any other could be exercised for the sole purpose of depriving a Negro citizen of a vote he had and would have retained but for the fact of his being Negro. This is quite the same as to hold that no congressional investigation may be conducted for the sole purpose of exposing a witness for the sake of exposure, or that no apportionment will be upheld whose sole purpose is to discriminate against a given class of voters. But the decisive difference is that in *Gomillion* it was possible to isolate a "sole" legislative purpose on the basis of an objective inquiry. The evidence, said Mr. Justice Frankfurter for the Court, was "tantamount . . . to a mathematical demonstration, that the legislation is solely concerned with segregating white and colored voters by fencing Negro citizens out of town so as to deprive them of their pre-existing municipal vote. . . ." No one, least of all counsel for Alabama, was able to invent any purpose at all that the gerrymander might have served other than the forbidden one. Fanciful suggestions might have been possible, and they might have included whim; but they would all have been disingenuous on their face given the meticulous care with which, running the line house-by-house, the legislature succeeded in not eliminating a single previous white resident of Tuskegee from the new city limits. Had the job been less meticulously done, or had the object of the legislature's discrimination been less readily observable than is the distinction of color, the case might have been different, and the way to the result might have led, of necessity, through an investigation of motive or a narrowing of the scope of the state's power to determine the boundaries of its political subdivisions.

Despite *Gomillion*, no doubt all sorts of "other manipulations to make the most of a majority"[11] will continue to pass muster, short of resort to psychoanalysis. *Gomillion* was extraordinary; as Bernard Taper has well said, the Alabama legislature, in going to the finical and vulnerable extreme of the Tuskegee gerrymander statute, was "like a child throwing a temper tantrum."[12] This does not happen often, but, like the "clear mistakes" of which Thayer speaks, it does occur. We have seen the like of *Gomillion* before and will no doubt see it again. If not a temper tantrum, the Alabama statute was an illustration of an unfortunate lay conception of the law as a jigsaw puzzle, a bag of tricks that can be managed to one's advantage if one is but tricky enough. But the law does not need to resort to the countertrick of motive analysis in order to vindicate itself. This is proved as well by some of *Gomillion's* predecessors in the annals of the Court.

In 1910, Oklahoma made literacy a qualification to vote, but it provided that no person who was a qualified voter on January 1, 1866 (before the effective date of the Fifteenth Amendment, when Negroes were, of course, not allowed to vote), nor any lineal descendant of such a person, should be required to pass a literacy test. This was known, naturally enough, as the Grandfather Clause. Said Solicitor General John W. Davis, arguing that it was unconstitutional: "The necessary effect and operation of the Grandfather Clause is to exclude practically all illiterate negroes [*sic*] and practically no illiterate white men, and from this its unconstitutional purpose may legitimately be inferred." And so it was inferred, and so it was held in 1915, in *Guinn* v. *United States*.[13] Oklahoma then tried again. It enacted that all those who had voted in the general election of 1914, which was held under the Grandfather Clause, remained automatically qualified voters. All others were given just twelve days, from April 30, 1916, to May 11, 1916, in which to register and thus qualify to vote. "All others" meant, in the circumstances, chiefly Negroes. This trick also fell. The Fifteenth Amendment, said the Court, "nullifies sophisticated as well as simple-minded modes of discrimination."[14] This sentence was prominently repeated in *Gomillion* v. *Lightfoot.*

One additional, quite early, and famous case to the same effect must not go unmentioned, for it builds a bridge to another aspect of the problem. This is *Yick Wo* v. *Hopkins,*[15] which was not a voting case and did not concern Negroes. It arose under an ordinance of the city of San Francisco, enacted in 1880, that made it unlawful for any person to establish or maintain a laundry in the city without having first obtained the consent of the Board of Supervisors, unless the laundry was located in a stone or brick building. One purpose of this ordinance is readily apparent. Laundries in wooden buildings are a fire hazard, and, as subsequent events made clear, San Francisco had reason to be wary of fire hazards. But certain further facts were also of record. There were about 320 laundries in the city. Of these, about 240 were owned and operated by Chinese aliens, and of the total of 320, about 310 were constructed of wood. The licenses of Yick Wo, the plaintiff, and some 150 of his countrymen, who like him operated laundries in wooden buildings, were withdrawn under the ordinance. When they did not quit their businesses, Yick Wo and his countrymen were arrested. Yet some 80-odd laundries owned by white men and operated under similar conditions, in wooden buildings, were left unmolested. Indeed, with a single exception, the Board of Supervisors granted all petitions of persons who were not Chinese to continue operating laundries in wooden buildings. The holding of the Supreme Court was as follows:

[T]he cases present the ordinances in actual operation, and the facts shown establish an administration directed so exclusively against a particular class of persons as to warrant and require the conclusion, that, whatever may have been the intent of the ordinances as adopted, they are applied by the public authorities charged with their administration, and thus representing the State itself, with a mind so unequal and oppressive as to amount to a practical denial by the State of that equal protection of the laws which is secured to the petitioners, as to all other persons, by the broad and benign provisions of the Fourteenth Amendment to the Constitution of the United States. Though the law itself be fair on its face and impartial in appearance, yet, if it is applied and administered by public authority with an evil eye and an unequal hand, so as practically to make unjust and illegal discriminations between persons in similar circumstances, material to their rights, the denial of equal justice is still within the prohibition of the Constitution.

Quite like *Gomillion* and the two Oklahoma voting cases, *Yick Wo* was decided on an objective determination of purpose. Like the Oklahoma cases, it is a constitutional adjudication, proscribing race as a standard of classification where the consequence is a deprivation, rather than—as in segregated facilities, which were then considered different and permissible—merely a separation. *Gomillion*, of course, forbids separation as well. Like all three of those cases, *Yick Wo* did not otherwise restrict, implicitly or explicitly, the scope of the governmental power in question; nor did it engage in psychoanalysis. It is different and can serve as a bridge only in that it concerned the action and purpose, not of a legislative body, but of officials charged with administering a legislative enactment. Now, as to officials as opposed to legislators, the position is significantly distinguishable. Although there was no occasion to make the point in *Yick Wo,* since on its facts the concept of purpose served well enough, the Marshall-Cooley-Cardozo strictures against attempting to diagnose motive do not have the same force when official action is concerned as they do with respect to legislation. Considerations of regard for "the station," so strong when the Court reviews the work of the legislature, are surely not of the same intensity in the relationship between the Court and administrative officials. The courts "will assume," says Cooley, in the same passage in which he speaks of the rule concerning motive, "that the legislature had before it any evidence necessary to enable it to take the action it did take." Courts do not generally make any such assumption about the evidence on which officials act. The short of it is that here as in other circumstances, and for obvious reasons, the Court accords to the responsible political institutions a degree of deference that it does not owe to officials. There is, moreover, a related and more telling difference. The traditional strictures against inquiries into motive subsume a certain difficulty of proof, which is in fact insuperable when legislative motive is in question but not necessarily so when it comes to "psychoanalyzing" administrative officials. But this point must take us on a rather lengthy excursus into legislative affairs before we can return to the distinguishable position with respect to officials.

Legislative motives are nearly always mixed and nearly never professed. They are never both unmixed and authoritatively professed on behalf of an entire legislative majority. Even assuming that considerations of "the station" are put aside and that the Court is to engage in a fact-finding process in order to diagnose motive as accurately as may be—through the use, to be sure, of the lower courts, which would be charged with conducting the actual trial— even on such assumptions, how is the fact to be found? It is true, of course, that though the Devil himself knoweth not the mind of man, the law often tries to know and claims that it can. Particularly in the criminal law, intent may well be decisive, and it is determined on the basis of circumstantial evidence—acts from which inferences are drawn backward to the state of mind of the actor—and on the basis of the credibility of the actor's own explanation of his actions. As to a legislative majority, the act is the vote for passage of a statute that has a given effect. Awareness of this effect may be imputed to the voting majority, because they should have had it even if in fact they did not. But by hypothesis, there will be more than one effect, else the whole problem is soluble quite simply through an objective assessment, as in *Gomillion* and the other cases I have discussed. And so the problem for the trier of fact is, not to draw an inference backward from an act to the state of mind of the actor, but to decide which of several acts is the one from which the inference to the state of mind is to be drawn. This is not quite the task that the criminal process commonly faces and performs. The only possibility of a solution— itself far from certain—is cross-examination of each individual legislator. In this posture of the problem, we may recur to Cooley's strictures. It is simply unthinkable that members of legislative majorities should from time to time be subject to cross-examination in various courts over the country regarding their state of mind when they voted. That is no more representative government than it would be judicial process for judges to be subject to cross-examination by legislative committees about their state of mind in deciding cases. It seems almost anticlimactic to add that legislatures whose members were subject to call for testimony in this fashion would be hard put to it to find the time to legislate. But it does not seem trivial to mention also that the upshot of continual inquiries into legislative motive would be a debasement of public morality, because—as in the administration of impossible divorce laws—it would surely lead to routine lying under oath.

The objection is often taken, however, that the Court does something very similar to motive analysis when it engages in statutory construction, and does it without manufacturing, and being deterred by, all the difficulties I have recited. This point is just barely substantial enough to deserve refutation. Ordinarily, statutory construction is tolerably well founded in realities. The Court imputes to a legislative majority knowledge of social and economic conditions that are generally known. It then proceeds to reason that if notice is authoritatively and publicly given, usually by legislative leaders, that a proposed statute is or is not to apply in a certain way, the legislators who then vote for its enactment at the very least acquiesce in the intentions so expressed. But if the same legislative leaders declare, not that the statute is to have this or that effect, but that one effect among many is the one that chiefly motivates them, how can that be imputed to every member of a legislative majority? Given the fact of my vote, you can deduce that I was at the very least willing to accept a consequence or a series of consequences of which I had notice. But so long as I may have been motivated by more than one possible consequence, how can the declared motive of someone else be imputed to me? Surely I can be charged with no more than a willingness to pursue my own motivation, regardless of that of others, which I may or may not have shared.

Statutory construction, however, as we have seen, is not always the comparatively realistic exercise I have just described—not that everyone would agree how realistic *that* is. The Court, as in *Kent* v. *Dulles,* may fail to apply a statute in the teeth of a reasonably well-determined legislative purpose, because it embarks upon a colloquy with the legislature, asking it to pass on certain consequences of the statute once more and more explicitly. This is in itself not altogether fictive. Something that is made explicit in the statute is more soundly imputable to the majority than if it is merely mentioned in debate or otherwise known. At any rate, the end to be achieved is quite clear and real; and that is to obtain a second legislative consideration. But the method of motive can lead to no similar colloquy, can produce no such end. If a statute is denied application for being impermissively motivated, how is the legislature to respond? It can respond to *Kent* v. *Dulles* by re-enacting the statute with certain explicit provisions in it. How can it respond so as to make sure that its statute is correctly motivated? Presumably only by imposing upon some of its members a requirement of less candor in debate. This is scarcely a desirable consummation. Even so, it may not suffice, since the wrong motive may be found in other materials than the debates; it is, after all, as difficult to disprove as it is to prove. As a colloquy, therefore, as a device of not doing which gives the legislature the opportunity to overrule the Court, the method of motive is euphemistic; it is an unacknowledged way, either of cutting off legislative power, or of leaving its specific exercise wholly to the discretion of judges to allow or forbid, with no relation to principle or, indeed, to articulable reason. It binds finally, without saying so and without being able to say why. For the same reason, there is no analogy between judicial attribution of improper motives to the legislature and those instances when, quite aside from the desire to avoid constitutional adjudication, the Court makes policy under a statute and arbitrarily imputes it to the legislature, because there are no materials available on which to base a finding of the legislature's actual intent. This is a function born of necessity; in any event, the legislative reprise is always open, and often forthcoming.

We may now turn again to the aspect of the problem of motive which the *Yick Wo* case suggested—that is, from legislatures to administrative officials, and to the difference in the position with respect to the latter. Unless they are performing quasi-judicial functions,[16] it cannot be very objectionable to subject such officials to cross-examination in court. The fact-finding process will deal, of course, with a limited and manageable number of persons. As for acts from which to draw inferences backward to the state of mind of the actors, there will, on the one hand, be a greater variety of them, not just the single act of the vote, for administration is a continuous operation; on the other hand, the range of effects flowing from each act is likely to be less broad and the fact-finder not so hard put to decide which particular effect motivated the action, for administration of a multipurpose statute takes place more at retail, whereas enactment is at wholesale. The fact-finding task thus begins to be possible.

The existence of this possibility is no matter of mere academic interest. On it will depend implementation of the decision in the *School Segregation Cases* beyond token integration, in the South and in some places in the North as well. The step following massive resistance, school closing, and the like has been legislation— usually pupil-placement laws—resembling more or less the San Francisco ordinance in the *Yick Wo* case, which was, as the saying goes, fair on its face.[17] Segregation in this or that degree is then maintained through administration with "an unequal hand"; an unequal hand, but not necessarily the "mind so oppressive" and the Victorian "evil eye" that made the discrimination objectively obvious in *Yick Wo*. Hence the motive of the administrators, found as a fact, will be decisive, although the motive of the legislature could not be. This was illustrated not long ago by an important litigation concerning the school system of New Rochelle, New York. The system was found by a federal court to have been administered so as to achieve and perpetuate segregation under statutes of the state of New York which are eminently fair on their face. An elaborate trial led the district judge to the conclusion that "the Board of Education of New Rochelle, prior to 1949, intentionally created Lincoln School as a racially segregated school . . . and . . . even since 1949 has been motivated by the purposeful desire of maintaining the Lincoln School as a racially segregated school." This conclusion, affirmed by the Court of Appeals, was derived in part from objective circumstantial evidence of the gerrymandering of school districts and the operation of transfer policies, and in part from testimony submitted subject to cross-examination.[18]

The possibility of a workable judicial method of "motivation research" with respect to administrative officials also puts in a somewhat different light the suggestion of Justices Black and Brennan for judicial control of congressional investigations. For the action of a congressional committee is the action of one or two senior staff officers and a quite limited number of Representatives or Senators—sometimes, when a subcommittee acts, a very small number indeed. It is the action, in most relevant aspects, of officials administering a legislative resolution rather than of the legislature itself. Thus a judicial fact-finding process is possible, and it has been attempted. Committee chairmen and staff officers have testified, in the course of contempt proceedings in court, on the issue of the pertinency of a question that a witness has refused to answer; they have been put on the stand to establish the purpose of the investigation, and thus the basis for a finding of pertinency of the question. But experience so far, while not generally denying the possibility of the process, has run into insuperable difficulties of proof. This is what happened in the recent *Wilkinson* and *Braden* cases, mentioned in Chapter 4.

The evidence in the *Wilkinson* case, for example, showed that Wilkinson had advocated abolition of the House Un-American Activities Committee, and that, at least in the mind of the committee's insufficiently notorious staff director, Mr. Richard Arens, this was one of the reasons for calling him to testify and asking him about Communist affiliation. Perhaps, then, the committee was embarked on a punitive expedition, which would be a thoroughly impermissible motive. But it could not be shown that this was Mr. Arens's sole or even dominant motive, let alone that of the other members of the committee. "It is the information of the committee," Mr. Arens told Wilkinson in opening the hearing,

or the suggestion of the committee that in anticipation of the hearings here in Atlanta, Georgia, you were sent to this area by the Communist Party for the purpose of developing a hostile sentiment to this committee and to its work for the purpose of undertaking to bring pressure upon the United States Congress to preclude these particular hearings. . . . Now, sir, if you will tell this committee whether or not, while you are under oath, you are now a Communist, we intend to pursue that area of inquiry and undertake to solicit from you information respecting your activities as a Communist on behalf of the Communist Party, which is tied up directly with the Kremlin; your activities from the standpoint of propaganda; your activities from the standpoint of undertaking to destroy the Federal Bureau of Investigation and the Committee on Un-American Activities. . . . So if you will answer that principal question, I intend to pursue the other questions with you to solicit information which would be of interest—which will be of vital necessity, indeed—to this committee in undertaking to develop legislation to protect the United States of America. . . . Now please answer the question: Are you now a member of the Communist Party?[19]

If no more emerges from this unedifying prose than that the committee was engaged in making a head count of Communists in the United States, and that it thought opposition to its own activities made it *prima facie* worth while to try to find out whether a man might be a Communist, this would be enough of a legitimate purpose, within the scope of the congressional informing function, on which to rest authority for this investigation. And since Mr. Arens denied on the stand, and maintained his denial under cross-examination, that his dominant motive was to punish Wilkinson, the inquiry was at a dead end and could come to anything only if one was willing to narrow the scope of the power to investigate.

Of course, political judgment, the judgment of the voter, might find such evidence sufficient. This is a judgment that often comes to rest necessarily on an imprecise balance of felt needs and apprehended dangers. It always involves rough classifications of men, causes, aims, and motives. In one of the few and not highly reputed cases in which the Court has essayed examination of legislative motives, it declared plaintively that the impermissible motive was one that "all others [meaning all others entitled to make the normal rough-and-ready political judgments] can see and understand." And the Court asked, virtually wailing: "How can we properly shut our minds to it?"[20] The answer is that the Court ought to shut its mind to much of what all others think they see. That is precisely what courts are for. They try things out on evidence, by the process of proof and refutation, and shut their minds to the kinds of surmise by which the general public may reach politically sufficient conclusions. No doubt, as I said in discussing the *Garner* sit-in case, courts as triers of fact draw inferences concerning matters of common knowledge in the shared experience of the community. But such common knowledge is not common gossip, or common political judgment. A court or a jury, along with the community, will infer without further proof that drunken driving is generally dangerous driving. But can it similarly infer, along with common gossip, that a legislature is corrupt, or that a politician is a self-seeking powermonger rather than a disinterested statesman?

The case from which I quoted in the previous paragraph concerned the congressional power to levy taxes. It held that a tax levied only on manufacturers who employed child labor was improperly motivated. The holding ultimately was based on an altogether untenable view of the scope of the taxing power. Under the guise of a finding of motive, the case attempted to narrow the power to regulate the economy, which inheres in the power to levy taxes, just as Justices Black and Brennan in the *Wilkinson* and *Braden* investigation cases would have restricted the scope of the informing function.

And so the mysteries of motive must remain largely, like Churchill's Russia, wrapped in their enigma. Inquiries into motive do afford a limited, if nevertheless fruitful, possibility of judicial control of administrative action. In such instances, the rule of the improper motive finds its place on the continuum of judicial power as a virtuous lesser doctrine, though, properly speaking, a constitutional one. Proceeding from a factual determination of its intended effect, the Court declares the action of administrative officials to be forbidden on principle. This is binding adjudication. It describes circumstances in which the power of government is cut off. But it does not reach broad ends; the circumstances it describes are narrowly confined, and no limitation is otherwise imposed on the scope of the governmental power that is in question. There is no decision generally limiting the power, for example, to assign pupils to schools not of their choice, or to maintain residentially districted schools. As applied to legislatures, however, or otherwise owing to impossibilities of proof, the doctrine of motive can produce only unacknowledged adjudications that do generally limit the scope of the governmental power in question; the doctrine does, then, reach broad ends, and it decides the issue in terms of those ends, though without facing it as such. Nor can the doctrine be viewed as a method of the colloquy, because it permits no effective legislative reprise.

The Mirage of Equal Protection

An ordinance of New York City prohibits the carrying of advertising for hire on the sides of vehicles traveling the streets of the city, except that owners of trucks may use the sides of their vehicles to advertise what they themselves sell. The Railway Express Agency, operating nearly two thousand trucks in New York City, was in the profitable habit of selling space on them for advertising unconnected with its own business. When it continued doing so after enactment of the ordinance, Railway Express was fined under it and wound up in the Supreme Court of the United States attacking the constitutionality of the ordinance. The attack failed. It was well within the police power of the state, said the Court, applying Thayer's rule of the clear mistake, to remove distractions to the drivers of vehicles and to pedestrians and thus to enhance their safety in the use of the streets. Railway Express argued, further, that it had been denied the equal protection of the laws guaranteed by the Fourteenth Amendment, because the ordinance did not forbid owner advertising or nonvehicular displays, such as the very common huge ones in Times Square, although these were surely as distracting and as menacing to traffic—if anything was —as what the ordinance forbade. Thus the ordinance discriminated. To this the Court made two replies. One was that the distinction between owner advertising and advertising for hire might relate rationally to the supposed purpose of the ordinance.

The local authorities may well have concluded that those who advertise their own wares on their trucks do not present the same traffic problem in view of the nature or extent of the advertising which they use. It would take a degree of omniscience which we lack to say that such is not the case. If that judgment is correct, the advertising displays that are exempt have less incidence on traffic than those of appellants.

The other answer, made in relation to the Times Square displays, was that it is "no requirement of equal protection that all evils of the same genus be eradicated or none at all."

All this provoked from the late Mr. Justice Jackson, although he agreed with the result, an expression of views concerning the Equal Protection Clause that deserves rather full exposition. He differed diametrically, said Justice Jackson, with the philosophy prevailing on the Court "as to the relative readiness with which we should resort" to the Due Process Clause and the Equal Protection Clause.

While claims of denial of equal protection are frequently asserted, they are rarely sustained. But the Court frequently uses the due process clause. . . . And I have frequently dissented. . . .

The burden should rest heavily upon one who would persuade us to use the due process clause to strike down a substantive law or ordinance. . . . Invalidation of a statute or an ordinance on due process grounds leaves ungoverned and ungovernable conduct which many people find objectionable.

Invocation of the equal protection clause, on the other hand, does not disable any governmental body from dealing with the subject at hand. It merely means that the prohibition or regulation must have a broader impact. I regard it as a salutary doctrine that cities, states and the Federal Government must exercise their powers so as not to discriminate between their inhabitants except upon some reasonable differentiation fairly related to the object of regulations. This equality is not merely abstract justice. The framers of the Constitution knew, and we should not forget today, that there is no more effective practical guaranty against arbitrary and unreasonable government than to require that the principles of law which officials would impose upon a minority must be imposed generally. Conversely, nothing opens the door to arbitrary action so effectively as to allow those officials to pick and choose only a few to whom they will apply legislation and thus to escape the political retribution that might be visited upon them if larger numbers were affected. Courts can take no better measure to assure that laws will be just than to require that laws be equal in operation.

This case affords an illustration. Even casual observations from the sidewalks of New York will show that an ordinance which would forbid all advertising on vehicles would run into conflict with many interests, including some, if not all, of the great metropolitan newspapers, which use that advertising extensively. Their blandishment of the latest sensations is not less a cause of diverted attention and traffic hazard than the commonplace cigarette advertisements which this truck-owner is forbidden to display. . . .[21]

In the vagueness and delegation cases, it will be recalled, the Court finds that the legislature, if it did anything, did too much all at once; and that is deemed too little. The proposition put forward by Justice Jackson is that sometimes the legislature does too little, and that the Court may find this, standing alone, to be too much. The transition appears not unlike the one that I made from vagueness to the doctrine of desuetude, with the object, as here, of ensuring the discharge of political responsibility.[22] But this is to design conceptual arabesques. Justice Jackson's proposition has for the most part a spurious attraction only, and as stated, with Jacksonian éclat and universality, it will not bear analysis. To be sure, it offers a way of not reaching one broad ultimate issue of power—in the *Railway Express* case, whether advertising in the streets may be regulated—and of leaving open, with respect to this issue, the possibility of a legislative reprise. But what it thus avoids does not, in most instances, need to be avoided. And, as is so often true of the doctrine of motive as well, the Jacksonian proposition decides in confusion another and more difficult broad ultimate issue of power and, failing to face it, decides it wrongly. As to this issue, far from provoking the political institutions into responsible discharge of their function, it cuts off political power.

Equal protection, overlapping quite a bit with due process, has been the umbrella under which the Court has sheltered a number of constitutional principles. Under it, the Court has evolved the proscription of race as a criterion of governmental classification. Other criteria may be so proscribed—for example, ancestral nationality and religion, though as to the latter one would certainly cite as well the First Amendment's guaranty of religious freedom. Thayer's rule of the clear mistake, prohibiting caprice, is also catalogued under due process and equal protection. Thus, in the present state of human knowledge, any kind of governmental classification of the populace, for any purpose, in accordance with color of hair or eyes would—if such a measure is imaginable—be forbidden as irrational, although we may some day learn that men are significantly to be differentiated along such lines, and the Court might then permit legislation to take account of the difference. Beyond are differences which we now know to be differences —aliens and citizens, literate and illiterate, poor and rich, big and small, powerful and weak, loyal and disloyal, joiners and loners; or, to recur to the *Railway Express* case, the difference between doing in self-interest and doing for hire, and between advertising on trucks and advertising on billboards. As to these, it is perfectly obvious that they will be rationally relevant in some respects but not in others. If a legislature distinguishes between the rich and the poor in levying taxes, or between the literate and the illiterate in conferring the franchise, it is making a rational discrimination. If, however, it grants to the rich but not to the poor, or vice versa, the right to become licensed as chiropractors, or to the citizen but not to the alien the right to run a laundry, or if it guarantees to the literate but not to the illiterate, or vice versa, the right to strike in order to better their conditions of labor, then one would deem the action capricious and a clear mistake under Thayer's rule.

But in these examples judgment is easy, because I have posited the purpose of the legislative action, on which rationality of the classification turns. Judgment may follow with equal ease when the legislature, as happens with increasing frequency, states its purpose in a statutory preamble. Finding the purpose, however, may itself be a task of some difficulty, complicated by the irrationality of the classification when viewed in light of some, perhaps of the most obvious, possible purposes. This difficulty was present in the *Railway Express* case, as Justice Jackson pointed out, although he came—not altogether with rigorous consistency—to agree that the distinction between self-interest advertising and advertising for hire may be rationally relatable to a traffic-safety purpose. But Justice Jackson, concurring in the result, ignored the other point made by Railway Express, namely, that the discrimination between display advertising in Times Square and truck advertising was wholly irrational. The difficulty is even more tellingly illustrated by an earlier case involving a Florida statute that required carriers for hire to post security against liability for injuries caused by their negligence but exempted carriers of farm products and of certain seafoods.[23] If the sole purpose of this statute was to protect the public against negligent truck drivers, and if the sole purpose of the New York ordinance was traffic safety, then it is hard to defend the rationality of the classifications. The legislative purpose, however, may have been, not merely to regulate traffic and protect the public, but also to discriminate. Two policies may have been served in tandem, one of them being to discriminate—that is, to foster farm production, owner operation of trucks, and certain commercial activity around Times Square. These are surely not capricious ends; they involve choices in the ordering of social activity, made along lines of significant differences. Yet to say that these ends are not irrational is to leave open the question whether they are good. It is not irrational either, in the present state of our society, to take account of differences between black and white or Jew and Catholic. We are prepared to lay it down as to the latter that it is bad and impermissible for government to favor the one over the other. For the rest, where a discrimination has no rational relation to the stated purpose of a governmental action, we dispose of it on that ground. But since the purpose may be to discriminate, we must face the question, as a matter of principle, whether that purpose is allowable, for it is in itself not irrational.

The problem may be put in another and no doubt more functional way. We require our legislatures to live up to a certain standard of rationality. But they are political institutions, and we should not require them also to be disinterested; they are, indeed, the forum for clashes of interests, contests of power, which produce sometimes a winner and a loser, and sometimes a compromise. The prohibition against legislative caprice sets some limit to the possible victory and circumscribes in some measure possible compromises. The winning and losing groups, or the line dividing the contestants that is drawn by compromise, must have a basis in reality. There are some conceivable groupings of victors and losers which we do not recognize as legitimate because they do not correspond to groups that actually operate as such, or that may be expected to operate as such, in society and that may therefore rationally be thought to need regulation or deserve protection. That would be the case with redheads and blue-eyed people. Everything else, however, is a rational discrimination. Of course, to want to foster farming, or Times Square displays, or small business, or the oil industry—always at some social cost, at the expense of some other desirable end—is not a rational choice in the sense that reason compels it. It is a choice, and perhaps it would be as well to call it arational. But the fostering of redheads would be counter-rational, the product of sheer unreasoned will or emotion.

Black and white, Catholic and Jew, are held exempt, as groups, from having to try out their strength in the political marketplace. Such an exemption and such a warranty of equal treatment extend in some measure also to other groups—the literate and illiterate, alien and citizen, rich and poor, joiners and loners, Communists and Republicans. But the balance of moral considerations and felt needs comes out in these instances so as to forbid mere discriminatory choices while, on the other hand, permitting the legislature to take account of observable differences that relate rationally to some independent purpose, which is itself permissible. Thus the rich are more highly taxed, and the illiterate may be denied the vote. However, in *Wieman* v. *Updegraff*, the loyalty case discussed in Chapter 2, the purpose simply to favor loners over a certain type of joiner is not allowed to the legislature, and the rationality of the classification is judged—and found lacking—solely in relation to the independently permissible purpose of attaining a loyal public service. And in *Yick Wo* v. *Hopkins*, a purpose to bestow economic favors on white citizens but not on alien Chinese is foreclosed. But as to farmers, fishermen, truckers, billboard advertisers, and other economic groups, the legislature may simply make discriminatory choices; they are subject to regulation as such and may be favored or disadvantaged. They ought to be so subject and currently as well as in its main tradition, though not without aberrations, the Court has held them to be. To follow Justice Jackson's suggestion is nothing more or less than to lay down the contrary principle, without quite acknowledging it. The upshot of a Jacksonian holding, to be sure, is not that advertising in city streets is left "ungoverned and ungovernable." But the result is, on analysis, that the choice whether farming or owner trucking or commercial activity in Times Square is to be fostered or deterred in one or another fashion—this choice is left "ungoverned and ungovernable," beyond possibility of legislative reprise.[24]

And yet, the argument against the Jacksonian proposition is quite conclusive only so long as the alternatives are as I have stated them in the illustrations I have adduced. A decision that advertising in city streets is not subject to governmental regulation and a judgment that all truckers or all advertising media or all advertising interests must be treated alike are, at the most, about equally consequential; if anything, the latter judgment, which the Jacksonian method would make, seems more far-reaching and difficult than the former, which it would avoid. A principle that would forbid regulation of advertising is, after all, scarcely imaginable, and the considerations against legitimating the regulatory power are not readily apparent. But suppose that a state were to close its public schools, but did so only in cities of 100,000 population or more.[25] Or suppose that the federal government, invoking national security, were to enact that private homes may be searched for atomic materials at any time of the day or night without warrant, but exempted homes located in communities of less than 100,000 population. Here, principles of the first magnitude would be in play: the possible obligation of the states to provide public education, and the privacy of the people's homes. A judgment either checking or legitimating the power of government to do such things at all would obviously be enormously far reaching. A judgment that urban localities, on the one hand, and suburban and rural ones, on the other, may not be so classified, to such an end, without more of a showing of relationship between purpose and the discrimination in fact made would be a less consequential decision. It would be a very different matter here not to be satisfied with the explanation that it is "no requirement of equal protection that all evils of the same genus be eradicated or none at all." Here, to hold that "the prohibition or regulation must have a broader impact" would indeed be to invite more responsible—extraordinarily responsible—political action before deciding an issue of principle that is extraordinarily difficult and far reaching. This would be to require, much as do the concepts of vagueness, delegation, and desuetude, "in the candid service of avoiding a serious constitutional doubt,"[26] that the political institutions "turn square corners" when they go about achieving certain very serious and unusual ends. A certain resemblance suggests itself, not only to *Rumely* but also to the *Garner* sit-in case. But it must be added that the "candid service" is performed when the Court is candid in the performance.

The Square Corners of the Commerce Clause and of Procedural Due Process

The phrase "turn square corners," used a few sentences ago, is taken from an essay of Professor Paul A. Freund. This essay leads us to certain lesser doctrines that have been developed under the Commerce Clause, to certain problems of free speech that Mr. Freund has found to be analogous, and thence to problems of due procedure. "If the Court," says Mr. Freund, "does require a local government to turn square corners when it deals with interstate commerce or trade in ideas, it is vindicating its responsibility as the guardian of structure and process." The consequences of such judgments, he points out, are quite unlike "those of the era of judicial vetoes of economic legislation. There, certain kinds of activity were held utterly immune—men's hours of labor, wages, and prices. . . . The analogy to the commerce cases, on the other hand, means that governments may do things in a right way and not in a wrong—a disproportionately repressive—way."[27]

The Constitution confides to Congress the power to regulate

commerce among the several states and with foreign nations, and from this has been deduced the Supreme Court's function as guardian of the freedom of interstate and foreign commerce from obstructive or otherwise burdensome state regulatory or taxing measures. The Court early formulated, and justly attributed to the Framers of the Constitution, the principled goal of an open national economy—a common market, to use the term now current in Europe. This is an extremely broad general principle, excruciatingly difficult to apply. Obviously, a goodly set of subprinciples was needed if the Court was to cope with, align, and bring to judgment the endless variety of state regulatory and taxing measures that affect the national economy. Obviously also, as the operation of the Commerce Clause was rewarded with success and commerce became national, an increasing number of things the states did affected that commerce, and so the initially sufficient principle of the open economy began to need modification, unless, indeed, it was to operate with ultimate and unintended success so as to obliterate the states as governmental units. If the states were to continue to be governments, it could not long remain true, as a flat proposition, that they were not allowed to regulate or tax interstate commerce. It had to be added, as the wit of T. R. Powell did add, that the states might regulate and tax interstate commerce, but not too much. The task of the Supreme Court, Powell said, was to decide how much is too much.

This task the Court has performed over the decades with rough effectiveness; the American common market is witness to that. It has performed it, as many think, better than Congress might have done, because Congress is busy and its performance would have been more episodic than that of the Court, thus allowing more state measures to stand simply by default. Further, as Mr. Freund has remarked, for Congress the task "might have been felt to call for a duty of insularity"—Congress, after all, is easily fragmented into its component parts, and its component parts are insular.[28] But in passing on hundreds of measures, in deciding in hundreds of cases whether a state may regulate the length and stopping places of interstate trains, whether it may regulate trains and trucks for safety, whether it may exact from interstate trucks taxes to pay their way on the state's roads, whether and how it may tax the sale or use of goods coming in from another state, whether and how it may tax the income derived by an out-of-state corporation from business done within the state, and so on without end—the performance of the Court has not always been the model of principled constitutional adjudication.[29]

Commerce Clause decisions are considered constitutional. For they purport to be and are in fact binding on the states. Yet, although this was for a time in doubt, they are not binding on Congress. Every decision forbidding this or that state regulatory or taxing measure in the name of the Commerce Clause is subject to congressional reprise. Congress may permit the states to do what the Court has forbidden. More significantly, Congress is always free to enact nationally an economic regulation which the Court has held to be foreclosed to the states under the Commerce Clause. Hence, theoretically in any event, Commerce Clause decisions amount only to allocations of power among the political institutions, distributions from local to national ones; these allocations are, moreover, as Professor Ernest J. Brown has written, "tentative and subject to reallocation by Congress."[30] In practice, however, one is less justified here than elsewhere in treating the congressional reprise as an ordinary possibility. Instances of it exist, to be sure,[31] and particularly by way of the enactment of national regulation. All economic measures that Congress has enacted may be so regarded, and some are immediately traceable to Commerce Clause adjudications.[32] But specific congressional replies, permitting the states to do what the Court has forbidden, are relatively rare, essentially for reasons I have mentioned, which make the Court a more suitable body than Congress to assume the primary responsibility of policing the integrity of the national economy. Great numbers and a great variety of state measures are involved. Each generally has a quite narrow impact in itself and is unlikely to rouse national interest. Only if Congress should ever legislate comprehensively in the field and delegate power to fill in the details to a quasi-judicial administrative agency would it in this respect achieve the full reality of a senior partnership with the Court in the discharge of the Commerce Clause function.

The congressional reprise in each specific case may thus be insufficiently open, as a practical matter, to enable us to look upon

Commerce Clause decisions as exemplifying a method of the colloquy; but it is open, it has been availed of, and the fact is significant. Commerce Clause decisions, with their great number, their long history, and the intricacy of their facts, are on occasion (more frequently than in other areas) found to embody conflicting principles—sometimes, indeed, no intelligible rule of judgment at all. Many commentators take them for no more than pragmatic, prudential adjustments. And the question is asked, if this unprincipled, pragmatically expedient course of adjudication has been tolerable these many years under the Commerce Clause, why insist on the rigor and the restraints of a principled process elsewhere; why, for example, resist the Court's assumption of a similarly pragmatic task in respect of the problem of legislative apportionment? The answer is that it is not clear why one should take pride in the Court's failures in Commerce Clause cases, or in their frequency; and that in the degree in which these failures have perhaps been inevitable, inhering in the function, they have been rendered tolerable by the possibility of congressional revision, which has been forthcoming when the shoe has pinched worst, and which has in any event come freely and frequently as to the most important aspects of the problem, by way of enactment of national regulations. Stewardship by the Court of legislative apportionment is proposed without such recourse, and that is a very different matter.

There is another distinguishing feature of Commerce Clause decisions, and it is the one to which Mr. Freund refers in the passage I have given. Even viewed as constitutional adjudications, most Commerce Clause decisions are extremely narrow, and their place on the continuum of judicial power is far removed from such judgments as are ultimately called for with respect, for example, to birth control, congressional investigations, or legislative apportionment, let alone segregation of the races. They do not commonly hold any kind of activity "utterly immune," leaving it, in Justice Jackson's phrase, "ungoverned and ungovernable." Rather, most Commerce Clause cases raise questions, as Mr. Freund says, of structure and method. The Court's decisions may require the turning of square corners, but they do not generally foreclose the achievement of this or that governmental end.

This is not merely to say that Commerce Clause decisions, like other judgments of the Court, are not driven beyond the natural limits of the rule of principle; it is not merely that, by reason of the episodic nature of its interventions, as well as through denials of certiorari and other conscious decisions not to intervene, the Court here as elsewhere allows what Mr. Freund has called "a little fuzziness and untidiness at the edges."[33] That is what the passive devices achieve in avowedly tolerating deviations from principle. And that happens here as well.[34] But the point here goes beyond that to the content of the adjudications themselves. These tend to prescribe and proscribe methods, not ends. Sometimes when the Commerce Clause forecloses an economic regulation by a state, and very often when a state tax is struck down, another measure, achieving much the same and sometimes precisely the same purpose, arises to take its place. This may not be true throughout. Some Commerce Clause decisions may effectively cut off to the state the possibility of raising revenue from certain economic interests or of regulating them. But the vast bulk of Commerce Clause decisions must be analyzed, subjected to empirical study, and ranged with this question in view—do they guard "structure and process" and prescribe "standards and methods," or do they foreclose ends? Most will be found to be of the former variety.

Mr. Freund has located among the former variety also certain decisions safeguarding the right to freedom of speech against restrictive local ordinances or statutes. These are, in every sense, theoretical and practical, constitutional decisions. But the infirmities which they uncover in municipal or state measures are, as Mr. Freund says, curable.

Sound trucks may not be subjected to an unfettered licensing power, but may be controlled in respect of time and place and volume. Jehovah's Witnesses may not be subjected to a license tax from the distribution and sale of their literature, but other forms of taxation, such as net-income tax or a general-property tax, are presumably applicable. The Witnesses may not be forbidden by ordinance to knock on doors, but presumably an ordinance may make it criminal to do so where the householder has posted a notice. In actuality, therefore, these momentous constitutional cases frequently come down to such alternatives as whether the City Fathers may place on receptive householders the burden of posting a welcome or must place on resistant householders the burden of posting a sign of inhospitality. The difference is by no means trivial, but it need not be inflated to the dimensions of irreconcilable principles.[35]

Structure and method and the turning of square corners are what procedural due process is generally about also. A distinction is commonly taken in constitutional law between procedural and substantive decisions, as they are called; and it is generally valid, because procedural decisions for the most part point to infirmities that are curable. They deal with the "how" of governmental action, whereas substantive decisions go to ends, dealing with the "what." At one extreme, the narrowest kind of procedural decision, such as that in the *Garner* case, can scarcely be deemed a constitutional adjudication; it is a passive device of avoidance. When there is nothing to avoid, procedural decisions, like other ones, must stand on their own feet and are inadequate if not principled. But having regard to their consequences—of which we need more empirical studies than we have—they are generally found nearer the passive sector of the continuum of judicial power than so-called substantive ones. And they are, therefore, less affected by rules of limitation drawn from the premise of distrust of judicial review. Said Mr. Justice Jackson in one of the last and one of the most brilliant of his opinions:

Procedural due process is more elemental and less flexible than substantive due process. It yields less to the times, varies less with conditions, and defers much less to legislative judgment. Insofar as it is technical law, it must be a specialized responsibility . . . of the judiciary on which they do not bend before political branches of the Government, as they should on matters of policy which comprise substantive law.

Yet, as Justice Jackson went on to say, "only the untaught layman or the charlatan lawyer" could believe "that procedures matter not." Rather:

Procedural fairness and regularity are of the indispensable essence of liberty. Severe substantive laws can be endured if they are fairly and impartially applied. Indeed, if put to the choice, one might well prefer

to live under Soviet substantive law applied in good faith by our com-
mon-law procedures than under our substantive law enforced by Soviet
procedural practices.[36]

Well one might, particularly because procedural rules are not all
the same in respect of their consequences; they are not broadcast
on a single wave length. Most uncover curable defects. Some,
however, will foreclose effective pursuit of the substantive policy
at hand, because as a practical matter, no process or method other
than the one the Court has forbidden will do. When this is true
we must be aware of it, and it should be a consideration entering
into the making of a judgment. Cases in which this is true cannot
be viewed as dealing merely with "structure and process"; their
place on the constitutional spectrum is elsewhere, as Justice Jackson would have been the first to admit.[37]

The congressional-investigation and perhaps also the security-
dismissal cases that I have discussed were such cases, in which the
distinction between procedural and substantive issues had little
practical significance. To hold that procedural rules applicable to
criminal or even civil or administrative trials must govern congressional investigations would be effectively to foreclose achievement of the ends which the informing function exists to achieve.
There are faint suggestions in the majority opinions in the *Barenblatt* and *Wilkinson* cases that one generally applicable procedural
safeguard may yet be imposed on congressional investigation—
namely, the requirement of probable cause.[38] The government does
not proceed criminally against an individual unless it has reason
to believe, on reliable evidence, that he has probably committed
the offense for which he is to be put to the trouble and notoriety of
a trial. And the substantive criminal law has not been rendered
ineffective by this procedural rule. Yet the congressional-investiga-
tive power would in large measure be so rendered. It is, after all,
a visitorial, informing power, not a prosecutorial one, and it relies
on the fishing expedition, which starts nowhere, or with the merest
suspicion, and may end nowhere also, having assured itself that
no remedial action is necessary. Could the census taker or the
public-opinion sampler operate if he had to show probable cause?
The mere labeling of the requirement as procedural will not
change its effect in these circumstances.

The Judgment of This Court

Judicial review, I said indiscriminately in Chapter 1, in the initial attempt to pose the question of its compatibility with democratic government, is the power to construe and apply the Constitution in matters of the greatest moment against the wishes of a legislative majority which is, in turn, helpless to affect the judicial decision. In every country that has an independent judiciary, as Judge Charles E. Wyzanski, Jr., has reminded us, the judges, whether or not they are clothed with the constitutional authority of ours, "mold the people's view of durable principles of government."[39] Yet the constitutional function makes for a significant difference. It is what distinguishes the American Supreme Court as the most powerful, not merely the most influential, judicial body in the world. But this is a function that looms, for the most part, in the background. I have therefore thought it important, in the previous chapter and in this one, to emphasize the foreground.

The Court, Brandeis wrote in 1936, has "avoided passing upon a large part of all the constitutional questions thrust upon it for decision."[40] Moreover, constitutional decisions are not fungible quantities. As to many, while it may remain true that the legislative majority cannot affect the judicial decision, it is not true that the consequences are similarly out of control; our system is more resourceful than that. But in the end there are issues of the first and of final importance—shall one say, a residue of ultimates, though some are more and some less far reaching in their consequences—which the Court may pick, define, and decide in fulfillment of its role as the constitutional authority of last resort. The occasions are few but they are sufficient in number and impact to save from absurdity the indiscriminate approach that I took for purposes of the analysis in Chapter 1. And so the nagging question cannot be ignored: How and whence do nine lawyers, holding lifetime appointments, devise or derive principles which they are prepared to impose without recourse upon a democratic society? The principle of Thayer's rule of rationality may speak for itself. But what of other ones? The judges do not draw them ready made, as I have argued and as is surely apparent, from the

constitutional text, from history, or from the record of their own—
which is to say, their predecessors'—prior decisions. These are
not irrelevant materials, not ever. They are empirical aids, being
deposits of experience; they are sources of inspiration, instigators
of reflection, producers of mood. In short, they are the setting for
judgment and they condition it, but they are not its wellspring.

Ending an opinion, a few years ago, in which he held that government may not force disclosure of certain political associations
from a university teacher in such a way as to inhibit his freedom
to teach and to learn as he thinks fit, Mr. Justice Frankfurter said:

> To be sure, this is a conclusion based on a judicial judgment in bal-
> ancing two contending principles—the right of a citizen to political
> privacy, as protected by the Fourteenth Amendment, and the right of
> the State to self protection. And striking the balance implies the exer-
> cise of judgment. This is the inescapable judicial task in giving sub-
> stantive content, legally enforced, to the Due Process Clause, and it is
> a task ultimately committed to this Court. It must not be an exercise of
> whim or will. It must be an overriding judgment founded on something
> much deeper and more justifiable than personal preference. As far as it
> lies within human limitations, it must be an impersonal judgment. It
> must rest on fundamental presuppositions rooted in history to which
> widespread acceptance may fairly be attributed. Such a judgment must
> be arrived at in a spirit of humility when it counters the judgment of
> the State's highest court. But, in the end, judgment cannot be escaped
> —the judgment of this Court.[41]

The function of the Justices—and there is no question but what
this accords with the great authoritative body of opinion on the
subject—is to immerse themselves in the tradition of our society
and of kindred societies that have gone before, in history and in
the sediment of history which is law, and, as Judge Hand once
suggested, in the thought and the vision of the philosophers and
the poets. The Justices will then be fit to extract "fundamental
presuppositions" from their deepest selves, but in fact from the
evolving morality of our tradition. No doubt, as the late Zechariah
Chafee, Jr., wrote, "the man himself is a part of what he decides."
But, as he concluded, if "law is the will of the Justices," it is "the
will of the Justices trying to do that which is right."[42]

Fundamental presuppositions are not merely to be alluded to

(Justice Frankfurter's paragraph quoted above came at the conclusion of a long argument) or even merely intoned, but are to be traced and evaluated from the roots up, their validity in changing material and other conditions convincingly demonstrated, and their application to particular facts carried to the last decimal. This was the great strength of Brandeis, master, Chief Justice Hughes said, of both microscope and telescope.[43] Only through this effort, prescribed by his craft, can the conscientious judge himself be assured that he is not at sea, buffeted by the wavelets of his personal predilections. And only thus can he hope for the ultimate assent of those whom otherwise he governs irresponsibly. It is by no means to be inferred, of course, that the life of the law is or has been logic. Holmes told us that it has not been, and we should now really stay told once and for all. But it may be inferred that the life of the law is reason, and *that* in no narrow or technical sense either. Writing about esthetic issues that I believe are cognate, Dwight Macdonald has indicated the appropriate method of verification. What standards, he asked, should apply to literary judgments? How does one prove that Faulkner was an important artist and that J. P. Marquand was not? "Faulkner's superiority," Mr. Macdonald answered,

cannot be proved, [but] it can be demonstrated, a quite different operation involving an appeal—by reason, analysis, illustration, and rhetoric—to cultural values which critic and reader have in common, values no more susceptible of scientific statement than are the moral values-in-common to which Jesus appealed but which, for all that, exist as vividly and definitely as do mercy, humility, and love.[44]

A judge, wrote Mr. Chafee in a similar vein, "is likely to be resorting to a body of principles which may have no physical location, but neither has courage nor loyalty nor love of truth."[45] I would suggest as a classic example of the constitutional function in full flight Brandeis' dissent in *Olmstead* v. *United States*[46] in which he sought to demonstrate that unauthorized wire-tapping violates a principle growing out of the Fourth Amendment's guaranty that the people shall be secure against unreasonable searches and seizures. I would assert that the rightness of the Court's decision in the *School Segregation Cases* can be demonstrated in like fashion. I would deny, however, that any similar demonstration can be or was mounted—could have been mounted even by a Brandeis —to show that a statute setting maximum hours or minimum wages violates fundamental presuppositions of our society.

But if there are fundamental presuppositions which men may— and which the Court should—seize and demonstrate, why cannot the Justices succeed in demonstrating them to one another? Why is there so much dissent on the Court? Why is the unanimity in the *Segregation Cases* such a celebrated rarity? Why did even Holmes and Brandeis come to differ in a case touching the rights of property owners?[47] Several sorts of answers are to be made. Men agreed on principle may differ in the acuity of their analysis of the concrete situation before them; men differ in capacity and learning. Truth, we may say with Renan, is constituted of nuances, and these are not equally visible to everyone. Moreover, as Mr. Chafee did not fail to observe in the essay from which I have quoted, "We cannot get outside ourselves to do our thinking and each of us inevitably puts something of himself into the general principles by which he shapes his conclusions about a set of facts, even undisputed facts."[48] Finally, although we collectively profess what Holmes, speaking individually, called "can't helps," yet there are no ineluctable, universal, timeless absolutes in the art of ordering society; hence, as I remarked before, the most fundamental of one man's fundamental presuppositions, most ideally arrived at, will not always be another's. That is why we prefer a nine-man Court.

The search for the deepest controlling sources, for the precise "how" and the final "whence" of the judgment that "cannot be escaped—the judgment of this Court," may, after all, end in the attempt to express the inexpressible. This is not to say that the duty to judge the judgment might as well be abandoned. The inexpressible can be recognized, even though one is unable to parse it. In any event, since we are talking about judgment by the Supreme Court in the American democracy, there is one element of it—the crucial element—which is somewhat more easily dealt with. Judgment must "rest on fundamental presuppositions rooted in history," Mr. Justice Frankfurter wrote, *"to which widespread accept-ance may fairly be attributed."* The qualifying clause is the thing.

And it is, indeed, a component of the judicial judgment that is easily dealt with, at least in theory—causing the other pieces of the puzzle to fall readily into place as well—if what is meant is that the Court is restricted to declaring an existing national consensus; that it is to enforce as law only the most widely shared values, so widely shared that they can be said to have the assent of something like Calhoun's concurrent majorities. But this would charge the Court with a function to which it is, of all our institutions, least suited. Surely the political institutions are more fitted than the Court to find and express an existing consensus—so long, at least, as the science of opinion sampling is no further developed than it is. What is meant, rather, is that the Court should declare as law only such principles as will—in time, but in a rather immediate foreseeable future—gain general assent. Very near the end of his life, the late Judge Learned Hand made the point in a moving passage (though he was speaking of the judicial function as a whole, not merely in constitutional cases):

After many years of effort to attain at once that degree of detachment in the discharge of what is inevitably a duty to fabricate, I have not yet lost a sense of joy when, for the moment anyway, I hope that in a given controversy I may have found a solution that will seem at least tolerable to those who are not committed in advance.[49]

The Court is a leader of opinion, not a mere register of it, but it must lead opinion, not merely impose its own; and—the short of it is—it labors under the obligation to succeed.

In one sense, we have thus got no nearer to parsing the inexpressible. "These judges," Mr. Justice Frankfurter was reduced to telling the American Philosophical Society in 1954, ". . . must have something of the creative artist in them; they must have antennae registering feelings and judgment beyond logical, let alone quantitative, proof."[50] But in another sense, the matter is far advanced once it is seen that the Court must pronounce only those principles which can gain "widespread acceptance," that it is at once shaper and prophet of the opinion that will prevail and endure. To be sure, there is still not much help in "quantitative proof"; it is still a question of "antennae."[51] But we can be much clearer concerning ways to go about the task, to limit its challenge and make it manageable. The first wisdom, as I have tried to show, is that the moment of ultimate judgment need not come either suddenly or haphazardly. Its timing and circumstances can be controlled. On the way to it, both the Court and the country travel the paths of the many lesser doctrines, passive and constitutional, that I have sought to describe and assess. Over time, as a problem is lived with, the Court does not work in isolation to divine the answer that is right. It has the means to elicit partial answers and reactions from the other institutions, and to try tentative answers itself. When at last the Court decides that "judgment cannot be escaped —the judgment of this Court," the answer is likely to be a proposition "to which widespread acceptance may fairly be attributed," because in the course of a continuing colloquy with the political institutions and with society at large, the Court has shaped and reduced the question, and perhaps because it has rendered the answer familiar if not obvious. In these continuing colloquies, the profession—the practicing and teaching profession of the law —plays a major role; the law, as Bentham long ago remarked, is made, not by judge alone, but by judge and company. But in American society the colloquy goes well beyond the profession and reaches deeply into the places where public opinion is formed.

I do not wish to maintain that this process is as deliberate, as well understood, or as well managed—by the judges, by the profession or by the public—as it might be. The modest effort of this book is to contribute to better understanding of it and to greater deliberation in its management. But my thesis is that such is in fact the process of judicial review carried on by the American Supreme Court. And perhaps one brief study in contrasts might serve further to illustrate both its imperfection and its actual operation. The judges have in the past decade declared and enforced the moral principle that the races must not be segregated by authority of the state. Many people, including judges—for example, as he has told us, Mr. Justice Frankfurter[52]—are equally opposed, on the profoundest of moral grounds, to capital punishment. Yet, as Professor Charles L. Black, Jr., has suggested[53] and as surely most lawyers would agree, it is just now quite unthinkable that the Supreme Court should, in the next death case to come before it, declare capital punishment unconstitutional—under the

Due Process Clause, let us say, or under the Cruel and Unusual Punishments Clause of the Eighth Amendment. But only a short-sighted and rather imprisoned lawyer would maintain that capital punishment can never be declared unconstitutional. It will be said that, of course, the difference is plain to see. Even as of 1954, national consensus on the racial problem was immanent; it is not on the abolition of capital punishment. But we do not really *know* this to be true, nor do we know how to find out, readily and reliably.[54] Moreover, if, or to the extent that, this is true, the important question is how it came to be in the one case, and whether similar conditions can be brought about in the other.

Events quite outside the Court's field of influence played their part, no doubt—chiefly the Second World War, consequent Negro economic and political emancipation, and presidential pressure during the Truman Administration. But for a generation, starting, as I have noted, before the War, the Court itself, while avoiding head-on collision with the practice of segregation, had put it in question and had eroded it, at least so far as higher education was concerned. It had gone even further with respect to segregation in housing.[55] And all this despite its own nineteenth-century error in engrafting the *principle* of segregation onto the mere *practice* of it. On the other hand, what of capital punishment? It has for some time been true, as the late Justice Jackson once remarked, and as Barrett Prettyman, Jr., has recently substantiated, that "When the penalty is death, we, like state court judges, are tempted to strain the evidence and even, in close cases, the law in order to give a doubtfully condemned man another chance."[56] It is currently, if not altogether satisfactorily, the law that the Court will require the states to provide counsel to indigent defendants in all capital cases, regardless of variant circumstances, whereas the same defendant may be convicted without counsel in a non-capital case, if in light of all the circumstances his trial has been fair and his other rights respected.[57] For a season it was the law that the United States could not subject dependents of military personnel overseas to trial by court-martial for capital offenses committed there but could do so in the case of lesser crimes. (The rule has since been corrected—if that is the right word—by the foreclosure of court-martial jurisdiction in all such cases.)[58] These attitudes and decisions are explained as groping efforts toward the shaping and reduction of the ultimate question, which is the moral admissibility of capital punishment itself.

Unfortunately, from the point of view of one who disbelieves in legal killing, and despite a history of past agitation and a present trend in the Western world toward abolition, the Court has missed or has willfully passed up its most signal opportunities to shape and reduce the issue. No sort of colloquy can be said to be in progress, and, barring spectacular extraneous events, the moment of judgment is therefore a generation or more away. The Court has legitimated the horror of a second (and successful) electrocution of the same man, which the sovereign state of Louisiana thought itself entitled to administer, because a first one had been accidentally botched.[59] The Court has twice legitimated the execution of men whose sanity was in question, leaving determination of their sanity to the private judgment of a governor and a warden, without benefit of any sort of procedural safeguard.[60] In the *Rosenberg* atom-spy case of 1953, the Court not only declined to "strain the law" but strained the other way and lent its acquiescence, if no more, to a proceeding of grisly speed, consummated in an atmosphere of the tumbril rolling to the guillotine and the heads being shown to the mob.[61] In the equally unspeakable *Chessman* case, the Court's role was less affirmatively discreditable, but its opportunity was greater. Owing to accident, irregularity, and error—some of it harmless and all of it, perhaps, curable and eventually cured—but in any event, accident chargeable to no one and irregularity and error for which the state was responsible, it took California, assisted by the federal courts including the Supreme Court, more than eleven years to summon up the certitude that Chessman might be put to a "just" death for an offense that was by then quite possibly, under amended statutes, no longer capital. It was nothing short of perverse to turn this course of events and its duration into a reproach against the condemned man. Yet that is exactly what many people did; the feeling came upon them that the choice was between Chessman and their institutions, that to allow the former to continue litigating was to threaten the latter, and that the only way to stop him was to kill him. And so it was done, and the Court declined to interfere.[62]

What the Court should have done was to declare that killing Chessman in 1960, after years in the death house, was a punishment infinitely more ghastly than killing him in 1948 would have been, and that under all the peculiar, hardly-to-be-repealed circumstances, the Constitution forbade it. Thus a process might have been set in motion to whose culmination in an ultimate broader judicial judgment, at once widely acceptable and morally elevating, we might have looked in the calculable future.

CHAPTER 6

The Supreme Court at the Bar of Politics

I have adverted repeatedly, at about every decisive point in the argument of this book, to the *School Segregation Cases,* for they at once epitomize and challenge all that I have tried to say about the role of the Supreme Court in American government. A direct and rather more comprehensive look at these cases is now called for, because their career since May 17, 1954, the date of decision, brings into view another element in the singular accommodation we have achieved between authoritarian judicialism and the practice of democracy. I have suggested that the rule of principle in our society is neither precipitate nor uncompromising, that principle may be a universal guide but not a universal constraint, that leeway is provided to expediency along the path to, and alongside the path of, principle, and, finally, that principle is evolved conversationally not perfected unilaterally. All this the decision in the *School Segregation Cases* illustrates. But it illustrates also what I have not yet touched on and what is commonly more obscure— another sort of colloquy that can take place after the declaration of governing principle by the Court, and another sort of reprise that is open to the political institutions and to society at large.

Everybody knows that the lifetime of applied principle is often no longer than one or two generations. Principle may endure beyond that, of course, but not necessarily as formulated in the application; if it does endure, it will often be through a process of renewal. And so what one means by the ultimate, final judgment of the Court is quite frequently a judgment ultimate and final for a generation or two.[1] That, however, is quite long enough to worry about, and the really interesting question, therefore, is what happens within the generation or two. Here the history of the *School Segregation Cases* sheds its light.

Composing for the Anthologies

The *School Segregation Cases* were five suits by individual Negro children praying that they be admitted to previously all-white schools, from which the local authorities had excluded them on the ground that they were Negroes and must attend schools reserved solely for Negroes. Thus was the issue raised whether separate schools for the two races are permissible in principle. The Court decided that they are not and that Negro children must have full entry to a common public-school system, free of restrictions or classifications based on race; so that, there being no other valid reason for excluding a Negro child from a school previously reserved for whites, race could not be erected into such a reason, and the Negro child must be admitted. That was the decision of May 17, 1954. But no decrees issued from the Court on that date. The formulation of appropriate decrees presented, the Court said, "problems of considerable complexity." Therefore, the Court called the parties to another argument at which they were to address themselves to these problems. Must it, the Court asked, order the immediate admission of Negro children to schools of their choice, within the limits of normal school districting, or may the Court "permit an effective gradual adjustment to be brought about from existing segregated systems to a system not based on color distinctions"?[2]

Like poetry, then, as a verse by Auden tells us, the great *School Segregation* decision of May 17, 1954, made nothing happen. But only like poetry. Only as it may sometimes seem that nothing but power, purposefully applied, can affect reality, only thus could it be said that this first decision had no consequences. And this is a species of romantic illusion. In fact, announcement of the principle was in itself an action of great moment, considering the source from which it came. Immediately, in the phrase Lincoln used about slavery, segregation was placed "where the public mind shall rest in the belief that it is in course of ultimate extinction"; and very shortly, in many places, there was a palpable effect. By early 1955, although there had as yet been no decree and there was thus no command outstanding which bound anyone to act, more than five hundred school districts had abandoned policies of segregation. This did not represent a large percentage of all segregated districts, and the number of Negro pupils actually admitted to white schools was even less impressive. Still, some 250,000 Negro pupils were affected. Although by far not all were now in white schools, some were, and, in any event, the racial barrier had been removed. This degree of integration had taken place in St. Louis and elsewhere in Missouri, in Baltimore, in West Virginia, Kentucky, Oklahoma, Tennessee, Texas, New Mexico, and Arizona, and in two school districts in Arkansas, where later the crisis of Little Rock was to strike. None of these cities and states was a party to the actual Supreme Court cases. Integration had taken place also in Delaware and Kansas, which were involved in the litigated cases, and most massively in Washington, D.C., also a litigant.[3]

In the fall of 1954, there had been some minor trouble. Segregation may be a way of life, but it subsumes racism, and that, in turn, is an idea, and it can be a fighting idea. So, provoked sometimes by itinerant agitators, a few riots flared up here and there in Delaware, Maryland, and West Virginia. They were promptly and easily quelled by local officials who knew what they were doing and why. One small community in Delaware, which had integrated eleven Negroes in a school with 665 whites, gave up in the face of some rioting.[4] But this was an isolated instance. On the whole, what followed immediately upon the Court's pronouncement of principle was encouraging and edifying. It spoke well for the effective role of the institution in the American system.

Very edifying, a demonstration of the spell the Court is capable of casting, a manifestation of its prestige, of the force of its mystique, and of the dominion of ideas. But the Court does not sit to make precatory pronouncements. It is not a synod of bishops, nor a collective poet laureate. It does not sit, Mr. Freund has remarked, "to compose for the anthologies."[5] If it did, its effectiveness would be of an entirely different order; and if it did, we would not need to worry about accommodating its function to the theory and practice of democracy. The Court is an organ of government. It is a court of law, which wields the power of government in disposing of concrete controversies. Therefore, although pronouncement of the principle of May 17, 1954, was in itself not an ineffectual act, it did not alone discharge the function of the Court. Jurisdiction having been assumed, that function required issuance of a legal decree.

All Deliberate Speed

In the vast majority of cases—barring those that are dismissed outright as not suitable for adjudication—the normal and expected judgment of the Court is a crisp and specific writing which tells one of the parties exactly what he must do, such as pay a judgment, deliver certain real estate, cease from doing something, or, indeed, go to jail. The equivalent in these cases would have been a decree ordering the named children, and perhaps, since these were class actions, all children in the five school districts affected who were similarly situated, to be admitted forthwith to the white schools of their choice. The question is, why should the Court not have issued such a decree? Indeed, one might have asked whether the Court could do other than issue such a decree?

If the Court, at the other extreme from merely composing for the anthologies, sat merely to render *ad hoc* judgments applicable solely to the precise circumstances of a controversy immediately before it, then also it would not be the powerful institution it is, and its function would need no elaborate justification. The matrix paradox of all paradoxes concerning the Court is, as I have noted, that the Court may only decide concrete cases and may not pronounce general principles at large; but it may decide a constitutional issue only on the basis of general principle. In the performance of this function—to use a fittingly lofty phrase of Chief Justice Hughes—the Court's "mental vision embraces distant scenes."[6] Hence, while the cases immediately before the Court exemplified and concretized the issue of principle, they could not be treated as if they involved only the admission of three or four dozen children to a dozen schools. Rather, these five cases did necessarily bring into view the total situation in all the states having school districts which are organized on a segregated basis. The admission of a few dozen children to a few dozen schools would have presented no very grave difficulties calling for a study of means of gradual adjustment. Seen in its totality, however, as involving some 5,000 school districts, nearly nine million white children and nearly three million colored, the situation exhibited great variety and complexity. To begin with, a vast number of statutes and regulations, incorporating centrally or marginally the rule of segregation, would require change in order to conform to the new principle. In most places, pupils are assigned to schools in accordance with the location of their homes. Where there were two schools, one white and one Negro, residential lines would now have to be drawn purely on a geographical basis, rather than, as previously, in accordance with both geography and race. But the two schools may not have been of equal size or otherwise of equal character. Thus elimination of the racial criterion may create a new and expensive problem before solving the old one. In general, running two segregated school systems is more expensive than running a single integrated one. But that is not to say that the process of integration might not require some immediate additional expenditures. And the cost of money is either money or time. Further complications: New assignments and other administrative arrangements for teachers, including Negro teachers, would have to be made. School transportation would have to be rearranged. No doubt, since Negro schools had seldom been fully equal to white ones, and since many Negro pupils came from economically and culturally depressed families, differences in educational background and aptitudes would be found between Negro and white pupils, and allowance might have to be made for these in the process of integration.

These and yet additional problems varied greatly from place to place, from cities to rural districts, and in relation, among other things, to the ratio of Negro to white pupils in a given district. No solution could be fabricated and made effective overnight, no matter what anyone might wish.[7] Moreover, the Court itself bore some responsibility for the situation it now faced. The practice of segregation was no invention of the Court, to be sure. But segregation had prospered and come to full flower at least partly in reliance upon the Court's decision, in 1896, that it conformed to constitutional principle. No one hearing the late John W. Davis, who argued to the Court in behalf of South Carolina, emphasize how pervasive and how solidly founded the present order was could fail to be sensible of the difficulties to be encountered in uprooting it. "Sometime to every principle," Mr. Davis remarked, "comes a moment of repose when it has been so often announced, so confidently relied upon, so long continued, that it passes the limits of judicial discretion and disturbance."[8] Mr. Davis was intimating that the existing order was no longer subject to judicial change, that no principle of its alteration could now be announced. This was to deny the essence of the Court's function, and on the basis of no more than an inadmissibly static view of society. But the suggestion that judicial alteration of so deep-rooted an order of things raises special problems to which the Court must have due regard—that could not be ignored.

It is unusual but not unheard of for the Court—for all courts, in the general run of business, constitutional and otherwise—to be faced with practical factors that make it impossible to achieve immediately a result called for by the Court's decision. Thus in applying the antitrust laws the Court may find—has in fact found —that a large corporation, the American Tobacco Company, for example, was a near-monopoly and violated the antitrust laws, and that it should be dissolved and split into its component parts. Or the Court may find, as it recently did, that ownership by the DuPont Corporation of a potentially controlling block of shares in the General Motors Corporation violates the antitrust laws, and that the relationship should be severed. But such things cannot be made to happen in a day.[9] Here is the elemental demonstration of the truth that very often society can only strive to attain the rule of principle through a tangle of perverse and intractable existing facts, which are themselves man-made but which are not any the less real for that. Pupil-assignment rules were willfully scrambled by men pursuing racist ends rather than ordained of God; but that does not render them any easier to unscramble overnight, once the racist principle has been extracted. There is

embedded in Anglo-American law, quite aside from the peculiar
function of constitutional adjudication, the recognition that, on
occasion, the law proposes but, for a time at least, the facts of life
dispose. The mainstream of Anglo-American legal development
has been the common law, administered by judges who evolved and
reasoned from principle. But there soon flowed alongside the
common law another stream, the equity jurisdiction, whose head-
waters were in the discretionary royal prerogative. Equity was a
more flexible process, more unprincipled, initially quite *ad hoc*. It
often worked the accommodation that made the rigorous principles
of the common law fit to live with. Our courts in general now
combine both functions—common law and equity—and so does
the process of judicial review.

The considerations I have recited are significant and would by
themselves have led the Court, in the exercise of equity discretion, to allow southern communities some time in which to comply
with the principle of integration; these considerations nevertheless leave out of account the most important factor. This is the
unpalatable but undeniable fact that the principle of the integration of the races ran counter to the views and the strong emotions,
not merely the customary practice, of a majority of the people to
whose way of life it was to be chiefly applicable; that is to say,
most southern whites. Despite the prefatory work that had been
in progress, as I have indicated, for over a generation, despite
many hopeful steps toward the integration of universities in the
South,[10] and, in any event, the absence of any concerted political
offensive against such integration or against other judicial measures enforcing equal treatment of the races—despite all that,
resistance could be expected. This does not mean that the principle
of integration was wrong or not suitable for pronouncement by the
Court in discharge of the constitutional functions, nor even that
the Court should have had more pause before announcing it,
fearing that it was not a fundamental presupposition "to which
widespread acceptance may fairly be attributed." First, even if the
task of the Court were, in Mr. Dooley's phrase, to follow the election returns, surely the relevant returns would be those from the
nation as a whole, not from a white majority in a given region.
Fragmented returns cannot count, any more than early ones.

Secondly, as we have seen, the Court's principles are required to gain assent, not necessarily to have it. Yet the fact of foreseeable opposition, like the fact of confident reliance, "so long continued," that Mr. Davis stressed, could not be ignored; it constituted an additional problem.

The problem was not simply one of enforcement. The task of the Court is to seek and to foster assent, and compliance through assent. Of course, we normally enforce some of our law—the criminal law, for example—forthwith and without recourse. But the analogy from the *Segregation Cases* to criminal statutes and the like fails completely. The latter are generally based on almost universal acceptance and need to be enforced only against an infinitesimal minority, consisting of the irreducible number of the antisocial. When they are not so based, they are commonly ineffective. Witness the great prohibition experiment. Witness also anti-gambling statutes, most sex laws, and other laws policing morals. Indeed, we have built-in devices for ensuring the ineffectiveness of such laws—for example, the discretion of prosecutors, who are most often politically sensitive officers, and the grand and petit jury systems. When we say, as we often do, that government should not try to enforce morality by law, we mean that in our system it cannot enforce it, if it is merely an idiosyncratic morality or a falsely professed morality, not the generally accepted one. It follows that in achieving integration, the task of the law—and all the more, the task of judicial rather than legislative law—was not to punish law breakers but to diminish their number. For what was to be foreseen was the resistance, not of a fringe of misfits, but of a populace. In such circumstances, it may not be prudent to force immediate compliance.

This brings me to a third and very closely connected reason that the Court did not order sudden execution of the principle pronounced in the *Segregation Cases*. The foreseeable opposition was localized, indeed isolated; but, by the same token, it was entrenched in a cluster of states, where it formed a majority. Thus concentrated, it could wield power disproportionate to what its numbers would give it if distributed nationwide. Hence, just possibly, the cooperation of the political branches might be needed in fostering the necessary acceptance; and it could well be looked for, since the Solicitor General of the United States, responding to the Court's request for an expression of views as *amicus curiae,* had appeared and supported the cause of the Negro plaintiffs. Normally, to be sure, the Court relies on its own great and mystic prestige and on the skilled exertion of its educational faculty, and finds them quite sufficient even to overcome or otherwise direct the will of the political branches. But here exceptional circumstances were in prospect. Moreover, there might be, not only resistance to the full reach of the new principle, but even difficulty with the enforcement of specific decrees. In an enforcement crisis of any real proportions, the judiciary is wholly dependent upon the Executive. The Court commands no significant police power of its own. It is true that both in practice and in theory the Executive is obliged to come to the judiciary's support in any such crisis. Good order demands it, regardless of the merits. But there are degrees of enthusiasm in rendering executive support, and there are ways of emphasizing order above, rather than alongside of, the decision that is to be enforced. If, then, one of those rare occasions was to be foreseen when the cooperation of the political institutions might be needed both in fostering consent and quite possibly in administering enforcement, the Court was entitled to consider that those institutions are uncomfortable in the presence of hard and fast principles calling for universal and sudden execution. They respond naturally to demands for compromise, and, of course, they contain within themselves representatives of the opposition that was to be foreseen. They can most readily be expected to exert themselves when some leeway to expediency has been left open. Therefore, time and an opportunity for accommodation were required not only for the other reasons I have mentioned; they were needed also to form part of the invitation that the Court might be extending to the political institutions to join with it in what amounted to a major enterprise of social reform.

It was argued to the Court by the National Association for the Advancement of Colored People, which represented the Negro children, that the task of making the Court's principle accepted and effective would be facilitated by a sort of shock treatment, an order of immediate and sudden execution, rather than by allowing time for accommodation. The argument was that "gradualism, far from facilitating the process, may actually make it more difficult; that, in fact, the problems of transition will be a good deal less complicated than might be forecast. . . . Our submission is that this, like many wrongs, can be easiest and best undone, not by 'tapering off' but by forthright action."[11] Conceivably this might have been so, but certainly it was not a broadly shared view. What the Court was more widely urged to do, especially by the Solicitor General, and what it did was in effect to require the local school boards to submit to the lower federal courts plans providing for a start toward integration—that is, to begin with, the admission of a few children here and there on some staged scheme. Any such plan would have to contain also the promise of eventual full compliance, meaning an eventually unified school system in which children would be assigned to schools without distinction of race, although other criteria, including residential ones, might still be effective. The Court set no deadlines. None was seriously urged, it being realized, as the Solicitor General pointed out, that conditions vary and "that maximum periods tend to become minimum periods."[12] The test for each plan would be whether it was moving in good faith toward integration "with all deliberate speed."

A most elusive phrase. Many have wondered—some among the literati have wondered a bit patronizingly—whether it was meant to bring to mind the refrain in "The Hound of Heaven," the magnificent devotional by the English Catholic poet Francis Thompson. That refrain is "Deliberate speed, majestic instancy," and the reference is to the Hound of Heaven's unrelenting pursuit of the sinner fleeing from grace. One may find here a suggestive allusion. However, the professional mind recognized, or thought it recognized, the phrase more readily as one familiar to ancient equity practice. Interestingly enough, the formula does not ring quite true to the language of English equity. The familiar phrase appears to have been "with all *convenient* speed." Further efforts to uncover the true origins of the formula have been unable to avoid the poets. Byron used the phrase in his correspondence, and, if one forces the translation a trifle, it can be found in Goethe.[13]

A phrase, then, that resembles poetry and resembles equity techniques of discretionary accommodation between principle and expediency, but that fits precisely one thing only, namely, the unique function of judicial review in the American system. The formula does not signify that the process of judicial review will involve itself in finding expedient compromises for a difficult situation. It means only that the Court, having announced its principle, and having required a measure of initial compliance, resumed its posture of passive receptiveness to the complaints of litigants. The political institutions might work out their compromises. Some of these might not return to be litigated at all. Some would. The Court placed itself in position to engage in a continual colloquy with the political institutions, leaving it to them to tell the Court what expedients of accommodation and compromise they deemed necessary. The Court would reply in the negative—and did eventually once so reply[14]—only when a suggested expedient amounted to the abandonment of principle. On the other hand, the Court would not approve, let alone itself work out, agreeable compromises, though the lower federal courts might take a hand. More typically, the passive devices of the colloquy precede, and prepare or avoid, the moment of constitutional judgment. Such was their role in most of the situations canvassed in Chapter 4. In the *Segregation Cases* the deliberate-speed formula opened a colloquy following judgment and called for employment of the passive devices to ease the way to its acceptance and effectuation.

Political Warfare and the Uses of Decisions of Courts

The initial reaction to the Court's decision, both in 1954 and in 1955, when the deliberate-speed decree came down, augured very well indeed for full acceptance, following a period of adjustment that would itself do no violence to principle. As I have indicated, the border states and especially the great border cities, as well as other marginal areas, began immediate compliance, even before issuance of the decree. In the rest of the South, the situation was this. There were some uncompromising, vaguely defiant comments by such as Herman Talmadge, then governor of Georgia, and Senator James O. Eastland, of Mississippi. But they were highly exceptional. Senator Richard B. Russell, of Georgia, attacked the Court rather sharply, but in substance went no farther than losing litigants often do. James F. Byrnes, then governor of South Carolina, was "shocked," but restricted himself to urging everyone "to exercise restraint and preserve order." These, too, were extremes, and they did not amount to a good-sized cloud on the horizon. Senator Harry F. Byrd, of Virginia, though imperiously critical, called only for "exercise of the greatest wisdom" and for "sober and exhaustive consideration," which—having regard to the Byzantine style of the Virginia machine—was taken as a signal to the faithful that they should avoid talk of abolishing the public schools. Senator Russell Long, of Louisiana, while regretting the decision, added: "My oath requires me to accept it as law. . . . I urge all Southern officials to avoid any sort of rash or hasty action." Senator Spessard L. Holland, of Florida, deplored spending "all our time in vain regrets." He advised "trying, as apparently the [Florida] State Cabinet has been doing along with officials and educators of both races at the local level, to learn how to bring it about." The governor of Arkansas, Francis Cherry, said: "Arkansas will obey the law. It always has." Governor Thomas Stanley, of Virginia, promised to "work toward a plan which will be acceptable to our children and in keeping with the edict of the Court. Views of the leaders of both races will be invited. . . ." The governor of North Carolina, William Ulmstead, though "terribly disappointed," said that "this is no time for rash statements or the proposal of impossible schemes." Texas, said Governor Allan Shivers, would comply, although it would take time to work out the details. Many school boards were beginning work on the details. The Virginia Superintendent of Public Instruction, Dr. Dowell J. Howard, foreswore any defiance. "We are trying to teach school children the law of the land," he said, "and we will abide by it."[15]

That was 1955. Three years later, by the fall of 1958, the segregation problem in the South looked like the American Algeria. It was pervasive, affecting the national posture in almost every aspect. It was a heavy drain on the sense of national purpose and integrity. And it was itself adrift. The judicial process had reached the limit of its capacity. The second battle of Little Rock had been fought to a Pyrrhic victory. Schools were closed in Little Rock and in Virginia. Congress and the presidency, each in its own way and for its own reasons, were immobilized. Four years later—a full seven years after the Court's decision—the situation appears very different again. In 1957 and 1958, the two battles of Little Rock seemed like First and Second Manassas. Today it is possible to see them as a Gettysburg, and to surmise that in the perspective of history they will represent the high-water mark of segregation. It is important to understand how this came about, because the crisis and its resolution—although, as at Gettysburg, we witness only resolution of the crisis, not settlement of the problem—served to illumine the role of the Supreme Court in our system, the capacities and the limitations of the institution.

In some indeterminate measure, the initial muted reaction to the Court's decision may have reflected simple shock. In some measure also, we witnessed the calm of incredulity. People could not bring themselves to believe that integration would really happen, and they entertained hopes of voluntary self-segregation by the Negro community. As reality bore down, some of the calm might have been dissipated in any event, and the unstructured individual in-fighting that characterizes southern politics might have helped to dispel it.[16] We really cannot tell. We do know, however, that a turning point came—distinctly and unmistakably, at least in retrospect—on March 11, 1956, with issuance of the Congressional Manifesto of that date by nearly the full membership of the southern delegation. This document was a calculated declaration of political war against the Court's decision. Formally, the Manifesto planted itself four-square on *Marbury* v. *Madison* and on modern literalist-absolutist attitudes, and rested there very comfortably indeed. I will quote the so-called legal argument of the Manifesto at some length and invite the reader, in a famous phrase, to lay these passages from the Manifesto beside the attitudes and views I explored in Chapter 2, and to decide whether the latter square with the former. The Founding Fathers, says the Manifesto, gave us a Constitution of checks and balances because they realized the inescapable lesson of history that no man or group of men can be safely entrusted with unlimited power. They framed this Constitution with its provisions for change by amendment in order to secure the fundamentals of government against the dangers of temporary popular passion or the personal predilections of public office holders.

We regard the decision of the Supreme Court in the school cases as clear abuse of judicial power. It climaxes a trend in the Federal judiciary undertaking to legislate, in derogation of the authority of Congress, and to encroach upon the reserved rights of the states and the people.

The original Constitution does not mention education. Neither does the Fourteenth Amendment nor any other amendment. The debates preceding the submission of the Fourteenth Amendment clearly show that there was no intent that it should affect the systems of education maintained by the states.

This was the form of the attack, in its own terms quite effective —an attack on the legitimacy of the decision, based on the conception of a plainly written Constitution, to be applied literally and not otherwise. The substance of the attack was quite another matter; it proceeded from different and highly sophisticated premises. In substance, the signers of the Manifesto declared that integration is wrong, unwise, intolerable, while segregation is just and convenient, and that this was why the Court's decision was wrong and should be overturned. They were quite clear about their purposes and about ways in which to achieve them. Putting the so-called legal argument behind them, they concluded as follows:

We commend the motives of those states which have declared the intention to resist forced integration by any lawful means.

We appeal to the states and people who are not directly affected by these decisions to consider the constitutional principles involved against the time when they too, on issues vital to them, may be the victims of judicial encroachment.

Even though we constitute a minority in the present Congress, we have full faith that a majority of the American people . . . will in time demand that the reserved rights of the states and of the people be made secure against judicial usurpation.

We pledge ourselves to use all lawful means to bring about a reversal of this decision which is contrary to the Constitution and to prevent the use of force in its implementation.

In this trying period, as we all seek to right this wrong, we appeal to our people not to be provoked by the agitators and trouble-makers invading our states and to scrupulously refrain from disorder and lawless acts.[17]

From the stand taken in this document, all else flowed. With few exceptions, moderate positions previously assumed were abandoned throughout the states that had been part of the Confederacy. Even along the border, the atmosphere changed. A year later, the violent crisis of Little Rock was upon us, in a state in which integration had begun three years earlier. The southern leaders understood and acted upon an essential truth, which we do not often have occasion to observe and which dawned on the southerners themselves somewhat late; hence the contrast between initial reactions and what followed. The Supreme Court's law, the southern leaders realized, could not in our system prevail—not merely in the very long run, but within the decade—if it ran counter to deeply felt popular needs or convictions, or even if it was opposed by a determined and substantial minority and received with indifference by the rest of the country. This, in the end, is how and why judicial review is consistent with the theory and practice of political democracy. This is why the Supreme Court is a court of last resort presumptively only. No doubt, in the vast majority of instances the Court prevails—not as a result of any sort of tacit referendum; rather, it just prevails, its authority is accepted more or less automatically, and no matter if grudgingly. It takes concerted effort at some risk, and hence not a little daring, to fight back, and then there is no guaranty of victory, as the Progressives and Populists found out. But given passion, vigor, and hard-headedness, it can be done and has been done. After all, as T. R. Powell once wrote, though by way of emphasis he reduced the matter somewhat too close to the vanishing point, what the Court can do is no more than "to say something. The effect depends upon others."[18] Broad and sustained application of the Court's law, when challenged, is a function of its rightness, not merely of its pronouncement. The southern purpose, therefore, was to organize and maintain unbroken the ranks of a determined and politically entrenched minority, and to test the convictions of the rest of the country. In opening this post-judgment colloquy, a colloquy searching not expedients of accommodation and compromise but the validity of the judgment itself, and in attempting this different sort of reprise, the southern leaders applied a lesson that Lincoln had taught, which seemed to have passed most northern politicians by.

I referred in Chapter 2 to Lincoln's general position in the years before the Civil War. He and the Republican party, and, as it turned out, a goodly majority of the nation were opposed to the Supreme Court's decision in 1857 in the *Dred Scott Case*. There the Court held that Dred Scott, a slave, did not gain his freedom when his master took him from a slave state into a free Territory because Congress, so the Court decided, lacked power to prohibit slavery in a Territory. The principle that the Court proclaimed was that slavery was not only legal in states which had it but was constitutionally guaranteed in unorganized territories as well. In the debates with Stephen A. Douglas in 1858, Lincoln said that he was against this decision, that he thought it wrong, that he feared its consequences, that he deemed it altogether deplorable. Douglas, on the other hand, without admitting that he necessarily thought the decision right, dwelt heavily on the argument that "whoever resists the final decision of the highest judicial tribunal aims a deadly blow at our whole republican system of government." "I yield obedience," Douglas said, "to the decisions of that Court—to the final determination of the highest judicial tribunal known to our Constitution." To this Lincoln countered by deriding the notion that a decision of the Supreme Court is a "Thus saith the Lord." The Court, he said, can be wrong. There is nothing sacred about the Court's decisions. Men may properly differ with them.

For a time, after Little Rock, there was a movement to draft Lincoln into the ranks of the "massive resisters," who were then going beyond the waging of political warfare against the Court's integration principle, to the raising of mobs against the enforcement of specific decrees. Lincoln never advocated disobedience of judicial decrees while they were in force. Such a position must lead to lawlessness of pestilential proportions, and Lincoln never took it. He was careful to point out that he and his party opposed the *Dred Scott* decision only in "a certain way." And he said explicitly: "We offer no *resistance* to it." But he did offer resistance to the principle, in the hope and with the expectation of overturning it. At Quincy, toward the end of the debates with Douglas, Lincoln said:

We do not propose that when Dred Scott has been decided to be a slave by the court, we, as a mob, will decide him to be free. We do not propose that, when any other one, or one thousand, shall be decided by that court to be slaves, we will in any violent way disturb the rights of property so settled; but we nevertheless do oppose that decision as a political rule which shall be binding on the voter, to vote for nobody who thinks it wrong, which shall be binding on the members of Congress or the President to favor no measure that does not actually concur with the principles of that decision. We do not propose to be bound by it as a political rule in that way, because we think it lays the foundation not merely of enlarging and spreading out what we consider an evil, but it lays the foundation for spreading that evil into the states themselves. We propose so resisting it as to have it reversed if we can, and a new judicial rule established upon this subject.

Earlier, Lincoln had gone as far as he ever did. "If I were in Congress," he said, "and a vote should come up on a question whether slavery should be prohibited in a new territory, in spite of that Dred Scott decision, I would vote that it should." Douglas poured scorn on Lincoln for saying that "if you elect him to the Senate he will introduce a bill to re-enact the law which the court pronounced unconstitutional. [Shouts of laughter, and voices, '*spot* the law.'] Yes, he is going to spot the law. . . . I never heard before of an appeal being taken from the Supreme Court. . . ." Lincoln was not deterred. Douglas, he said,

would have the citizen conform his vote to that decision; the member of Congress, his; the President, his use of the veto power. He would make it a rule of political action for the people and all the departments of the government. I would not. By resisting it as a political rule, I disturb no right of property, create no disorder, excite no mobs.

And further:

What are the uses of decisions of courts? . . . First—they decide upon the question before the court. They decide in this case that Dred

Scott is a slave. Nobody resists that. Not only that, but they say to everybody else, that persons standing just as Dred Scott stands are as he is. That is, they say that when a question comes up upon another person it will be so decided again, unless the court decides in another way, unless the court overrules its decision. Well, we mean to do what we can to have the court decide the other way. That is one thing we mean to do.[19]

One need hardly add that all this, summed up in only somewhat milder form in Lincoln's First Inaugural, was heresy against the theoretical basis of *Marbury* v. *Madison.* Public officers swear to support the Constitution of the United States, and, according to *Marbury* v. *Madison,* as Douglas was quick to point out, the Constitution is in the Supreme Court's keeping and must be supported as declared by the Court. There can be no pursuit of contrary "political rules" except in contravention of the oath to support the Constitution, meaning the oath to support the Supreme Court's invocations of it. But that is *Marbury* v. *Madison;* it does not describe the system, as it is or has been. To be sure, quite aside from *Marbury* v. *Madison* the Court is the institution best fitted to give us a rule of principle, which we strive to attain along with the principle of self-rule. Hence principle, called constitutional law, is in the Court's charge, and the other institutions are expected to defer to the Court with respect to it. Anything else would probably not work. So it is generally thought, and so I argued in Chapter 1. But, as I suggested, there are two qualifications. First, on the supreme occasion, when the system is forced to find ultimate self-consistency, the principle of self-rule must prevail. Secondly, it is no use taking a mechanistic view of the separation of powers. One may refer to the machinery of government, but one must not—to borrow a witticism of Chief Justice Taft—think that it really is machinery. The functions cannot and need not be rigidly compartmentalized. The Court often provokes consideration of the most intricate issues of principle by the other branches, engaging them in dialogues and "responsive readings"; and there are times also when the conversation starts at the other end and is perhaps less polite. Our government consists of discrete institutions, but the effectiveness of the whole depends on their involvement with one another, on their intimacy, even if it often is the sweaty intimacy of creatures locked in combat.

Lincoln's position did not lack precedent. President Jackson thought himself thoroughly entitled to make his own decision on the constitutionality of the Bank of the United States, regardless of what John Marshall had held. Chief Justice Taney, when Attorney General in 1832, giving an opinion, admittedly, on a somewhat hypothetical case, made clear his view that though a judgment pronounced by the Supreme Court may be conclusive of the case in which it is rendered, "it does not follow that the reasoning or principles which [the Court] announces in coming to its conclusions are equally binding and obligatory" on the legislative and executive branches; those branches need not conform to and adopt the Court's principle "in every other case . . . although all of them may unite in believing it erroneous." In a later day, President Franklin Roosevelt did not feel himself bound by the Court's principles in economic matters and successfully urged Congress to follow a different "political rule," thus producing not only the New Deal but in time new constitutional principles as well. Hernando D. Money, of Mississippi, stated the position a bit inelegantly, or if you will colorfully, but with fair accuracy, in the course of a Senate debate in 1909 on proposed income-tax legislation, which would have been very similar to a measure the Court had declared unconstitutional fourteen years earlier (in the famous *Pollock* case, which was eventually overcome by the Sixteenth Amendment, itself then under debate). Said Mr. Money:

I am not one of those who regard the judgment of the Supreme Court as an African regards his deity. I respect such a decision just exactly to the extent that it is founded in common sense and argued out on reasonable logic, but when it violates the law of common sense, then I cease to so regard it, except that as a citizen I am bound by it.

Putting thus aside and distinguishing, as Lincoln had, his duty as a peaceable citizen, the Senator added for good measure: "As a legislator, I have no more regard for it [a decision that violates the law of common sense] than I have for the decision of a magistrate in one of the counties of the State of Mississippi. . . ."

Two aspects of the Franklin Roosevelt episode deserve additional notice. One, not without some interest, is that among the leading supporters of the President's constitutional position and of the Guffey-Snyder Bituminous Coal Bill, which brought it to a head, was Representative Fred M. Vinson, of Kentucky, later Chief Justice of the United States. The other, of a different sort of significance, bespeaks a characteristic ambivalence on the part of the political branches in the conduct of their relations with the Court. Both the President and Mr. Vinson suggested well enough that Congress has its responsibilities also, and that it may take for a "political rule" its own principles rather than the Court's. This was unmistakably the position on any fair reading of what the Court had quite recently said and of what Congress was proposing to do, although no one, of course, intended "to decide Dred Scott to be free"; no disturbance of the Court's specific judgments was in question. But there was a second bow to the string, as there generally will be. Factual distinctions could be made out, and there was a chance that the Court would not find its established principle applicable to the new legislation, as well as the chance, of course, that it would reverse itself. Hence the President could conclude by saying no more than: "I hope your committee will not permit doubts as to constitutionality, however reasonable, to block the suggested legislation." Hence the positions could be blurred and even reversed. Mr. Vinson and others could urge also that constitutional decision is the province of the Court, which Congress should not usurp by voting this bill down on the basis of its own view of its unconstitutionality. And Republicans and other opponents could argue, in long and learned speeches, that the Constitution was everyone's business, that Congress was responsible for its own judgment on the constitutionality of this bill, and, finding it unconstitutional, should not enact it. But this is the rhetoric of caution, on the one hand, and of advantageous political alliance with the Court, on the other. Though not wishing to negate a normal deference to the Court's function as constitutional oracle of last resort, the President and the future Chief Justice were in fact urging Congress to act on its own principles, in contravention of the Court's; and their opponents were conceding the function of principled decision wholly to the Court, for their judgment of constitutionality was in no way an independent one.[20]

Following the Lincoln-Jackson-Roosevelt tradition, southern politicians were perfectly within their rights in declining to accept the Court's decision in the *School Segregation Cases* as a political rule. They were within their rights in deploring it and arguing against it. They could hope to convert public opinion. They could vote for laws that failed to advance its principle and even failed to concur with it. They could refuse to consider the issue settled and could relitigate it at every opportunity that the judicial process offered, and of course it offers a thousand and one. They could reject as laughable statements that they were bound by their oaths to put the decision into effect in all situations in which it was applicable, without waiting for the constraint of litigation. If they succeeded in turning public opinion, they could realistically look to the day when the principle announced by the Court would be rescinded or allowed to lapse without enforcement. Until that day, the decision was law, in accordance with the uses of decisions of courts. But this meant only that specific decrees ordering certain children to be admitted to certain schools had to be obeyed, and that until public opinion could be turned, children standing in the same position would be similarly treated, though only following litigation and more litigation.

Success has eluded the southern leaders, but narrowly. For a moment it seemed within reach, while the main body of northern opinion, led by President Eisenhower, mounted no defense. The chief response that was made was in terms of *Marbury* v. *Madison;* the President sounded almost verbatim like Stephen A. Douglas. This was an argument that could not be won—at the most it could be brought to a standstill. The Court, said the southerners just about unanswerably, had botched the job that Marshall describes in *Marbury* v. *Madison;* pretty obviously, the Court had performed some other function, not the one there indicated. But under *Marbury* v. *Madison,* ran the reply on a parallel rail, the Court is empowered to lay down the law of the land, and citizens must accept it uncritically. Whatever the Court lays down is right, even if wrong, because the Court and only the Court speaks in the name of the Constitution. Its doctrines are not to be questioned; indeed, they are hardly a fit subject for comment. The Court has spoken. The Court must be obeyed. There must be good order and peaceable submission to lawful authority. The Court itself, rising to its own defense for the only time in 1958, took the same tack. The Supremacy Clause, said the Court in an opinion issued, in unusual fashion, in the name of all its members, not merely in the name of one Justice as authorized spokesman, makes the Constitution the supreme law of the land. In *Marbury* v. *Madison,* Marshall had said: "It is emphatically the province and duty of the judicial department to say what the law is." Thus it came to be, the Court now added, "that the federal judiciary is supreme in the exposition of the law of the Constitution," and this is "a permanent and indispensable feature of our constitutional system." Hence the principle announced in the *School Segregation Cases* is the supreme law of the land, and "every state legislator and executive and judicial officer is solemnly committed by oath taken pursuant to Article VI, Section 3, 'to support this Constitution.'" To war against the Court was to war against the Constitution itself, and the Court made clear that by this it intended to proscribe not only resistance to specific decrees but resistance to the principle of integration as a political rule.[21]

The debate was at a standstill. Both sides were right, both sides were wrong, and it didn't matter. The decisive issue, to which the southerners amply devoted their attention, going beyond the fictions of *Marbury* v. *Madison,* was whether what the Court had done was right or wrong, good or bad. As to this, President Eisenhower had nothing to say, except for one or two very damaging, though sheepish, admissions that he entertained some doubts of his own.[22] And so the real point of the southern attack was missed. At best, the President—and, for its own reasons, also the Congress —politely declined the Court's invitation to join with it in ensuring the success of its now hazardous undertaking. At best, the President made a faint attempt to support the Court by drawing on *its* resources, *its* prestige and mystique, not by bringing to its aid those of the political institutions. This constituted no particular support at all. No wonder the southerners thought for a season that success was within their grasp. No one had joined the decisive issue with them. There was hardly a contest.

Having scented victory, the southern leaders, or at least a sufficient number of them, sought to assure it by turning from litigation and agitation to direct action by the use of mobs. Thus they abandoned the tradition in which they had been acting. For this no support could be found in the position of Lincoln or of those who preceded and followed him. And it was therefore a crucial mistake, though, it must be said, an understandable one. It was an acceptance of a calculated risk, which, after all, only hindsight shows up to have been wholly mistaken. The action at Little Rock, following upon a visit from Marvin Griffin, then governor of Georgia, and his associates, was certainly not Mr. Faubus' alone, whether or not a full council of war was ever held, and whether or not it was unanimously agreed to. In the event, it raised in much bolder fashion than before the issue of order, the peace of the community as against mob rule, and it caused President Eisenhower to react. Too much cannot be made of this, however. The Executive is obliged to aid in the enforcement of specific judicial decrees that have been flouted. It is a matter of maintaining the peace. But this is an indifferent omen, at best, for the endurance of the Court's principle, if the merits of the decision are not themselves defended as right and good; and Mr. Eisenhower did not so defend them. For enforcement is a crisis of the system, not its norm. When the law summons force to its aid, it demonstrates, not its strength and stability, but its weakness and impermanence. The mob, like revolution, is an ambiguous fact. The mob is bad when it is wrong; it may be heroic when it is right. It is surely a deeply ingrained American belief that mobs of our people do not generally gather to oppose good laws, and the very fact of the mob, therefore, puts the law in question. Fear of the mob, moreover, the interest in good order, is an ambivalent feeling, for it is more easily satisfied, everything else being equal, by conceding what the mob wants, by redressing its grievances, than by fighting it. And so a few enforcement crises like Little Rock, rather than hurting their cause, might well have gone far to win the southern leaders' battle for them. The Court's integration principle would have been in train of being reversed, directly or by desuetude. *On peut tout faire avec les baionnettes, sauf s'y asseoir.*

But there was another factor in play, and it roused northern opinion, whose latent temper the southern leaders had gravely misestimated. It is this factor that lent decisive consequence to the riots in Little Rock, abetted by such later skirmishes as in New Orleans in the fall of 1960, at the University of Georgia during the following winter, and in connection with the freedom rides in the spring of 1961 in Montgomery. Compulsory segregation, like states' rights and like "The Southern Way of Life," is an abstraction and, to a good many people, a neutral or sympathetic one. These riots, which were brought instantly, dramatically, and literally home to the American people, showed what it means concretely. Here were grown men and women furiously confronting their enemy: two, three, a half dozen scrubbed, starched, scared, and incredibly brave colored children. The moral bankruptcy, the shame of the thing, was evident. Television, it should be emphasized, as in the Army-McCarthy hearings, played a most significant role. There was an unforgettable scene, for example, in one CBS newscast from New Orleans, of a white mother fairly foaming at the mouth with the effort to rivet her distracted little boy's attention and teach him how to hate. And repeatedly, the ugly, spitting curse, NIGGER! The effect, achieved on an unprecedented number of people with unprecedented speed, must have been something like what used to happen to individuals (the young Lincoln among them) at the sight of an actual slave auction, or like the slower influence on northern opinion of the fighting in "Bleeding Kansas" in 1854-55.

And so the southern leaders had overplayed their hand. Mob action led to the mobilization of northern opinion in support of the Court's decision—not merely because the mob is disorderly, but because it concretized the abstraction of racism, somewhat in the manner in which the cases and controversies in whose context the Court evolves its principles concretize all abstractions. The essence of Lincoln's analysis now became clear to all. Political opposition could defeat the Court's decision. Given the force and determination of the southern opposition and its acute understanding of "the uses of decisions of courts," the principle of integration could be saved only by the active engagement of northern opinion in the political war. One of those supreme occasions had been brought about when a decisive reprise is open to the political branches; it was for them to make the Court's decision their rule of political action, or not to do so, and thus to make or break the decision itself. The political branches, and most particularly the President and aspirants to the presidency, had independently, on their own responsibility, to speak their moral approval of the Court's decision, to support it by drawing on their own resources, and to act in pursuance of it. This was one time when hiding behind the judges' skirts would not do. The political institutions had a decision of their own to make.

The presidential campaign of 1960 marked the assumption of political responsibility for the principle of racial integration. And there has since been a world of difference between the tone of the Kennedy Administration on this subject and that of its predecessor, and a difference as well in the vigor and imagination of the litigating activity undertaken by the Department of Justice. This has made it possible for southern moderates to be effective, as in the University of Georgia case in the winter of 1961 and in Atlanta, New Orleans, Dallas, Little Rock, and elsewhere the following fall.[23] Southern moderates could not be heard to any substantial purpose while the issue was in doubt, while a realistic chance of overturning the Court's principle seemed to remain. Only now—though perhaps romantic illusions still linger on the fringes of southern opinion—is it at last quite clear that the issue is settled, the principle established and immutable.

This was the great achievement symbolized by an opening of schools in the fall of 1961, for the first time in some years without any acute crisis. It is a great achievement because the settlement and broad acceptance of a governing principle is a matter of the first importance in our society. And it is an achievement not shaken or diminished by the insurrection at the University of Mississippi in September 1962, which ended—if, as these lines are written, it can be said to have quite ended—in deep tragedy, with two dead and many injured. Indeed, the events in Mississippi, ugly though they were, and paradoxical as this assertion may seem, confirmed the earlier achievement.

That latter-day Daniel Shays, Governor Ross R. Barnett of Mississippi, gave timely and utterly clear notice, early in September, of his intention to rise against a specific decree of the local federal courts, which ordered the admission of James Meredith, a Negro, to the State University. Yet, just as clearly, no sense of impending tragedy was abroad in the land. A minor crisis seemed in prospect, not without its element of comic posturing. For the serious crisis had been one of the national will. It was behind us, and it had determined the outcome of this one. There was room for doubt about the outcome when Governor Faubus of Arkansas embarked upon his course of defiance in 1957. There was none now. Governor Barnett had the sympathy of a majority of his white constituents, no doubt, but he stood relatively alone before a mildly intrigued public as twice—on September 20 and 25—he barred the way to Mr. Meredith and two federal officers. Neither the Mississippi Congressional delegation nor other Southern Congressmen and Governors rallied publicly to his side at this time. It was a gesture, and it would end.

But the Administration permitted it not to end. It gave Mr. Barnett time for what could not have been a simple task, namely, the mobilization and concentration in Oxford of a force of several hundred men, somewhere near the full strength, very likely, of the law-enforcement apparatus of Mississippi and its political subdivisions. It gave time for mobs to gather from far and near, to form on the campus, to feel protected, to be agitated and perhaps organized. It made it practically necessary for other politicians who could not or would not lose face to Mr. Barnett eventually to come to his support. The outcome was still certain. But—and this was the heart of its error—the Administration permitted the rise, as from the swamps, of a faint miasma of illusion that things might yet be adjusted otherwise. For the Administration said very little, and nothing formally or on the highest authority. The President, at this time, was held in the background. The state, almost by default, dug itself in psychologically.

Attorney General Kennedy was represented as feeling that the use of force, and especially military force, is a terrible last resort, and that results obtained by the use of force are far from unmixed blessings. It would be dense to deny this. But the Administration ended by ensuring what it justly feared most—the use of regular troops, and in very large numbers. On Wednesday, September 26, five days before the dénouement, the third and last peaceable attempt to enroll Mr. Meredith was made. The federal force that presented itself at the gates of "Old Miss" with Mr. Meredith consisted of one Justice Department attorney and one federal marshal. It was repulsed, after a bit of unarmed shoving, by the Lieu-

tenant Governor of Mississippi, assisted by twenty state policemen. Some fifteen sheriffs from surrounding counties were present
in reserve. It bears repeating that this was a third attempt. Should
there not by then have been a personal, public intervention by the
President, invoking the bonds of the Union, declaring the abiding
moral conviction of a vast majority of his and Governor Barnett's
countrymen that the law whose protection Meredith claimed is
a just law, and announcing that troops were at the ready, to be
used only if necessary, but, if necessary, to be used? Might not a
couple of hundred marshals—thus backed by the solemn word of
the President—have more or less politely shoved their way past
the Lieutenant Governor and his platoon and got Mr. Meredith
registered at this time? By the next day and the day after, many
more state policemen and uglier mobs were on the scene. They
might have been anyway. But the accomplished fact of registra-
tion and the demonstrated national will would have changed the
position enormously, as in fact they ultimately did.

This is not to place a shred of responsibility for the final tragedy
on the Administration. The responsibility rests fully and heavily
where it belongs. It was from Governor Barnett that the mob derived the half frivolous, half insanely frustrated spirit out of which
fatal violence erupted on Sunday night, September 30; and perhaps the event will give pause in future to grown men in responsible positions before they abandon themselves to secessionist
hysteria. The Administration's reaction in the end was sure and
balanced, even as it had been in face of the Montgomery freedom-
ride riots of the spring of 1961.

With this in mind, and recognizing that the Kennedy Administration's other actions with respect to civil rights have been generally energetic, creative, and principled, it remains important to
note that for some crucial days the crisis was mishandled and thus
magnified. This is important because, although the settlement of
principle achieved earlier is now reaffirmed, yet that is all that has
been settled. The races are in principle to be integrated, in the
school systems as in other facilities provided or supported by government. School authorities are to work toward this end, and are in
any event to do nothing inconsistent with its eventual attainment.
The position is restored to what it was during the first year and a
half after the Court's initial judgment, when southern reaction was

for the most part calm and reluctantly acquiescent, and before the decision was challenged in the attempt to overturn it. Now the decision stands, the challenge is over, and the problem of achieving the goal of integration is before the country. Difficulties persist and crises may recur. The process demands heroic men and women, but the Negro community seems miraculously able to produce them. To the end that these men and women may succeed with all deliberate speed—as it is now clearly the national will that they shall—enforcement crises must be resolved by the use of the minimum force necessary, but above all decisively and promptly, so that the futility of resistance is never in the slightest doubt. Those who pass from litigation and political obstruction to overt insurrection must not be led to expect that they will be negotiated with.

The problem area is not small, and its problems are deep. It embraces not only Alabama, Mississippi, and South Carolina, but the great bulk of southern rural counties. In the Black Belt of the South—some hundred rural counties—the Negro's civil rights are scarcely being abridged, for he has none; there are not enough rights or anything else to go around. This is an underdeveloped area, quite like those we hear so much of elsewhere. None of the many recent advances in civil rights, from the earliest to the latest, with the single possible exception of the formal abolition of slavery, has had an appreciable impact here. And that is because the problem is not yet in its essence political or moral; it is fundamentally economic. Here a federal school-aid bill and programs for the development of what is now a sick one-crop economy may be more important than principles declared by the Supreme Court or the Civil Rights Acts of 1957 and 1960. What is needed above all is that the government in Washington should negotiate an *Alianza para Progreso* with the Black Belt.[24]

This is the area of the gravest immediate difficulties. Looking beyond it, however, it is evident that the chief consequence of the settlement of principle which has occurred will shortly be that the problem has been nationalized, and that it will have to be attacked in the North in much the same way as in the South.

Future movement in the South beyond token integration—once that has taken place throughout—will put in issue, as I noted in Chapter 5, the administration of the pupil-placement laws under which Negro children are sparingly assigned to formerly all-white schools. How soon that will happen will depend on the amount of massive pressure that southern Negro communities are ready to exert. The question in each case will be whether the administration of these laws is racially neutral. This line of litigation will before long reach the point where the problem assumes a national scope and is no longer specifically southern. For it is notorious that by far the larger number of colored children in northern metropolitan areas attend schools that are *de facto* segregated, or very nearly so. As an able study by Will Maslow has reported, segregation may be effectuated by present or past gerrymandering of a school district, "by arbitrary site selection, by manipulating transfer policies, by under-utilization of certain schools," and by like practices that will prove vulnerable in litigation.[25]

Segregation was the national pattern for many generations following the Civil War. Until 1938, it was permitted by law in New York school districts that chose to have it.[26] It existed in Kansas until it was struck down in one of the *School Segregation Cases* in 1954. Only since then has it been abolished in at least one city each in California, Michigan, and Ohio and in a number of communities in Illinois, Pennsylvania, and New Jersey.[27] During the past generation, the South has lagged behind the rest of the country by insisting upon an explicit, legally enforced policy of segregation. This made no small difference. The goals we acknowledge determine the direction in which our society moves. Therefore, the seven years' struggle to establish the principle of racial integration, in the South as well as elsewhere, was a matter of enormous importance. The problem now broadens to encompass the entire position of the Negro throughout American society. It opens up, oddly enough, in circles that are at once concentric and intersecting—schools, housing, employment, political participation. It is unnecessary to point out that neither the courts alone nor the federal government by itself are equal to finding and enforcing solutions. No doubt, the southern states will continue to lag behind in practice, as they did in principle. But they must be led forward by northern communities, as well as pushed by federal authorities.

Notes

Chapter 1

1. R. G. McCloskey, *The American Supreme Court* (Chicago: University of Chicago Press, 1960), pp. 40, 42, 43. (Copyright 1960 by The University of Chicago.)
2. See L. Hand, *The Bill of Rights* (Cambridge: Harvard University Press, 1958), p. 11; T. R. Powell, *Vagaries and Varieties in Constitutional Interpretation* (New York: Columbia University Press, 1956), pp. 12-23; O. W. Holmes, Jr., *Collected Legal Papers* (New York: Harcourt, Brace, 1920), p. 270; J. B. Thayer, *John Marshall* (Boston: Houghton Mifflin, 1901), pp. 57, 84.
3. *Field v. Clark*, 143 U.S. 649 (1892).
4. 6 Cranch 87 (1810).
5. See W. W. Crosskey, *Politics and the Constitution in the History of the United States*, Vol. 2 (Chicago: University of Chicago Press, 1953), chs. XXVII-XXIX; cf. H. M. Hart, Jr., "Professor Crosskey and Judicial Review," 67 *Harvard Law Review* 1456 (1954).
6. See, e.g., C. L. Black, Jr., *The People and the Court* (New York: Macmillan, 1960), p. 6; H. Wechsler, *Principles, Politics and Fundamental Law* (Cambridge: Harvard University Press, 1961), p. 7; E. V. Rostow, "The Supreme Court and the People's Will," 33 *Notre Dame Lawyer* 573, 575-76 (1958); cf. L. H. Pollak, "Racial Discrimination and Judicial Integrity: A Reply to Professor Wechsler," 108 *University of Pennsylvania Law Review* 1, 3 (1959).
7. See p. 2.
8. 1 Wheaton 304.
9. 6 Wheaton 264.
10. 4 Wheaton 316.
11. F. Frankfurter, "A Note on Advisory Opinions," 37 *Harvard Law Review* 1002-03, n. 4 (1924).
12. See M. DeW. Howe, *Justice Oliver Wendell Holmes: The Shaping Years* (Cambridge: Belknap Press of Harvard University Press, 1957), p. vii; O. W. Holmes, Jr., "The Path of the Law," 10 *Harvard Law Review* 457, 469 (1897).
13. See D. B. Truman, *The Governmental Process* (New York: Knopf, 1951).
14. R. A. Dahl, *A Preface to Democratic Theory* (Chicago: University of Chicago Press, 1956), pp. 125, 132. (Copyright 1956 by the University of Chicago.)
15. See E. V. Rostow, "The Democratic Character of Judicial Review," 66 *Harvard Law Review* 193, 195 (1952).
16. L. Hand, *op cit. supra* n. 2, at pp. 73-74. (Copyright © 1958 by The President and Fellows of Harvard College. Reprinted by permission of the publishers.)

17. See, *e.g.,* Black, *op. cit. supra* n. 6, at pp. 23 *et seq.,* 210 *et seq.*
18. Thayer, *op. cit. supra* n. 2, at pp. 103-04, 106-07.
19. See Rostow, *op. cit. supra* n. 15, at p. 201.
20. H. Finer, "Congressional Investigations: The British System," 18 *University of Chicago Law Review* 521, 522 (1951).
21. Rostow, *op. cit. supra* n. 15, at p. 205.
22. L. Hand, "The Contribution of an Independent Judiciary to Civilization," in I. Dilliard, ed., *The Spirit of Liberty* (New York: Knopf, 1953), pp. 155-65.
23. *Eakin* v. *Raub,* 12 S. & R. 330, 343, 355 (1825).
24. J. B. Thayer, "The Origin and Scope of the American Doctrine of Constitutional Law," in *Legal Essays* (Boston: The Boston Book Co., 1908), pp. 1, 39.
25. See p. 2.
26. H. F. Stone, "The Common Law in the United States," 50 *Harvard Law Review* 4, 25 (1936).
27. *Eakin* v. *Raub,* supra n. 23, at p. 354.
28. Rostow, *op. cit. supra* n. 15, at p. 208.
29. H. M. Hart, Jr., "Foreword: The Time Chart of the Justices," 73 *Harvard Law Review* 84, 99 (1959).
30. H. J. Muller, *The Uses of the Past* (New York: Oxford University Press, 1957), pp. 364-65, 367.
31. See Black, *op. cit. supra* n. 6, at pp. 34 *et seq.*
32. See L. Hartz, *The Liberal Tradition in America* (New York: Harcourt, Brace, 1955), pp. 9 *et seq.;* B. F. Wright, "Editor's Introduction," in *The Federalist,* John Harvard Edition (Cambridge: Harvard University Press, 1961), p. 41.
33. See C. Fairman, "Joseph P. Bradley," in A. Dunham and P. B. Kurland, eds., *Mr. Justice* (Chicago: University of Chicago Press, 1956), pp. 69, 80-82; C. Fairman, "Mr. Justice Bradley's Appointment to the Supreme Court and the Legal Tender Cases," 54 *Harvard Law Review* 977 (1941).

Chapter 2

1. 7 *Harvard Law Review* 129. It is printed also in J. B. Thayer, *Legal Essays* (Boston: The Boston Book Co., 1908), p. 1.
2. L. K. Cohen, ed., *The Legal Conscience—Selected Papers of Felix S. Cohen* (New Haven: Yale University Press, 1960), p. 44.
3. 208 U.S. 412 (1908).
4. See *First National Bank* v. *Fellows,* 244 U.S. 416 (1917); C. Warren, *The Supreme Court in United States History,* Vol. 1 (Boston: Little, Brown, 1926), p. 501.
5. See, *e.g., Bates* v. *Little Rock,* 361 U.S. 516 (1960); *Butler* v. *Michigan,* 352 U.S. 380 (1957); *Tot* v. *United States,* 319 U.S. 463 (1943).
6. *Dennis* v. *United States,* 341 U.S. 494, 517, 525 (1951).
7. 344 U.S. 183.
8. *Poe* v. *Ullman,* 367 U.S. 497, 522, 539, 554 (1961).

9. "Legal Tender," 1 *Harvard Law Review* 73; reprinted in Thayer, *op. cit. supra* n. 1, at p. 60.
10. See *Hepburn* v. *Griswold*, 8 Wallace 603 (1869); *Legal Tender Cases*, 12 Wallace 457, 570, 587, 634 (1870).
11. 12 *Harvard Law Review* 464; reprinted in Thayer, *op. cit. supra* n. 1, at p. 153.
12. L. Hand, *The Bill of Rights* (Cambridge: Harvard University Press, 1958).
13. H. Wechsler, "Toward Neutral Principles of Constitutional Law," in Wechsler, *Principles, Politics and Fundamental Law* (Cambridge: Harvard University Press, 1961), p. 5. This important paper is also printed in 73 *Harvard Law Review* 1 (1959). (Copyright © 1961 by The President and Fellows of Harvard College. Reprinted by permission of the publishers.)
14. R. H. Jackson, *The Supreme Court in the American System of Government* (Cambridge: Harvard University Press, 1955), p. 76.
15. F. Frankfurter, "Chief Justices I Have Known," in P. Elman, ed., *Of Law and Men* (New York: Harcourt, Brace, 1956), p. 138.
16. H. Wechsler, *Principles, Politics and Fundamental Law*, p. xiii.
17. *Ibid.*, pp. xiii-xiv.
18. 364 U.S. 479 (1960); for a defense of the decision, see 75 *Harvard Law Review* 127 (1961).
19. *Terminiello* v. *Chicago*, 337 U.S. 1, 11 (1949).
20. B. N. Cardozo, *The Nature of the Judicial Process*, paperback ed. (New Haven: Yale University Press, 1960), pp. 138-40.
21. L. H. Pollak, "Racial Discrimination and Judicial Integrity: A Reply to Professor Wechsler," 108 *University of Pennsylvania Law Review* 1, 33 (1959).
22. See Speech at Chicago, July 10, 1858, in R. P. Basler, ed., *The Collected Works of Abraham Lincoln*, Vol. 2 (New Brunswick, N.J.: Rutgers University Press, 1953), pp. 484, 500.
23. See G. K. Gardner, "Liberty, the State, and the School," 20 *Law and Contemporary Problems* 184 (1955).
24. Wechsler, *op. cit. supra* n. 16, at p. xiv; see V. S. Navasky, "The Benevolent Housing Quota," 6 *Howard Law Journal* 30 (1960); Note, "Benign Quotas: A Plan for Integrated Public Housing," 70 *Yale Law Journal* 126 (1960). See also B. I. Bittker, "The Case of the Checker-Board Ordinance: An Experiment in Race Relations," 71 *Yale Law Journal* 1387 (1962).
25. H. V. Jaffa, *Crisis of the House Divided* (Garden City, N.Y.: Doubleday, 1959), pp. 22, 37. (Copyright © 1959 by Harry V. Jaffa. Reprinted by permission of Doubleday & Co., Inc.) Speech at Peoria, Oct. 16, 1854, in *The Collected Works of Abraham Lincoln*, Vol. 2, pp. 247, 266, 255-56; Speech at Springfield, June 16, 1858, *ibid.*, p. 461.
26. See S. E. Morison and H. S. Commager, *The Growth of the American Republic*, Vol. 1 (New York: Oxford University Press, 1942), p. 245; E. S. Morgan, *The Birth of the Republic* (Chicago: University of Chicago Press, 1956), pp. 96-97.
27. Last Speech at Springfield, Oct. 30, 1858, *The Collected Works of Abraham Lincoln*, Vol. 3, p. 334.
28. Jaffa, *op. cit. supra* n. 25, at pp. 237, n. 1, 416-17; Speech at Peoria,

Oct. 16, 1854, *The Collected Works of Abraham Lincoln*, Vol. 3, pp. 247, 255; Jaffa, *op. cit.*, p. 232.
29. C. E. Wyzanski, Jr., "Constitutionalism: Limitation and Affirmation," in A. E. Sutherland, ed., *Government Under Law* (Cambridge: Harvard University Press, 1956), pp. 473, 485-86.
30. See *Naim* v. *Naim*, 197 Va. 734, 90 S.E. 2d 849, *appeal dismissed*, 350 U.S. 985 (1956); L. H. Pollak, "The Supreme Court and the States; Reflections on *Boynton* v. *Virginia*," 49 *California Law Review* 15, 45, n. 79 (1961).
31. See A. M. Bickel, "The Original Understanding and the Segregation Decision," 69 *Harvard Law Review* 1, 9-10 (1955).
32. *Plessy* v. *Ferguson*, 163 U.S. 537 (1896).

Chapter 3

1. See, e.g., G. Gilmore, "Legal Realism: Its Cause and Cure," 70 *Yale Law Journal* 1037 (1961).
2. M. Lerner, "The Great Constitutional War," 18 *Virginia Quarterly Review* 530, 545 (1942).
3. 81 *Congressional Record Appendix* 362-63 (1937); *New York Times*, March 12, 1956, p. 19, col. 2 (late city ed.).
4. *New York Times*, Feb. 3, 1957, "News of the Week."
5. See J. F. Byrnes, "The Supreme Court Must Be Curbed," *U.S. News and World Report*, May 18, 1956, pp. 50, 52.
6. A. T. Mason, *The Supreme Court from Taft to Warren* (Baton Rouge: Louisiana State University Press, 1958), pp. 36-37, 189-90.
7. L. K. Cohen, ed., *The Legal Conscience—Selected Papers of Felix S. Cohen* (New Haven: Yale University Press, 1960), pp. 37, 25-26.
8. *Ibid.*, p. 67.
9. *Ibid.*, p. 128.
10. J. P. Frank, *Marble Palace—The Supreme Court in American Life* (New York: Knopf, 1958), pp. 60, 62, 238.
11. T. Arnold, "Professor Hart's Theology," 73 *Harvard Law Review* 1298, 1310-13 (1960); H. M. Hart, Jr., "Foreword: The Time Chart of the Justices," 73 *Harvard Law Review* 84, 99 (1959).
12. See, e.g., A. M. Bickel, *The Unpublished Opinions of Mr. Justice Brandeis: The Supreme Court at Work* (Cambridge: Belknap Press of Harvard University Press, 1957), pp. 66-68, 97, 111-13, 212; A. N. Whitehead, *Symbolism* (New York: Macmillan, 1927), p. 69.
13. H. L. Stimson and McGeorge Bundy, *On Active Service in Peace and War* (New York: Harper, 1947), quoted in E. E. Morison, *Turmoil and Tradition* (Boston: Houghton Mifflin, 1960), p. 651.
14. Mason, *op. cit. supra* n. 6, at pp. 192, viii, 36-37.
15. H. L. Black, "The Bill of Rights," 35 *New York University Law Review* 865 (1960).
16. F. Frankfurter, "John Marshall and the Judicial Function," in P. Elman, ed., *Of Law and Man* (New York: Harcourt, Brace, 1956), p. 3.
17. *Trop* v. *Dulles*, 356 U.S. 86 (1958); *Weems* v. *United States*, 217 U.S. 349, 382, 413 (1910).

18. See *Olmstead* v. *United States*, 277 U.S. 438, 478 (1928); *Boyd* v. *United States*, 116 U.S. 616 (1886).
19. *Smith* v. *California*, 361 U.S. 147, 157 (1959).
20. *Wilkinson* v. *United States*, 365 U.S. 399, 415, 422 (1961); *Braden* v. *United States*, 365 U.S. 431, 438, 444-45 (1961).
21. *United States* v. *Butler*, 297 U.S. 1, 62 (1936).
22. T. R. Powell, *Vagaries and Varieties in Constitutional Interpretation* (New York: Columbia University Press, 1956), p. 43.
23. *Konigsberg* v. *California*, 366 U.S. 36, 56, 65, 77 (1961); *Braden* v. *United States*, 365 U.S. 445-46.
24. C. L. Black, Jr., "Mr. Justice Black, the Supreme Court and the Bill of Rights," *Harper's*, February 1961, p. 63.
25. Cf. T. R. Adam, "The Queen as Political Symbol in the British Commonwealth," in L. Bryson *et al.*, eds., *Symbols and Society* (New York: Harper, 1955), p. 9; A. Salomon, "Symbols and Images in the Constitution of Society," *ibid.*, pp. 103, 104-05.
26. See *Board of Education* v. *Barnette*, 319 U.S. 624, 632-33, 662 (1943); H. S. Thomas, *Felix Frankfurter, Scholar on the Bench* (Baltimore: Johns Hopkins Press, 1960), pp. 42-68; Whitehead, *op. cit. supra* n. 12, at p. 61.
27. H. J. Muller, "Acknowledgments," in *The Uses of the Past* (New York: Oxford University Press, 1957).
28. *Whitney* v. *California*, 274 U.S. 357, 372, 375-77 (1927).
29. Z. Chafee, *Free Speech in the United States* (Cambridge: Harvard University Press, 1948), p. 21, quoted in L. W. Levy, *Legacy of Suppression* (Cambridge: Belknap Press of Harvard University Press, 1960), p. 2.
30. See A. M. Bickel, "The Original Understanding and the Segregation Decision," 69 *Harvard Law Review* 1 (1955).
31. 332 U.S. 46, 68, 71-72 (1947); see C. Fairman, "Does the Fourteenth Amendment Incorporate the Bill of Rights?" 2 *Stanford Law Review* 5 (1949).
32. *Hepburn* v. *Griswold*, 8 Wallace 603 (1870); *Legal Tender Cases* 12 Wallace 457, 570, 587, 634 (1871) (dissenting opinions); *Juilliard* v. *Greenman*, 110 U.S. 421, 451 (1884) (Field, J., dissenting).
33. *Burns* v. *Wilson*, 346 U.S. 137, 150 (1953) (Douglas, J., dissenting); G. D. Henderson, "Courts Martial and the Constitution: The Original Understanding," 71 *Harvard Law Review* 293 (1957); F. B. Wiener, "Courts Martial and the Bill of Rights: The Original Practice," 72 *Harvard Law Review* 1, 266 (1958).
34. S. E. Morison and H. S. Commager, *The Growth of the American Republic*, Vol. 1 (New York: Oxford University Press, 1942), p. 292; C. P. Curtis, "A Modern Supreme Court in a Modern World," 4 *Vanderbilt Law Review* 427, 428 (1951); see W. Mendelson, *Justices Black and Frankfurter: Conflict in the Court* (Chicago: University of Chicago Press, 1961), p. vii.
35. H. Thomas, *The Spanish Civil War* (New York: Harper, 1961), p. 47.
36. *Home Building and Loan Assn.* v. *Blaisdell*, 290 U.S. 398, 453, 442-443 (1934); see also remarks of Stone, J., dissenting, in *Dimick* v. *Schiedt*, 293 U.S. 474, 488, 495 (1935).
37. *United States* v. *Moreland*, 258 U.S. 433, 441, 451 (1922); Brandeis

Papers, Harvard Law School; W. H. Taft Papers, Library of Congress.
38. Quoted in Muller, *op. cit. supra* n. 27, at p. 373.
39. Cf. C. J. Becker, *The Heavenly City of the Eighteenth-century Philosophers,* paperback ed. (New Haven: Yale University Press, 1959), pp. 88-118.
40. *Gompers* v. *United States,* 233 U.S. 604, 610 (1914).
41. J. Burckhardt, *Judgments on History and Historians* (Boston: Beacon Press, 1958), p. 163; J. C. Levenson, *The Mind and Art of Henry Adams* (Boston: Houghton Mifflin, 1957), p. 133; Muller, *op. cit. supra* n. 27, at pp. 32-33.
42. Levy, *op. cit. supra* n. 29, at p. 175.
43. Muller, *op. cit. supra* n. 27, at p. 31; see also E. H. Carr, *What Is History?* (New York: Knopf, 1962), pp. 3-35.

Chapter 4

1. P. A. Freund, *On Understanding the Supreme Court* (Boston: Little, Brown, 1949), pp. 11, 9, 43.
2. Quoted in J. C. Levenson, *The Mind and Art of Henry Adams* (Boston: Houghton Mifflin, 1957), p. 129.
3. L. K. Cohen, ed., *The Legal Conscience—Selected Papers of Felix S. Cohen* (New Haven: Yale University Press, 1960), p. 37.
4. 2 Dallas 409 (1792).
5. See H. M. Hart, Jr., and H. Wechsler, *The Federal Courts and the Federal System* (Brooklyn: Foundation Press, 1953), pp. 75-77.
6. Quoted in J. B. Thayer, *Legal Essays* (Boston: The Boston Book Co., 1908), p. 53.
7. F. Frankfurter, "Advisory Opinions," in *Encyclopedia of the Social Sciences,* 1, pp. 475, 478 (1930).
8. F. Frankfurter, "A Note on Advisory Opinions," 37 *Harvard Law Review* 1002, 1006 (1924).
9. Thayer, *op. cit. supra* n. 6, at p. 10.
10. 6 Wheaton 264, 404 (1821).
11. H. Wechsler, "Toward Neutral Principles of Constitutional Law," in Wechsler, *Principles, Politics and Fundamental Law* (Cambridge: Harvard University Press, 1961), pp. 5, 9-10; see also H. Wechsler, "Comment," in A. E. Sutherland, ed., *Government Under Law* (Cambridge: Harvard University Press, 1956), pp. 134, 138; cf. L. Hand, *The Bill of Rights* (Cambridge: Harvard University Press, 1958), p. 15.
12. 297 U.S. 288, 341 (1936).
13. F. Frankfurter and A. S. Fisher, "The Business of the Supreme Court at the October Terms, 1935 and 1936," 51 *Harvard Law Review* 577, 623 (1938).
14. 306 U.S. 118 (1939).
15. 268 U.S. 510 (1925).
16. 341 U.S. 123 (1951).
17. Cf. *Doremus* v. *Board of Education,* 342 U.S. 429 (1952); P. A. Freund, "Foreword: The Year of the Steel Case," 66 *Harvard Law*

Review 89, 95 (1952); E. Cahn, ed., *Supreme Court and Supreme Law* (Bloomington: Indiana University Press, 1954), pp. 34-36.
18. 262 U.S. 447 (1923).
19. *Steward Machine Co.* v. *Davis*, 301 U.S. 548 (1937).
20. L. L. Jaffe, "Standing to Secure Judicial Review: Public Actions," 74 *Harvard Law Review* 1265, 1266; Jaffe, "Standing to Secure Judicial Review: Private Actions," 75 *Harvard Law Review* 255, 305, n. 152 (1961).
21. E.g., *Muskrat* v. *United States*, 219 U.S. 346 (1911); *International Longshoremen's Union* v. *Boyd*, 347 U.S. 222 (1954); *Rescue Army* v. *Municipal Court*, 331 U.S. 549 (1947); *United Public Workers* v. *Mitchell*, 330 U.S. 75 (1947); cf. *Gritts* v. *Fisher*, 224 U.S. 640 (1912); *Cherokee Intermarriage Case*, 203 U.S. 76 (1906). Compare *Public Affairs Associates, Inc.*, v. *Rickover*, 369 U.S. 111 (1962), and *FCC* v. *Sanders Bros. Radio Station*, 309 U.S. 470 (1940) (nonconstitutional issues).
22. Hand, *op. cit. supra* n. 11, at p. 15.
23. See, e.g., *Harmon* v. *Brucker*, 355 U.S. 579 (1958); H. M. Hart, Jr., "The Power of Congress to Limit the Jurisdiction of Federal Courts: An Exercise in Dialectic," 66 *Harvard Law Review* 1362 (1953); L. L. Jaffe, "The Right To Judicial Review," 71 *Harvard Law Review* 401, 769 (1958). But see *Schilling* v. *Rogers*, 363 U.S. 666 (1960).
24. Wechsler, *op. cit. supra* n. 11, at pp. 11, 13-14. See also M. F. Weston, "Political Questions," 38 *Harvard Law Review* 296 (1925). But see Jaffe, *op. cit. supra* n. 20, at 74 *Harvard Law Review* 1302-07.
25. See Wechsler, *op. cit. supra* n. 11, at pp. 14-15; H. M. Hart, Jr., "Foreword: The Time Chart of the Justices," 73 *Harvard Law Review* 84, 89, n. 13 (1959).
26. Address of Chief Justice Warren, American Law Institute Meeting, May 19, 1954, quoted in F. B. Wiener, "The Supreme Court's New Rules," 68 *Harvard Law Review* 20, 51 (1954). See *Naim* v. *Naim*, 197 Va. 734, 90 S.E. 2d 849, *appeal dismissed*, 350 U.S. 985 (1956); L. H. Pollak, "The Supreme Court and the States: Reflections on *Boynton* v. *Virginia*," 49 *California Law Review* 15, 45, n. 79 (1961). And see Note, "The Insubstantial Federal Question," 62 *Harvard Law Review* 488, 492-93 (1949); Hart and Wechsler, *op. cit. supra* n. 5, at pp. 572-76.
27. See, e.g., *Pennsylvania* v. *Board of Directors of City Trusts of Philadelphia*, 391 Pa. 434, 138 A. 2d 844, *certiorari denied*, 357 U.S. 570 (1958); *Rice* v. *Sioux City Memorial Park*, *affirmed by equally divided court*, 348 U.S. 880 (1954), on rehearing, *certiorari dismissed*, 349 U.S. 70 (1955); *Baltimore Radio Show, Inc.*, v. *Maryland*, 193 Md. 300, 67 A. 2d 497 (1949), *certiorari denied*, 338 U.S. 912 (1950); *Dorsey* v. *Stuyvesant Town Corp.*, 299 N.Y. 512, 87 N.E. 2d 541 (1949), *certiorari denied*, 339 U.S. 981 (1950). See R. L. Stern, "Denial of Certiorari Despite a Conflict," 66 *Harvard Law Review* 465 (1953); L. L. Jaffe, "Foreword, The Supreme Court, 1950 Term," 65 *Harvard Law Review* 107, 109-10 (1951); Frankfurter and Fisher, *op. cit. supra* n. 13, at pp. 596 *et seq.*; Wechsler, *op. cit. supra* n. 11, at p. 14.
28. Quoted in F. Frankfurter and J. M. Landis, *The Business of the Supreme Court* (New York: Macmillan, 1928), p. 276.

29. Acting Attorney General Beck to the President, Feb. 12, 1925, File No. 72868-2, Justice and Executive Branch, Archives of the United States.
30. C. P. Curtis, "A Modern Supreme Court in a Modern World," 4 *Vanderbilt Law Review* 427, 433 (1951).
31. Frankfurter, *op. cit. supra* n. 7, at p. 478.
32. 323 U.S. 214, 242, 245-46 (1944); and see R. H. Jackson, *The Supreme Court in the American System of Government* (Cambridge: Harvard University Press, 1955), pp. 75-76; but cf. E. V. Rostow, "The Japanese American Cases—A Disaster," 54 *Yale Law Journal* 489, 510-12 (1945).
33. See Freund, *op. cit. supra* n. 17, esp. at p. 91; Hart and Wechsler, *op. cit. supra* n. 5, at pp. 1203, 1211; *Youngstown Sheet and Tube Co.* v. *Sawyer,* 343 U.S. 937-38 (1952).
34. 365 U.S. 43 (1961).
35. *Times Film Corp.* v. *City of Chicago,* 180 F. Supp. 843, 844 (N.D. Ill. 1959); 272 F. 2d 90, 91, 92 (7th Cir. 1959).
36. *Joseph Burstyn, Inc.,* v. *Wilson,* 343 U.S. 495 (1952); *Gelling* v. *Texas,* 343 U.S. 960 (1952); *Commercial Pictures Corporation* v. *Regents of the University of New York,* 346 U.S. 587 (1954); *Superior Pictures, Inc.,* v. *Department of Education,* 346 U.S. 587 (1954); *Holmby* v. *Vaughn,* 350 U.S. 870 (1955); *Times Film Corp.* v. *City of Chicago,* 355 U.S. 35 (1957); *Kingsley International Pictures Corp.* v. *Regents of the University of New York,* 360 U.S. 684 (1959).
37. See F. S. Siebert, *Freedom of the Press in England 1476-1776* (Urbana: University of Illinois Press, 1952), generally and at p. 383; L. W. Levy, *Legacy of Supression* (Cambridge: Belknap Press of Harvard University Press, 1960); M. DeW. Howe, "Juries as Judges of Criminal Law," 52 *Harvard Law Review* 582 (1939); J. Kelly, "Criminal Libel and Free Speech," 6 *University of Kansas Law Review* 295, 304 (1958).
38. *Myers* v. *Bethlehem Shipbuilding Corp.,* 303 U.S. 41, 51-52 (1938).
39. See *Kingsley Books, Inc.,* v. *Brown,* 354 U.S. 436 (1957); P. A. Freund, "The Supreme Court and Civil Liberties," 4 *Vanderbilt Law Review* 533, 538-39 (1951).
40. Brief for Respondents, No. 34, at p. 12, *Times Film Corp.* v. *City of Chicago,* 365 U.S. 43 (1961).
41. *American Civil Liberties Union* v. *City of Chicago,* 3 Ill. 2d 334, 121 N.E. 2d 585 (1954).
42. See *Brattle Films, Inc.,* v. *Commissioner of Public Safety,* 333 Mass. 58, 121 N.E. 2d 891 (1955); *RKO Radio Pictures* v. *Ohio,* 162 Ohio St. 263, 122 N.E. 2d 769 (1954). Springfield, Mo., Palo Alto, Calif., and Pine Bluff, Ark., all repealed censorship ordinances in 1954. See Brief of Motion Picture Association of America, Inc., as Amicus Curiae, No. 34, at pp. 3-4, and see Brief for the Petitioner, No. 34, at p. 15, *Times Film Corp.* v. *City of Chicago,* 365 U.S. 43 (1961).
43. See T. I. Emerson, "The Doctrine of Prior Restraint," 20 *Law and Contemporary Problems* 648, 658-60 (1955).
44. See *Rogers* v. *Missouri Pacific Railroad,* 352 U.S. 500, 524, 527, 529, 559 (1957); J. M. Leiman, "The Rule of Four," 57 *Columbia Law Review* 975 (1957).
45. 318 U.S. 44.
46. 367 U.S. 497.

47. 29 *U.S. Law Week* 3258-60 (1961); see Brief for Appellants, Nos. 60, 61, at p. 17, *Poe* v. *Ullman,* 367 U.S. 497 (1961); N. St. John-Stevas, *Birth Control and Public Policy* (Santa Barbara, Calif.: Center for the Study of Democratic Institutions, 1960), p. 25.

48. 29 *U.S. Law Week* 3260 (1961).

49. 367 U.S. at 528. Cf. *United States* v. *Fruehauf,* 365 U.S. 146 (1961).

50. St. John-Stevas, *op. cit. supra* n. 47, at pp. 53-57.

51. See *New York Times,* Nov. 3, 1961, p. 37, col. 4; Nov. 11, 1961, p. 25, col. 1; Nov. 25, 1961, p. 25, col. 8; Dec. 9, 1961, p. 12, col. 4; cf. Comment, "Threat of Enforcement—Prerequisite of a Justiciable Controversy," 62 *Columbia Law Review* 106, 131 (1962).

52. Cf. *United States* v. *Raines,* 362 U.S. 17 (1960).

53. See *Tileston* v. *Ullman,* 129 Conn. 84, 98, 26 A. 2d 582, 589 (1942) (dissenting opinion).

54. J. B. Thayer, *John Marshall* (Boston: Houghton Mifflin, 1901), pp. 106-07.

55. Cf. *Girouard* v. *United States,* 328 U.S. 61 (1946).

56. 346 U.S. 100, 113-18; but cf. *District of Columbia* v. *John R. Thompson Co.,* 203 F. 2d 579, 592 (D. C. Cir. 1953).

57. Scrutton, L. J., in *Rex* v. *London County Council* [1931] 2 K.B. 215, 226, quoted in C. K. Allen, *Law in the Making,* 6th ed. (Oxford, England: Clarendon Press, 1958), p. 463.

58. J. C. Gray, *The Nature and Sources of the Law,* 2d ed. (New York: Macmillan, 1921), pp. 190, 192; see also H. Kelsen, *General Theory of Law and State* (Cambridge: Harvard University Press, 1945), p. 119; A. Ross, *On Law and Justice* (Berkeley: University of California Press, 1959), p. 78; Note, "Judicial Abrogation of the Obsolete Statute: A Comparative Study," 64 *Harvard Law Review* 1181 (1951).

59. A. G. Amsterdam, "The Void for Vagueness Doctrine in the Supreme Court," 109 *University of Pennsylvania Law Review* 67 (1960).

60. Cf. *Cramp* v. *Florida,* 368 U.S. 278 (1961).

61. 341 U.S. 494, 497, 515 (1951).

62. *McBoyle* v. *United States,* 283 U.S. 25, 27 (1931). See J. Goldstein, "Police Discretion Not to Invoke the Criminal Process: Low-Visibility Decisions in the Administration of Justice," 69 *Yale Law Journal* 543, 547-48, n. 9 (1960). Compare the Court's sensitivity to the problem of notice in *Lambert* v. *California,* 355 U.S. 225 (1957), and *James* v. *United States,* 366 U.S. 213 (1961).

63. *Nash* v. *United States,* 229 U.S. 373, 377 (1913).

64. Amsterdam, *op. cit. supra* n. 59, at pp. 108, 90, 80.

65. Gray, *op. cit. supra* n. 58, at pp. 192-93; see Goldstein, *op. cit. supra* n. 62, at 587, n. 95.

66. *Hearings on Nomination of Robert H. Jackson to Be an Associate Justice of the Supreme Court,* 77th Congress, 1st Session, pp. 47-69 (1941), quoted in H. M. Hart, Jr., and A. M. Sacks, *The Legal Process,* tent. ed. (Cambridge: 1958), pp. 1085-87; see A. M. Cates, Jr., "Can We Ignore Laws?—Discretion Not to Prosecute," 14 *Alabama Law Review* 1 (1961); W. R. La Fave, "The Police and Nonenforcement of the Law—Part I," [1962] *Wisconsin Law Review* 104.

67. Cf. Allen, *op. cit. supra* n. 57, at pp. 463-66.

68. See W. O. Douglas, "Vagrancy and Arrest on Suspicion," 70 *Yale Law*

Journal 1, 7 (1960); J. Goldstein, *op. cit. supra* n. 62, at pp. 580-81; Note, "Interstate Immorality: The Mann Act and the Supreme Court," 56 *Yale Law Journal* 719, 729 (1947).

69. Cf. Comment, 62 *Columbia Law Review*, *supra* n. 51, at p. 128.
70. See St. John-Stevas, *op. cit. supra* n. 47, at pp. 53-57.
71. Jackson, J., dissenting in *Korematsu* v. *United States*, 323 U.S. 246. The use of a similar method of the colloquy in the somewhat different context of the Court's relationship with federal administrative agencies and with state courts is represented by *Secretary of Agriculture* v. *United States*, 347 U.S. 645 (1954); *Securities and Exchange Commission* v. *Chenery Corp.*, 318 U.S. 80 (1943); *Harrison* v. *NAACP*, 360 U.S. 167 (1959); compare *Kent* v. *Dulles*, 357 U.S. 116 (1958), discussed in text, *infra* pp. 164-66, with *Jacob Siegel Co.* v. *Federal Trade Commission*, 327 U.S. 608 (1946).
72. 345 U.S. 41, 43, 46, 47.
73. Cf. *United States* v. *Josephson*, 165 F. 2d 82 (2d Cir. 1947), *certiorari denied*, 333 U.S. 838 (1948); *Barsky* v. *United States*, 167 F. 2d 241 (D.C. Cir. 1948), *certiorari denied*, 334 U.S. 843 (1948).
74. W. Wilson, *Congressional Government* (Boston: Houghton Mifflin, 1901), p. 303.
75. 354 U.S. 178, 187, 200-06, 216.
76. 103 U.S. 168, 195.
77. See *Quinn* v. *United States*, 349 U.S. 155, 165 (1955); *Bart* v. *United States*, 349 U.S. 219 (1955); *Scull* v. *Virginia*, 359 U.S. 344 (1959). Compare N. L. Nathanson, "The Supreme Court as a Unit of the National Government: Herein of Separation of Powers and Political Questions," 6 *Journal of Public Law* 331, 345-58 (1957).
78. 360 U.S. 109, 112 (1959).
79. 365 U.S. 399, 431.
80. See L. L. Jaffe and N. L. Nathanson, *Administrative Law*, 2d ed. (Boston: Little, Brown, 1961), pp. 33-34; K. C. Davis, *Administrative Law Treatise* Vol. 1, Sec. 2.02 (St. Paul, Minn.: West Publishing Co., 1958).
81. Cohen, *op. cit. supra* n. 3, at p. 37.
82. 293 U.S. 388; 295 U.S. 495.
83. See R. W. Ginnane, "The Control of Federal Administration by Congressional Resolutions and Committees," 66 *Harvard Law Review* 569 (1953).
84. L. L. Jaffe, "An Essay on Delegation of Legislative Power: II," 47 *Columbia Law Review* 561, 592 (1947).
85. *Olmstead* v. *United States*, 277 U.S. 438, 471, 478 (1928) (Brandeis, J., dissenting).
86. See *Quinn* v. *United States*, 349 U.S. 155 (1955); *Emspak* v. *United States*, 349 U.S. 190 (1955). But see *Rogers* v. *United States*, 340 U.S. 367 (1951).
87. See *Sweezy* v. *New Hampshire*, 354 U.S. 234 (1957).
88. J. M. Landis, "Constitutional Limitations on the Congressional Power of Investigation," 40 *Harvard Law Review* 153, 221 (1926).
89. *Ibid.*, p. 217.
90. Cf. Note, "The Grand Jury as an Investigatory Body," 74 *Harvard Law Review* 590 (1961).

91. 363 U.S. 420 (1960); see 71 Stat. 634, 636 (1958).
92. 357 U.S. 116 (1958).
93. Cf. A. M. Bickel and H. H. Wellington, "Legislative Purpose and the Judicial Process: The Lincoln Mills Case," 71 *Harvard Law Review* 1 (1957).
94. See C. H. Pritchett, *Congress Versus the Supreme Court* (Minneapolis: University of Minnesota Press, 1961), pp. 86-95.
95. 360 U.S. 474, 502, 506-07.
96. 367 U.S. 886, 888, 892, 894; Transcript of Record, No. 97, at p. 32, *Cafeteria Workers* v. *McElroy*, 367 U.S. 886 (1961); *Cafeteria Workers* v. *McElroy*, 284 F. 2d 173, 176 (D.C. Cir. 1960).
97. Cf. 367 U.S. 894 with 367 U.S. 898.
98. H. M. Hart, Jr., "Foreword: The Time Chart of the Justices," 73 *Harvard Law Review* 84, 99 (1959).
99. See, e.g., G. K. Gardner, "The Great Charter and the Case of *Angilly* v. *United States*," 67 *Harvard Law Review* 1 (1953). See *Wong Yang Sung* v. *McGrath*, 339 U.S. 33 (1950); but cf. *Cafeteria Workers* v. *McElroy*, 284 F. 2d 173, 181-82, 183 (D.C. Cir. 1960).
100. Cf. *Missouri ex rel. Gaines* v. *Canada*, 305 U.S. 337 (1938); *Sipuel* v. *Board of Regents*, 332 U.S. 631 (1948); *Sweatt* v. *Painter*, 339 U.S. 629 (1950). See also *McLaurin* v. *Oklahoma State Regents*, 339 U.S. 637 (1950). See Brief for the United States as Amicus Curiae, Nos. 1, 2, 4, 8, 10, at pp. 8-17, *Brown* v. *Board of Education* (*The School Segregation Cases*), 347 U.S. 438 (1954).
101. Pollak, *op. cit. supra* n. 26, at p. 17.
102. *Machinists* v. *Street*, 367 U.S. 740, 785 (1961); *Communist Party of the United States* v. *Subversive Activities Control Board*, 367 U.S. 1, 137, 144 (1961).
103. *Naim* v. *Naim, supra* n. 26.
104. *Frank* v. *Herter*, 269 F. 2d 245; *Worthy* v. *Herter*, 270 F. 2d 905; *Porter* v. *Herter*, 278 F. 2d 280 (D.C. Cir. 1959), *certiorari denied*, 361 U.S. 918 (1959).
105. 368 U.S. 157. Cf. *Wolfe* v. *North Carolina*, 364 U.S. 177 (1960); *Boynton* v. *Virginia*, 364 U.S. 454 (1960); *Burton* v. *Wilmington Parking Authority*, 365 U.S. 715 (1961).
106. Cf. Pollak, *op. cit. supra* n. 26, at p. 26, n. 33.
107. *Lanzetta* v. *New Jersey*, 306 U.S. 451 (1939); see Amsterdam, *op. cit. supra* n. 59, at pp. 90-93.
108. See, e.g., *United States* v. *Witkovich*, 353 U.S. 194 (1957); *United States* v. *Minker*, 350 U.S. 179 (1956); *Association of Westinghouse Salaried Employees* v. *Westinghouse Electric Corp.*, 348 U.S. 437 (1955); *Girouard* v. *United States*, 328 U.S. 61 (1946); *United States* v. *Macintosh*, 283 U.S. 605, 627 (1931) (Hughes, C. J., dissenting).
109. *Apex Hosiery Co.* v. *Leader*, 310 U.S. 469 (1940); *Screws* v. *United States*, 325 U.S. 91 (1945); see Note, "Interstate Immorality: The Mann Act and the Supreme Court," *supra* n. 68. Cf. *Duplex Printing Press Co.* v. *Deering*, 254 U.S. 443, 488 (1921) (Brandeis, J., dissenting). See Comment, "Deportation and Exclusion: A Continuing Dialogue Between Congress and the Courts," 71 *Yale Law Journal* 760 (1962).
110. See, e.g., *Musser* v. *Utah*, 333 U.S. 95 (1948); but cf. *Yick Wo* v. *Hopkins*, 118 U.S. 356 (1886) (*semble*).

111. *Rumely* v. *United States, supra* n. 72.
112. *Greene* v. *McElroy*, 254 F. 2d 944, 953-54 (D.C. Cir. 1958).
113. M. Finkelstein, "Further Notes on Judicial Self-Limitation," 39 *Harvard Law Review* 221, 243 (1925); 7 Howard 1 (1849).
114. See A. M. Schlesinger, *Political and Social Growth of the American People 1865-1940*, 3d. ed. (New York: Macmillan, 1941), p. 95, n. 1.
115. C. Fairman, "Mr. Justice Bradley," in A. Dunham and P. B. Kurland, eds., *Mr. Justice* (Chicago: University of Chicago Press, 1956), pp. 69, 83.
116. L. L. Jaffe, "Standing to Secure Judicial Review: Public Actions," 74 *Harvard Law Review* 1265, 1303 (1961).
117. See, e.g., *Atlantic Freight Lines, Inc.*, v. *Summerfield*, 204 F. 2d 64 (D.C. Cir. 1953); *Joint Anti-Fascist Refugee Committee* v. *McGrath*, 341 U.S. 123, 187 (1951) (Reed, J., Vinson, C. J., and Minton, J., dissenting); *Colegrove* v. *Green*, 328 U.S. 549, 552 (1946) (*semble*); *Massachusetts* v. *Mellon*, 262 U.S. 447, 482-86 (1923) (*semble*); cf. *Frothingham* v. *Mellon*, 262 U.S. 447, 486-89 (1923), where standing in the pure sense was in question.
118. See *Oetjen* v. *Central Leather Co.*, 246 U.S. 297 (1918); The *Chinese Exclusion Case*, 130 U.S. 581, 602 (1889); *Steward Machine Co.* v. *Davis*, 301 U.S. 548 (1937); *Massachusetts* v. *Mellon, supra* n. 117; R. H. Jackson, *op. cit. supra* n. 32, at p. 60; *supra* n. 104; *Fong Yue Ting* v. *United States*, 149 U.S. 698 (1893); but cf. *Wickard* v. *Filburn*, 317 U.S. 111 (1942).
119. See R. Neustadt, *Presidential Power* (New York: John Wiley, 1960), pp. 34-35.
120. C. E. Wyzanski, Jr., "Constitutionalism: Limitation and Affirmation," in A. E. Sutherland, ed., *Government Under Law* (Cambridge: Harvard University Press, 1956), pp. 473, 485-86.
121. Compare, e.g., *Everson* v. *Board of Education*, 330 U.S. 1 (1947), with President Kennedy's conclusion on the constitutional principle to be drawn from the case, *New York Times*, March 2, 1961, p. 12, col. 8 (late city ed.); see also, e.g., *Whitney* v. *California*, 274 U.S. 357, 372 (1927) (Brandeis, J., concurring); *Abrams* v. *United States*, 250 U.S. 616, 624 (1919) (Holmes, J., dissenting).
122. See *Anderson* v. *Dunn*, 6 Wheaton 204 (1821); *Watkins* v. *United States*, 354 U.S. 178, 216 (1957) (Frankfurter, J., concurring); *Braden* v. *United States*, 272 F. 2d 653, 661 (5th Cir. 1959); Transcript of Record, No. 54, at 66, 69 (charge to the jury), *Braden* v. *United States*, 354 U.S. 431 (1961).
123. 328 U.S. 549, 552, 553-54, 556, 566-67; see J. D. Lucas, "Dragon in the Thicket: A Perusal of *Gomillion* v. *Lightfoot*," in *1961 Supreme Court Review* (Chicago: University of Chicago Press), pp. 194, 220.
124. See, e.g., *Myers* v. *Anderson*, 238 U.S. 368 (1915); *Smith* v. *Allwright*, 321 U.S. 649 (1944); *Terry* v. *Adams*, 345 U.S. 461 (1953); *Gomillion* v. *Lightfoot*, 364 U.S. 339 (1960).
125. See A. Lewis, "Legislative Apportionment and the Federal Courts," 71 *Harvard Law Review* 1057 (1958).
126. See J. W. Hurst, *The Growth of American Law—The Law Makers* (Boston: Little, Brown, 1950), pp. 39-45.

127. H. Wechsler, "The Political Safeguards of Federalism," in *Principles, Politics and Fundamental Law* (Cambridge: Harvard University Press, 1961), pp. 49, 50.
128. *Baker v. Carr,* 369 U.S. 186, 323 (1962) (Frankfurter, J., dissenting).
129. *Supra* n. 128.
130. W. H. Taft, Informal remarks delivered before the alumni of the Yale Law School, June 18, 1928. Manuscript in the Yale Law Library.

Chapter 5

1. "My intellectual furniture consists of an assortment of general propositions which grow fewer and more general as I grow older. I always say that the chief end of man is to frame them and that no general proposition is worth a damn." M. DeW. Howe, ed., *Holmes-Pollock Letters,* Vol. 1 (Cambridge: Harvard University Press, 1946), p. 118.
2. See H. J. Friendly, "The Federal Administrative Agencies: The Need for Better Definition of Standards," 75 *Harvard Law Review,* 863, 1055, 1263 (1962).
3. See, e.g., J. M. Landis, *The Administrative Process* (New Haven: Yale University Press, 1938), pp. 55-57.
4. E.g.: compare *Panama Refining Co. v. Ryan,* 293 U.S. 388 (1935), with 49 Stat. 30 (1935); *United States v. South-Eastern Underwriters Assn.,* 322 U.S. 533 (1944), with 59 Stat. 33 (1945); *United States v. Cardiff,* 344 U.S. 174 (1952), with 67 Stat. 477 (1953); *United States v. California,* 332 U.S. 19 (1947), with 67 Stat. 29 (1953) (two previous congressional attempts vetoed in 1946 and 1952); *Jencks v. United States,* 353 U.S. 657 (1957), with 71 Stat. 595 (1957); *Kent v. Dulles,* 357 U.S. 116 (1958), with Department of State Passport Regulations, 27 *Federal Register* 344-45 (1962); *Greene v. McElroy,* 360 U.S. 474 (1959), with Executive Order No. 10865, 25 *Federal Register* 1583 (1960). See Note, "Congressional Reversal of Supreme Court Decisions: 1945-1957," 71 *Harvard Law Review* 1324 (1958); C. H. Pritchett, *Congress Versus the Supreme Court* (Minneapolis: University of Minnesota Press, 1961), Chs. 6, 7, 8; W. F. Murphy, *Congress and the Court* (Chicago: University of Chicago Press, 1962), Ch. 3.
5. Comment, "Deportation and Exclusion: A Continuing Dialogue Between Congress and the Courts," 71 *Yale Law Journal* 760, 767 (1962).
6. See H. H. Wellington, "*Machinists v. Street:* Statutory Interpretation and the Avoidance of Constitutional Issues," *1961 Supreme Court Review* (Chicago: University of Chicago Press), p. 49.
7. *Barenblatt v. United States,* 360 U.S. 109, 134, 153, 166 (1959); *Wilkinson v. United States,* 365 U.S. 399, 429 (1961).
8. *United States v. Constantine,* 296 U.S. 287, 298-99 (1935) (Cardozo, J., dissenting).
9. T. M. Cooley, *Principles of Constitutional Law,* 2d ed. (Boston: Little, Brown, 1891), pp. 160-61, quoted in J. B. Thayer, *Cases on Constitutional Law,* Vol. 1 (Cambridge: C. W. Sever, 1895), p. 175.
10. 364 U.S. 339, 341, 342, 347 (1960).

11. J. D. Lucas, "Dragon in the Thicket: A Perusal of *Gomillion* v. *Light-foot*," *1961 Supreme Court Review* (Chicago: University of Chicago Press), pp. 194, 244.

12. B. Taper, *Gomillion versus Lightfoot* (New York: McGraw-Hill, 1962), p. 96.

13. 238 U.S. 347, 352.

14. *Lane* v. *Wilson*, 307 U.S. 268, 275 (1939).

15. 118 U.S. 356, 373-74 (1886).

16. See *United States* v. *Morgan*, 313 U.S. 409, 422 (1941).

17. See, e.g., *Shuttlesworth* v. *Birmingham Board of Education*, 162 F. Supp. 372 (N.D. Ala. 1958), *affirmed*, 358 U.S. 101 (1958).

18. *Taylor* v. *Board of Education of New Rochelle*, 191 F. Supp. 181, 183 (S.D. N.Y. 1961), *affirmed*, 294 F. 2d 36 (2d Cir. 1961), *certiorari denied*, 368 U.S. 940 (1961); but cf. *Jones* v. *School Board of Alexandria, Va.*, 278 F. 2d 72 (4th Cir. 1960). See W. Maslow, "De Facto Public School Segregation," 6 *Villanova Law Review*, 353 (1961).

19. *Wilkinson* v. *United States*, 365 U.S. 399, 423-24 (1961).

20. *Child Labor Tax Case*, 259 U.S. 20, 37 (1922); but cf. *Sonzinsky* v. *United States*, 300 U.S. 506 (1937); *United States* v. *Sanchez*, 340 U.S. 42 (1950); *United States* v. *Kahriger*, 345 U.S. 22 (1953).

21. *Railway Express Co.* v. *New York*, 336 U.S. 106, 110, 111-13 (1949). See Note, "Suitable Home Tests Under Social Security: A Functional Approach to Equal Protection," 70 *Yale Law Journal*, 1192, 1197-1203 (1961).

22. See, e.g., *Adams* v. *City of Park Ridge*, 293 F. 2d 585 (7th Cir. 1961).

23. *Smith* v. *Cahoon*, 283 U.S. 553 (1931).

24. Cf. *Morey* v. *Doud*, 354 U.S. 457 (1957); but cf. *Liggett Co.* v. *Lee*, 288 U.S. 517, 541 (1933) (Brandeis, J., dissenting); see P. G. Kauper, *Constitutional Law—Cases and Materials* (Boston: Little, Brown, 1960), pp. 1384-87.

25. Cf. *James* v. *Almond*, 170 F. Supp. 331 (E.D. Va. 1959); *Hall* v. *St. Helena Parish School Board*, 197 F. Supp. 649 (E.D. La. 1961); *Allen* v. *County School Board, Prince Edward County*, 198 F. Supp. 497 (E.D. Va. 1961).

26. *United States* v. *Rumely*, 345 U.S. 41, 47 (1953).

27. P. A. Freund, "The Supreme Court and Civil Liberties," 4 *Vanderbilt Law Review*, 533, 550 (1951); P. A. Freund, *The Supreme Court of the United States* (Cleveland and New York: World Publishing Co., Meridian Books Original, 1961), pp. 57, 87.

28. P. A. Freund, "Umpiring the Federal System," in Freund, *The Supreme Court of the United States, op. cit. supra* n. 27, at pp. 92, 93; see H. Wechsler, "The Political Safeguards of Federalism," in Wechsler, *Principles, Politics and Fundamental Law* (Cambridge: Harvard University Press, 1961), p. 49.

29. See, e.g., E. J. Brown, "The Open Economy: Justice Frankfurter and the Position of the Judiciary," 67 *Yale Law Journal* 219 (1957); A. M. Bickel, *The Unpublished Opinions of Mr. Justice Brandeis—The Supreme Court at Work* (Cambridge: Belknap Press of Harvard University Press, 1957), pp. 110-118; Note, "Developments in the Law—Federal Limitations on State Taxation of Interstate Commerce," 75 *Harvard Law Review* 953 (1962).

30. Brown, *op. cit. supra* n. 29, at p. 221; see L. H. Pollak, "The Supreme Court and the States: Reflections on *Boynton* v. *Virginia*," 49 *California Law Review* 15, 48 (1961).
31. Compare, e.g., *Leisy* v. *Hardin*, 135 U.S. 100 (1890), with *In re Rahrer*, 140 U.S. 545 (1891); see *Clark Distilling Co.* v. *Western Maryland Railway*, 242 U.S. 311 (1917); *Whitfield* v. *Ohio*, 297 U.S. 431 (1936); *Kentucky Whip & Collar Co.* v. *Illinois Central R.R.*, 299 U.S. 334 (1937); compare *Northwestern States Portland Cement Co.* v. *Minnesota*, 358 U.S. 450 (1959), with 73 Stat. 555 (1959).
32. *Wabash, St. Louis and Pacific Railway* v. *Illinois*, 118 U.S. 557 (1886), led to enactment of the Interstate Commerce Act. See C. Fairman, *Mr. Justice Miller and the Supreme Court* (Cambridge: Harvard University Press, 1939), p. 314, n. 31.
33. P. A. Freund, "Umpiring the Federal System," 54 *Columbia Law Review* 561, 572 (1954).
34. See Note, 75 *Harvard Law Review*, *supra* n. 29, at p. 956, n. 12.
35. Freund, *op. cit. supra* n. 27, 4 *Vanderbilt Law Review*, at pp. 553-54.
36. *Shaughnessy* v. *Mezei*, 345 U.S. 206, 218, 224 (1953).
37. See *Watts* v. *Indiana*, 338 U.S. 49, 57 (1949) (Jackson, J., dissenting).
38. 360 U.S. 109, 134 (1959); 365 U.S. 399, 412 (1961).
39. C. E. Wyzanski, "Constitutionalism: Limitation and Affirmation," in A. E. Sutherland, ed., *Government Under Law* (Cambridge: Harvard University Press, 1956), pp. 473, 486.
40. *Ashwander* v. *Tennessee Valley Authority*, 297 U.S. 288, 341, 346 (1936).
41. *Sweezy* v. *New Hampshire*, 354 U.S. 234, 255, 266-67 (1957).
42. Z. Chafee, "Do Judges Make or Discover Law?" 91 *Proceedings of The American Philosophical Society* 405, 420 (1947).
43. C. E. Hughes, "Mr. Justice Brandeis," in F. Frankfurter, ed., *Mr. Justice Brandeis* (New Haven: Yale University Press, 1932), p. 3.
44. D. Macdonald, "The Triumph of the Fact: An American Tragedy," *The Anchor Review*, Vol. 2 (New York: Doubleday, 1957), pp. 113, 124.
45. Chafee, *op. cit. supra* n. 42.
46. 277 U.S. 438, 471 (1928).
47. *Pennsylvania Coal Co.* v. *Mahon*, 260 U.S. 393 (1922).
48. Chafee, *op. cit. supra* n. 42, at p. 419.
49. *Proceedings in Honor of Mr. Justice Frankfurter and Distinguished Alumni. Occasional Pamphlet Number 3. Harvard Law School* (1960), p. 62.
50. F. Frankfurter, in P. Elman, ed., *Of Law and Men* (New York: Harcourt, Brace, 1956), pp. 31, 39.
51. See S. H. Kadish, "Methodology and Criteria in Due Process Adjudication—A Survey and Criticism," 66 *Yale Law Journal* 319 (1957).
52. See Frankfurter, *op. cit. supra* n. 50, at pp. 77, 81.
53. C. L. Black, "Old and New Ways in Judicial Review," *Bowdoin College Bulletin* No. 328 (1958).
54. See Frank, J., in *United States* v. *Rosenberg*, 195 F. 2d 583, 608 (2d Cir. 1952); *Repouille* v. *United States*, 165 F. 2d 152 (2d. Cir. 1947).
55. See *Shelley* v. *Kraemer*, 334 U.S. 1 (1948).
56. *Stein* v. *New York*, 346 U.S. 156, 196 (1953); see B. Prettyman, *Death and the Supreme Court* (New York: Harcourt, Brace & World, 1961).

57. Compare *Powell* v. *Alabama,* 287 U.S. 45 (1932), with *Betts* v. *Brady,* 316 U.S. 455 (1960).
58. Compare *Reid* v. *Covert,* 354 U.S. 1 (1957), with *Kinsella* v. *Singleton,* 361 U.S. 234 (1960). And see *Grisham* v. *Hagan,* and *McElroy* v. *Guagliardo,* 361 U.S. 278, 281 (1960).
59. *Francis* v. *Resweber,* 329 U.S. 459 (1947).
60. *Solesbee* v. *Balkcom,* 339 U.S. 9 (1950); *Caritativo* v. *California,* 357 U.S. 549 (1958).
61. *Rosenberg* v. *United States,* 346 U.S. 273, 324 (1953).
62. *People* v. *Chessman,* 38 Cal. 2d 166, 238 P. 2d 1001 (1951); *Chessman* v. *Teets,* 354 U.S. 156 (1957); *People* v. *Chessman,* 52 Cal. 2d 467, 341 P. 2d 679 (1959); *Chessman* v. *California,* 361 U.S. 871, 892, 925 (1959); 361 U.S. 941 (1960); *Chessman* v. *Dickson,* 361 U.S. 955, 965 (1960); *Chessman* v. *Teets,* 362 U.S. 966 (1960).

Chapter 6

1. See R. A. Dahl, "Decision-Making in a Democracy: The Supreme Court as a National Policy-Maker," 6 *Journal of Public Law* 279 (1957).
2. *Brown* v. *Board of Education,* 345 U.S. 972-73 (1953), 347 U.S. 483, 495-96 (1954).
3. See *Southern School News,* March 1956, p. 2; *U.S. News and World Report,* May 27, 1955, pp. 75-76; *The Reporter,* Dec. 30, 1954, p. 12; Brief of the Attorney General of Arkansas as Amicus Curiae, Nos. 1, 2, 3, 4, and 5, at p. 6, and Brief of the Attorney General of Maryland as Amicus Curiae, Nos. 1, 2, 3, 4, and 5, at p. 11, *Brown* v. *Board of Education,* 349 U.S. 294 (1955).
4. See *Time,* Oct. 4, 1954, p. 49; *U. S. News and World Report,* Oct. 8, 1954, p. 42.
5. P. A. Freund, "The Supreme Court and Civil Liberties," 4 *Vanderbilt Law Review* 533, 552 (1951); also printed in P. A. Freund, *The Supreme Court of the United States* (Cleveland and New York: World Publishing Co., Meridian Books Original, 1961), pp. 57, 89.
6. C. E. Hughes, "Mr. Justice Brandeis," in F. Frankfurter, ed., *Mr. Justice Brandeis* (New Haven: Yale University Press, 1932), p. 3.
7. See Brief for the United States on the Further Argument of the Questions of Relief, Nos. 1, 2, 3, 4, and 5, at pp. 8-22, *Brown* v. *Board of Education,* 349 U.S. 294 (1955).
8. 22 *U. S. Law Week* 3160 (1953); see also 21 Id. 3165 (1952).
9. *United States* v. *American Tobacco Co.,* 221 U.S. 106 (1911); *United States* v. *E. I. duPont de Nemours & Co.,* 366 U.S. 316 (1961).
10. See G. B. Johnson, "Progress in the Desegregation of Higher Education," 32 *Journal of Educational Sociology* 254 (1959); *Southern School News,* Dec. 1959, p. 1; but cf. *Lucy* v. *Adams,* 134 F. Supp. 235 (N.D. Ala. 1955).
11. Brief for Appellants in Nos. 1, 2, and 3 and for Respondents in No. 5 on Further Reargument, at p. 17, *Brown* v. *Board of Education,* 349 U.S. 294 (1955).
12. *Op. cit. supra* n. 7, at p. 25.

13. See A. Thaler, "With All Deliberate Speed," 27 *Tennessee Law Review* 510 (1960).
14. *Cooper v. Aaron*, 358 U.S. 1 (1958); cf. *Shuttlesworth* v. *Birmingham Board of Education*, 162 F. Supp. 372 (N.D. Ala. 1958), *affirmed*, 358 U.S. 101 (1958).
15. See *New York Times*, May 18, 1954, p. 1, cols. 5, 7; *Time*, May 24, 1954, p. 22; *The Nation*, Dec. 18, 1954, p. 528; Amicus Curiae Brief of the Attorney General of Florida, Nos. 1, 2, 3, 4, and 5, at p. 44, *Brown* v. *Board of Education*, 349 U.S. 294 (1955); B. Muse, *Virginia's Massive Resistance* (Bloomington: Indiana University Press, 1961), pp. 4-5; J. W. Peltason, *Fifty-eight Lonely Men* (New York: Harcourt, Brace & World, 1961), pp. 31-32.
16. See B. Collier, "Segregation and Politics," in D. Shoemaker, ed., *With All Deliberate Speed* (New York: Harper, 1957), p. 110.
17. *New York Times*, March 12, 1956, p. 19, col. 2 (late city ed.).
18. T. R. Powell, *Vagaries and Varieties in Constitutional Interpretation* (New York: Columbia University Press, 1956), p. 8; see G. Patric, "The Impact of a Court Decision: Aftermath of the McCollum Case," 6 *Journal of Public Law* 455 (1957).
19. P. M. Angle, ed., *Created Equal?—The Complete Lincoln-Douglas Debates of 1858* (Chicago: University of Chicago Press, 1958), pp. 23, 56, 58, 36, 78, 333; C. Sandburg, *Abraham Lincoln—The Prairie Years and the War Years*, one-vol. ed. (New York: Harcourt, Brace, 1954), p. 134; R. P. Basler, ed., *The Collected Works of Abraham Lincoln*, Vols. 2 and 3 (New Brunswick: Rutgers University Press, 1953), pp. 495, 516, 255.
20. See J. D. Richardson, *Messages and Papers of the Presidents*, Vol. 2 (New York: Bureau of National Literature, Inc., 1898), pp. 575, 582; C. B. Swisher, "Mr. Chief Justice Taney," in A. Dunham and P. B. Kurland, eds., *Mr. Justice* (Chicago: University of Chicago Press, 1956), pp. 203, 212; 44 Cong. Rec. Part 4, p. 4115, 61st Cong. 1st Sess. (1909); 79 Cong. Rec., Part 12, pp. 13449 *et seq.*, 74th Cong., 1st Sess. (1935); J. W. Hurst, *The Growth of American Law—The Lawmakers* (Boston: Little, Brown, 1950), pp. 33-34; A. T. Mason, *The Supreme Court from Taft to Warren* (Baton Rouge: Louisiana State University Press, 1958), p. 19.
21. *Cooper v. Aaron*, 358 U.S. 1, 18 (1958).
22. See Peltason, *op. cit. supra* n. 15, at pp. 46-48.
23. See *Holmes v. Danner*, 191 F. Supp. 394 (M.D. Ga. 1961); *New York Times*, Jan. 14, 1962, p. 58, col. 1.
24. See *1961 United States Civil Rights Commission Report*, Vol. 1, Voting (Washington: Govt. Printing Office), pp. 143-98.
25. W. Maslow, "De Facto Public School Segregation," 6 *Villanova Law Review* 353, 357 (1961).
26. See A. M. Bickel, "The Original Understanding and the Segregation Decision," 69 *Harvard Law Review* 1, 37, n. 71 (1955).
27. See Maslow, *op. cit. supra* n. 25, at p. 353, n. 4.

Table of Cases

Cases listed in *italics* are discussed in some detail. Those listed in ordinary type are merely cited. References are to pages and, where appropriate, to end notes pertaining to the page references immediately preceding them.

291

Index